Careless People

Careless People

A Cautionary Tale of
Power, Greed, and
Lost Idealism

Sarah Wynn-Williams

FLATIRON
BOOKS
NEW YORK

CARELESS PEOPLE. Copyright © 2025 by Sarah Wynn-Williams.
All rights reserved. Printed in the United States of America.
For information, address Flatiron Books, 120 Broadway,
New York, NY 10271.

www.flatironbooks.com

The Library of Congress Cataloging-in-Publication Data is available
upon request.

ISBN 978-1-250-39123-0 (hardcover)
ISBN 978-1-250-39124-7 (ebook)

Our books may be purchased in bulk for promotional,
educational, or business use. Please contact your local bookseller
or the Macmillan Corporate and Premium Sales Department
at 1-800-221-7945, extension 5442, or by email at
MacmillanSpecialMarkets@macmillan.com.

First Edition: 2025

10   9   8   7   6   5   4   3   2   1

For Tom

I'm sorry I dragged you into all this.

&

For my grandmother Eileen

Who regularly reminds us to "live an ordinary life"
and "enjoy the good times."

They were careless people, Tom and Daisy—they smashed up things and creatures and then retreated back into their money or their vast carelessness, or whatever it was that kept them together, and let other people clean up the mess they had made.

—F. SCOTT FITZGERALD, THE GREAT GATSBY

Contents

Careless People

Prologue

We're in the middle of an archeological ruin somewhere on the Panamanian coast. It's me, two guys I work with, clusters of people who are basically naked, and Mark Zuckerberg. Mark is not happy. This is the 2015 Summit of the Americas, an international meeting of world leaders. This particular event is a state dinner that—other than Mark—is supposed to be exclusively heads of state of various countries: Brazil, Colombia, Cuba, Canada, the US, over thirty other nations. I wrangled Mark an invitation because I've been trying to convince him that he needs to have relationships with these people.

But somehow we are the only ones at this party.

Under dark skies and low clouds, a red carpet stretches into the distance in the ruins, dimly lit by the open fires. It's flanked by guards in ancient costumes with frilly collars and colorful silk pants, wielding swords and ax-type things. Plus the naked people, who—on closer inspection—are seminaked, wearing abbreviated, ancient, flesh-toned costumes. On one side, a group of people wearing only tiny loincloths and holding crops. Farther down, people who appear to be dressed as members of a kind of primeval Ku Klux Klan. All in front of these ancient fortifications, the site of the oldest European settlement on the Pacific coast of the Americas.

"Why are there naked people at a state dinner?" Mark whispers.

"Honestly," I say, searching for a reasonable response, "I couldn't say. This is my first state dinner with naked people."

We trudge down the endless red carpet past weird scenes of ritual, trading, fighting, and who knows what else, the Facebook men I'm with mostly averting their eyes because of the nakedness. And because any time you look directly at one of the noncostumed extras, they meet your eyes and stare back at you. It's unnerving.

When we get to the empty dining area, I see who's sitting where and it's dreadful. Because he isn't a head of state, Mark is assigned a table between two people who seem to be random relatives of the president of Panama. I mean, they might also have been ministers, and I'm trying to google them and simultaneously pretend that everything about the evening is okay and normal, and of course I have no internet signal because we're in archeological ruins on the coast of Panama.

Seeing few other options, I casually switch out Mark's name card with that of a minor president on a better table. I ferry the name cards inconspicuously in my handbag so the staff who have emerged and are milling around don't notice, and then breathe a sigh of relief and let the team know what I've done.

"He wants to sit next to Castro," Javi says.

"Not happening," I respond.

Javi's my favorite of the coworkers here tonight—Javier Olivan, in charge of "growth" at Facebook, which means he's the person responsible for getting the billions who still aren't on the platform to sign up. Javi's a laid-back Spaniard and one of the few people in top management with a sense of humor.

When the heads of state finally start arriving, my job is to manage "pull-asides." I used to work at an embassy, and "pull-asides" is diplomatic jargon for exactly what you'd think: pulling to one side the person you want to talk to. Mark waits on the edge of the crowd, not convinced about any of this. It's my job at Facebook to run international policy, and to make this matter I need to get Mark engaged in the issues and politics Facebook encounters and creates in the world. Some things that a company needs done on the international stage, only the CEO can do. It's just that this CEO doesn't want to. Mark is deeply skeptical of all this. And he plainly does not enjoy it.

My first target is the prime minister of Canada, Stephen Harper. I take a breath, steel myself, and approach.

"Hello, Prime Minister Harper," I say. "I'm Sarah Wynn-Williams from Facebook. You'll remember me from all the data center and privacy stuff." Look, it's not a great start but it's all I've got, and yes, "remember me" is definitely a stretch. We've never met personally, and if he does remember our data center negotiations, he might feel we screwed his government over. Facebook got them to agree to a bunch of concessions and then we built the data center in Iowa.

He just stares blankly at me like I'm a wart on his foot. Out of the periphery of my eye I see Javi looking relieved that I'm sourcing heads of state for Mark.

"Anyway, I'm here with Mark Zuckerberg." I pause. His expression is inscrutable. "I was wondering whether you wanted to meet him?"

"No," Prime Minister Harper says firmly. "I wouldn't."

I hear the deflating sound of "Oooooh" beside me, and realize that Javi has brought Mark over with him, and he is standing right next to me for this exchange. Prime Minister Harper moves off to mingle with other heads of state. Mark and I just stand there, looking at each other. I turn to Javi, who declares, "I'm getting mojitos for all of us," and strides off to the bar, leaving me and Mark in an uncomfortable silence. "Make sure they're doubles," I call after him.

For the rest of the cocktail hour, the political leaders avoid us. No one approaches Mark. He's not used to this, to being ignored. Usually, he's hounded by people who think he's the most interesting person in the room. Now he stands awkwardly in the middle of this fancy party, a fish out of water. The three of us down the mojitos Javi has gotten, and I send him back for more.

I go to double-check that Mark's table seating is secure and realize I've been rumbled and the seats switched back. I try swapping the name cards again with an even lesser-known president's and stand by and watch as they get switched back within minutes. The lights start to dim, signaling the end of the drinks and the beginning of the dinner, and I quickly lay out the situation to Mark.

"Do I have to stay?" he asks earnestly.

"No," I answer, conscious that his night has been rather peculiar already.

"Then let's leave."

And right at that moment the lights go out, except for one lone spotlight, pointed at a tunnel near us. A stream of horses adorned with colorful silks rushes out, ridden by performers in elaborate costumes.

How do we get out of here?

We can't go back down the endless red carpet. At the end of the carpet there's a large media contingent, and we can't have the international press capturing Mark Zuckerberg fleeing from a state dinner. But there's no other discernible exit. It's ruins and fortifications in all directions except for the red carpet and the tunnel the horses are streaming out of.

The president of Panama stands up and urges people to take their seats. I take one last look around and make a terrible choice, urging Mark and the Facebook team, "Run! Follow me!"

I sprint straight into where the horses are emerging from. I figure wherever the horses are galloping in from, there has to be an exit. But it's only as I see the looks of terror from Javi and Mark as they race past me sprinting in my heels that I realize my mistake. Horses take evasive action around us, looking equally terrified, and probably not expecting a young tech CEO to charge at them through the tunnel of a ruined castle or church or fort or whatever it is we're running through. This is madness. There's a whooshing of hooves and tails and silks, warm mammals, fear, hot breath, and expressions of surprise in Spanish. And then, abruptly, miraculously, the tunnel ends. We pop out the other side into darkness.

I double over, partly to catch my breath, partly because I can't bear to look at Mark and partly because I have no idea what the security arrangements are for that many world leaders and I'm afraid that at any second we're all going to be taken out by snipers.

When I force my head up, I can see that we're standing in the middle of a ginormous field next to some ancient wall, near some straggling horses in silk that shimmers in the moonlight. Mark gives me a wan smile. Not sure what else to do, we set off into the darkness, across the fields, dressed in our formal state dinner outfits, with no cell reception or any sense at all of where we are other than Panama. We trudge through the black wilderness for what feels like miles, hoping to come to a road. Eventually, I get one bar on my phone and call for a car. When they ask me where to send it, I tell them, "Honestly, I have no idea." Mark hears this and starts to laugh, and the others cautiously join in.

That's pretty much what my early years at Facebook were like. It was a lot of launching ourselves at various things that did not quite work out like we expected. I was there for seven years, and if I had to sum it up in a sentence, I'd say that it started as a hopeful comedy and ended in darkness and regret. I was one of the people advising the company's top leaders, Mark Zuckerberg and Sheryl Sandberg, as they were inventing how the company would deal with governments around the world. By the end, I watched hopelessly as they sucked up to authoritarian regimes like China's and casually misled the public. I was on a private jet with Mark the day he finally understood that Facebook probably did put Donald Trump in the White House, and came to his own dark conclusions from that. But most days, working on policy at Facebook was way less like enacting a chapter from Machiavelli and way more like watching a bunch of fourteen-year-olds who've been given superpowers and an ungodly amount of money, as they jet around the world to figure out what power has bought and brought them.

That's the story I'm here to tell.

1

Simpleminded Hope

It was idealism that originally led me to Facebook. Looking back, I'm a little ashamed to admit that. This was in 2009, back when it still was possible to be optimistic about Facebook, in those innocent days when it still was possible to be hopeful about the internet.

It's hard to admit you wanted to "save the world" without putting it in quotation marks, but that's what I thought I'd been doing since my midtwenties. During those years, I was a diplomat for New Zealand at the United Nations.

I grew up in Christchurch, which is an agricultural services town, the biggest city in the South Island and about the size of Lincoln, Nebraska. To give you a sense of what it's like, every November there's a holiday everyone calls Show Day, where the whole city comes out to see sheep and vegetables and there's a dog show and horse racing and a lot of drinking. I loved Show Day.

I grew up in a family of four kids. The eldest. The responsible one. My childhood was pretty normal, I guess, except for the time I was attacked by a shark.

I was thirteen when this happened. We were on vacation at a beach where my family camped every year. I'm standing in the water with a friend. I don't see it. I feel it. A force so powerful and unexpected. A shark attack is like being hit by a knife attached to a freight train. I've never been on the receiving end of such searing pain as its teeth go deeper and deeper.

It locks its mouth around my torso, just above my waist on my right side. It feels like it's trying to get inside me, pushing deeper, trying to rip my stomach, that chunk of me, away. I'm trapped. It starts shaking me the way a dog shakes a toy, back and forth, trying to force me under the water. I go under once and struggle to my feet, then a second time and a third. This third time I start to take in ocean water and the thought occurs to me, "Oh, it's trying to drown me. I could drown." Like, I thought in a shark attack you die from the attack, but now there's a whole new way to die I hadn't realized. I'm in its mouth, clenched between its teeth, under the water. I need air desperately.

My animal instincts kick in. I'm scratching, kicking, punching, pulling, doing whatever I physically can to escape. It's like hand-to-hand combat. I fight with everything I have to try to get my head above the surface.

Whatever I did, it is enough to give the shark a fright. It lets go and swims away.

I struggle toward the shore and send my friend for help. My swimsuit is tattered. I look down and see two big puncture wounds and a chunk of skin missing. Gone. There's blood pouring out. I'm worried that's going to bring the shark back or maybe some other sharks so I stumble through the water as fast as I can. But once I get to shallow water, I collapse and lie there alone, feeling the blood oozing out of me, the sting of the salt water, the hole in my body.

I don't know how long I've been there when some fishermen come along.

"Are you all right?"

I'm patently not all right. But the other issue is that I'm exposed; the shark has ripped off enough of my swimsuit that I'm quite naked. I'm also thirteen. So I try to tell them I'm fine, just hoping they'll go away. They're like, "Um, you don't look fine." And I'm all, "I'm okay. I'll figure it out, you carry on." Maybe it's the blood, or the shreds

of swimsuit but they don't buy it. "We'll get you out of the water."
And I'm still telling them I'm fine when at a certain point they just
stop negotiating, pick up my seminaked body and carry me up to the
shoreline. I am dying of shame. Absolutely dying of shame. On the
beach a small crowd starts to form, to my horror. My parents arrive and
lift me into the back of our family car. The beach is in a remote part
of New Zealand and there's no hospital nearby. We set off to the
closest town, a twenty-minute drive away.

There's no hospital in the town, so we have to call the local
doctor to open up his medical office, which is a small, single-story
building. Once we get there everyone seems relieved, like the crisis
has passed. It's almost jovial as my dad and the doctor discuss the
cricket and plans for the weekend. My dad cheerfully explains that
yesterday we'd tried to refloat whales that had stranded on a beach
nearby, that I had been in charge of two small whales we'd nick-
named Moby and Maybe, not knowing if the smaller one would
make it. No one is in a hurry. No one asks me what happened. The
doctor cleans the wound, pulls the skin around the jaw marks together, and stitches it up so there's no longer a chunk missing. He
gives me a tetanus shot and warns my parents that I might be a little
dramatic that night because I might be in shock but I'd be fine. I
obviously was a fighter. Everyone laughs.

We return to the campground. I'm allowed to stay in the camper
rather than head under the attached awning with my three siblings
because I'm in pain, which the doctor had told me and my parents
to expect, some mild pain from the stitches. Very quickly I realize
this pain is not mild. It's searing. I start vomiting up blood and these
thick, dark, sticky clots that look like coffee grounds, which I assume is stomach lining but I know nothing about the human body. I
pull out a large red plastic cup to collect it so I don't get the camper
dirty.

Everyone else goes to bed but I can't sleep. It keeps getting worse
and worse. I feel like I'm on fire. I wait, quiet as possible so I don't

wake anyone. After a while, the red cup is full and I'm onto another. The pain is excruciating.

Eventually I wake my parents.

"I'm on fire. I'm burning up inside."

"Go back to sleep. You'll be fine."

This continues throughout the night: I wake my parents, they tell me that the doctor said I'd be fine. We'll all learn later what actually is happening. The shark had bitten through my bowel in several places, so it's like I've been stabbed multiple times. The blood and the contents of my bowel are leaking into my gut, basically poisoning me. I have sepsis, acute peritonitis. Eventually there is so much of this toxic blood liquid that it floods through my body and flows into my lungs, making it increasingly difficult to breathe. Like I'm suffocating.

I wake my parents again.

"I can't breathe. I can't breathe. I can't get the air in."

My mother—tired of being woken—responds in an authoritative voice, "Mind over matter. Stop that hyperventilating." This has become a family joke. Now anytime one of us mentions anything, a cold or a cut or appendicitis, we respond, "Mind over matter. Stop that hyperventilating."

We later learn that my left lung has collapsed from a pulmonary edema. And my right lung is damaged.

By morning, I realize I'm losing my ability to keep going.

I wake my parents one more time and say:

"I'm dying."

But I cannot convince them. And my life depends on convincing them. I have no Plan B. I can't drive. I don't have my own phone. This is 1993.

The next morning, after my family wakes and starts getting breakfast, I'm barely getting in enough air to breathe. Then my eyes roll into the back of my head. My mother told me later that when she saw the whites of my eyes, she felt like she was falling through the surface of the earth. Now she believes me. And wants to rush me to the doctor.

Problem is, my dad's MIA. Utterly unworried about how badly I'm doing, he's taken the car to show fishermen the scraps of my swimsuit, hoping they can identify the type of shark and, I suspect, secretly hoping that they'll go hunting for it.

When he returns, we get in the car. By now, with one collapsed lung and fluid rapidly accumulating in the other, it's taking all my concentration to keep enough air going in and out. I'm lying prone in the back seat of the car, and as we make our way toward town, for the first time I start to doubt whether I can keep doing what I've been doing to keep myself alive.

My dad, meanwhile, seems not to be rushing at all. He's a keen fisherman. I swear that when we cross any bridge, I can feel the car slow down while he scans the river for fish, like he always does. From the back seat my mother tells him to hurry.

Eventually we get stuck behind a farmer who's moving his sheep across a short bridge, which is a regular New Zealand thing. I hadn't factored this into my estimate of "this is how long I have to keep myself going until I reach help" and now I completely lose it. I start to lose consciousness. It's like lifting off in an airplane. It feels good, weightless and painless. Floating into unconsciousness where there's no suffering. But I fight it. I think, "I've got to get back."

We finally get to town. Back at the same medical office with the doctor who told my parents I'd be fine. By now I can't speak, can't move, and I'm drifting in and out of consciousness. My dad carries me inside and the doctor from the day before approaches us. Not this guy, I think, as I'm hoisted onto a table. He and two other doctors crowd around to examine me, poking me this way and that, and then they leave abruptly to talk to my parents off in the corner. I hear one of them say something that I can't quite make out but sounds like "she's dying" or "she's dead."

My dad howls, "She was my favorite daughter." I enjoy that for a moment. I have two sisters. I can't wait to tell them. I'd always suspected it. Then my mother wails, "Just like the cat!" Because our cat Winkels had recently met an untimely end. Just like the cat. Brutal.

After this my dad gets very angry, yelling at the doctors to do something, to find out what had gone wrong.

Next thing I know, the doctor comes back. Gets out a very large blade like a mini ax and starts thwacking it down, carving into my left arm. Then my right arm. It's like I'm a piece of meat being hacked open. No anesthesia. No warning. And I'm beyond the point where I have any control over my own body. I can't move or speak. I can't raise any alarm.

I'd thought the shark attack was more pain than a person can bear, the worst that could happen. I was wrong.

The doctor repositions himself near my ankle and brings the blade down with force, splitting the skin and plunging the blade to the bone. Why is the doctor hacking open my ankles? The only explanation I can muster is that he thinks I'm already dead. I'm experiencing my own autopsy. The mortal terror I felt during the shark attack returns, that feeling like, I could die right this second. Painfully. Hacked to death. Is it weirder to die from a shark attack or an autopsy? Will they even know they killed me? The fear chokes me as I anticipate the next ax strike across my neck or skull or some other vulnerable part of me, delivering the final blow.

Instead the next blow lands on the bone in my left ankle. It's agonizing enough that my body spasms. This sparks a change in the room, like they see me as a person again. Not some inanimate object. They realize I'm alive. Someone calls for a helicopter to take me to a hospital.

I later learned it wasn't an autopsy. They knew I was alive. I'd lost so much blood that the doctors believed if they didn't get intravenous blood into me immediately, I would die. In severe trauma cases where it's impossible to find a vein, because blood pressure is so low, it's standard ER procedure to slice into the arms or ankles. That's why I have one-inch scars on my arms and legs. (They're positively delicate compared with the scars on my stomach from the jaw marks.) There wasn't time to give me anesthetic or explain. I don't think the doctors expected me to live. By the time they loaded me up into the helicopter, I don't think anyone did. And later, after hours of surgery, the doctors at the hospital tell my parents I'm unlikely to make it. They started to plan my funeral.

Days later I wake up from a coma in an intensive care unit. I can hear a nurse calling my mother as I slowly take in my surroundings.

My mother leans over me, looks into my eyes, and says, "Aren't you lucky the doctors saved you?"

I can't talk because I'm on life support and a ventilator is helping me breathe. So I gesture for a pen and paper. I make eye contact with her to be sure she's watching, and write slowly and deliberately, drawing a thick black line under each word for emphasis:

I SAVED MYSELF

I'm not sure I can name all the ways this experience changed me, but I think at the very least it probably made me bolder. Any time I glimpse a possible adventure and have to decide, do I go for this? I do.

I forced myself back in the water, same beach, same time of day, one year later. I didn't want to give up swimming in the ocean for the rest of my life. I liked it too much. Which is to say, I bounced back.

I spent my teenage years having a good time, singing in bands, hanging out with other kids who liked music, but there was always a sense of, why did this happen to me? If I survived against the odds, surely there had to be a reason? Every time someone told me I was lucky to survive, I thought, Shouldn't I be doing something with this life? Devoting myself to changing the world in some way? How do you do that?

In law school, the stuff I was drawn to was human rights and international environmental treaties, thinking maybe this was the way to make a difference? In New Zealand, it's easy to feel like you're on the edge of the world. A time zone ahead of everyone else but somehow always behind. Everything is shaped by other countries. It's easy to feel adrift in a sea that others make. After becoming an attorney, I ended up in the foreign service because it seemed like a way to change the world, and I wanted an adventure. I ended up at the UN because I genuinely believed it was the seat of global power. The place you go when you want to change the world. Which is to say I was young, a New Zealander, and very naive.

My issues at the UN? A lot of protecting. Protecting biodiversity, protecting oceans, protecting whales, protecting endangered species. Climate change.

At first, I loved every minute of it, digging into the kinds of big, global problems that cross borders, stuff you can only make a dent in with international cooperation. But after years of endless negotiations and discussion that didn't seem to result in much change in the world, I found myself in the bowels of the United Nations' New York headquarters, a charmless warren of cramped meeting rooms with cheap furniture and dated décor, enduring another grueling late-night session on conserving ocean life. We were drafting the annual report on the "law of the sea," dozens of lawyers sitting in a circle, and the delegates were literally arguing over punctuation. I know it's a cliché, but it's a cliché for a reason. Norwegian, Russian, and Chinese lawyers tussled over whether to insert a semicolon or a comma after some word in a paragraph deep in a document no one would ever read.

I'd struck up an unlikely friendship with the aging Argentinian diplomat I was seated next to. During a pause in the proceedings, he leaned over and casually asked, "Do you know what the single most impactful thing to actually protect the oceans over the last decade is?"

"That's a hard one. You mean a United Nations meeting?" I guessed.

He laughed.

"No. Nemo."

Thinking "Nemo" might be a Spanish word that I was unfamiliar with, I laughed too, playing along, not exactly comprehending.

"The fish," he added. "That little fishy they have to find."

"Ah." I finally got it. *Finding Nemo.*

I had to concede that he was right. The system was broken. I was wasting my twenties toiling long hours with a collection of bureaucrats in their fifties in the twilights of their careers, arguing about punctuation but telling ourselves we were saving the environment. When you realize a cartoon fish can achieve more than the United Nations, it's time to go.

I moved to a job at the New Zealand embassy in Washington, DC, hoping I could get closer to where important decisions about the world were actually made. DC seemed like the center of the world. The place where important decisions get made. The funniest thing about that job was the number of times state officials would comment, "Wow, your English is really good." I never had the heart to admit that it's my mother tongue. I'd just take the compliment.

The embassy was a tiny operation—just eight diplomats—and I was responsible for anything Congress or any US government agency might do that would affect New Zealand, except military or intelligence stuff. I quickly discovered that the American politicians and officials regarded New Zealand as a harmless place they might like to visit on vacation but not relevant to world affairs in any way. That's how everyone saw us. In 2008, after Zimbabwe's president Robert Mugabe refused to leave office following an electoral defeat, the State Department called in diplomats from many countries to its headquarters in Foggy Bottom to coordinate a response. On my way into the meeting, I read my instructions out loud to my South African counterpart; this was a cable I'd gotten from my bosses telling me that New Zealand should take a leadership position in opposing Mugabe. She laughed so hard she could barely catch her breath. "Oooh! I'm sure after decades of despotic rule Mugabe will be quaking in his boots! New Zealand's taking a leadership position in opposing Mugabe!"

Then, in early 2009, I was overcome by what I can only describe as a Facebook fever. It started small enough. Facebook was a lifeline for me, a way to connect to my life back home. Washington, DC, still felt foreign and I was a bit lost in it. Logging on to Facebook was like going to a new but familiar place where my friends, my family, and scraps of my old life continued. Facebook had been around since 2004 and by this point, in 2009, around four hundred million people were using it globally. It was still a pretty scrappy outfit, and still seen by lots of people as a place for college kids to waste time—that's what made this crazy. I urged my sisters, brother, and friends who weren't on Facebook to join, and followed friends' new babies, new relationships, and old photos back home in Christchurch. Then I noticed politicians started showing up. I remember looking at a New Zealand politician's vacation photos, seeing him on holiday, pictures of himself and his kids, and how new that seemed. Then I saw my real-life friend Chris Hipkins, who'd just been elected to parliament, responding to voters directly on his Facebook profile. I think it's hard to remember how radically new that felt, seeing powerful people, celebrities, athletes, writers, and all the rest of us side by side in this new digital common ground. Everyone was there, on equal footing, in this massive public square, talking and sharing information. Like a database of everyone in the world. It seemed obvious that at some point someone was going to use this for persuasion, for rallying people together, for politics. I wondered how long it would be.

While working my embassy job, my fascination with Facebook evolved into an unshakable belief that Facebook was going to change the world. But whenever I tried to explain why I believed this, I failed. Worse, I just sounded utterly insane.

This site was opening up the world. It seemed obvious that politics was going to happen on Facebook, and when it did, when it migrated to this enormous new gathering place, Facebook and the people who ran it would be at the center of everything. They'd be setting the rules for this global conversation. I was in awe of its ineffable potential.

The vastness of the information Facebook would be collecting was unprecedented. Data about everything. Data that was previously entirely private. Data on the citizens of every country. A historic amount of data and so incredibly valuable. Information is power.

At some point, governments would want to control it. I'd seen at the UN how things that cross borders, that are valuable and touch many countries, raise questions like, Who gets the fish in the sea? I'd seen this with technology especially. When genetically modified organisms became widespread, the UN wanted to set global rules for this new tech. For years I worked on treaties that tried to figure out the rules, who got the benefits, how to manage the risk, and who would pay if something went wrong.

Facebook was going to be a way bigger thing, especially in politicians' lives—and their constituents' lives—than genetically altered crops. I could only imagine the scale of the global battle to set boundaries that was sure to come.

After years of looking for things that would change the world, I thought I'd found the biggest one going. Like an evangelist, I saw Facebook's power confirmed in every part of everyday life. Whatever Facebook decided to do—what it did with the voices that were gathering there—would change the course of human events. I was sure of it.

This was a revolution.

What do you do when you see a revolution is coming? I decide I will stop at nothing to be part of it. At the center of the action. Once you see it, you can't sit on the sidelines. I'm desperate to be part of it. I can't remember ever wanting anything more.

There's one problem. No one at Facebook seems to think this way. As best as I could tell, Facebook sees itself as a way for people to waste time on the internet. Facebook does not seem to think of itself as an explosive force that's about to tear apart and remake politics all over the world. It doesn't even seem to have people working on politics, or policy, or relations with governments outside the US, or any of the things that consume me. It doesn't seem to know that the revolution is coming and that Facebook is it.

So how do I convince them of that? I've never been to Silicon Valley. I've never previously identified a revolution or a new form of politics, and I am what can only be described as a random New Zealander. So . . . how do I get to people inside Facebook and persuade them to take my advice? How do I convince them to give me a job?

That's the task I set out on.

2

Pitching the Revolution

Pitching a job at Facebook would not have been possible without Facebook. I see this as yet another confirmation of its importance. I've also never pitched a job before and I have no idea how to do it, especially a job that doesn't exist.

The first roadblock is that Facebook the company prides itself on being difficult to reach. It has hundreds of millions of users and ensures that not a single one of them can reach its tiny staff with random emails or phone calls. So in my spare time I start to internet-stalk all possible connections: contact numbers listed on the site and any email for any staff member vaguely connected to the issues I'm consumed by.

Initially there really isn't anyone to pitch to. The only political staff they have are teaching Congress how to use Facebook, which isn't the revolution I'm looking for. Then I learn that Facebook has hired Marne Levine as vice president of global public policy in the summer of 2010. I don't know who she is but I know her hire means that Facebook is starting to think seriously about politics for the first time. I'm thrilled.

The problem is that it's impossible to figure out how to reach her. There's no contact information on the website, of course. So I spend hours tracking down Marne's home phone number and address, and consider cold-calling her to pitch. Fortunately, in this round of the battle between desire and reality, the few remaining shreds of common sense, the last vestiges of social norms, and that final gatekeeper, shame, stop me from phoning her.

I've learned enough about America in my time here that it's clear to me that it operates on a "who you know" basis. Armed with that knowledge, I look for someone connected to Marne who's also connected to me. I scour every single person on her Facebook friends list, which mercifully is public. (I can't believe Facebook provides a detailed list of everyone's social connections—to anyone.) We have one friend in common. That's it. One shot.

That mutual friend—Ed Luce—is remarkably good humored about introducing me to Marne. They both worked for Larry Summers at the Treasury Department. He offers to put me in touch with another ex-Treasury colleague, Sheryl Sandberg—the number two at Facebook—but after hours of research I'm sure Marne's the right person.

My conversation with Ed happens at his home in DC. I can tell he's bemused by the idea of recommending someone for a job that doesn't exist. Over a cold beer, he quizzes me on why I'm fixated on working for the company, what I know of its leadership, and why I'm convinced that Facebook is going to change the world. In retrospect, I can see he was also gently probing me to understand whether I knew what I was getting myself into. I plainly didn't.

Ed sends an embarrassingly generous email to Marne in which he suggests that I have something very valuable to offer Facebook and concludes, "You'll be amused to know that she worked out I knew you after perusing your friends on Facebook!"

When I don't hear back from Marne immediately, I draft a manifesto of sorts outlining how Facebook should be engaging politically around the world. My boyfriend convinces me not to send it, certain that the only thing it will convince Marne of is that I'm a crazy person.

Months pass following Ed's email to Marne, and my evangelical belief that I have to work on geopolitical issues at Facebook only hardens and intensifies. This manifests in diligent follow-ups that are diligently ignored. Finally, as 2010 is about to draw to a close, I'm standing outside a Loft clothing shop on Connecticut Avenue just before New Year's Eve. Marne has finally agreed to hear my pitch, but I'm fairly certain from the holiday timing months after my original email that it's a polite favor to Ed rather than an indication of any interest in what I'm pitching.

The tiny Facebook office is perched on the fourth floor of a building that looks more like a house than the office of an actual company. I live about three blocks away, so I arrive far too early. The biting cold winter wind forces me to duck inside Loft and peruse the vast array of pantsuits—the political costume of women seeking power—that the store has curated for its DC clientele. Ten minutes before our scheduled meeting, I punch the access code into the elevator and seconds later I'm dislodged into a cramped office space.

The difference between the elegant embassies that I'm used to and this office is stark. It's unlike any office space I've ever seen. There are cords, monitors, food, swag, and toy Nerf guns littering the tiny open-plan space. A friendly brunette with a Texas accent introduces herself as Marne's assistant Meredith and guides me to some couches jammed up against an internal column. We're meeting a few days before the New Year, so the office isn't busy, but there are a few guys scattered around the place who work at their desks with large headphones on.

My mind swings between "this is simply an insane thing to do" and "Facebook needs this—they need it so much" every few seconds. I feel nervous.

When I first had my revelation about Facebook, it seemed so obvious to me that I'd assumed I'd have to beat out a line of bright, connected Americans making their way to the company to be part of the same revolution. Instead I'm having to pitch the revolution *to* Facebook.

Meeting Marne, I'm struck by her eyes; they're hazel, intense. Her blond hair is cut into a sharp bob. I spent so much time devouring everything about her on the internet that it's somehow a surprise to actually be sitting in front of her.

I manage to get out the start of my opening line, "Facebook needs a diplomat . . . ," before Marne interrupts me with her first question.

"What do you mean by 'diplomat'?"

Followed quickly by her second, "Why would Facebook need someone like that?" And then, "How would you rank that need against the other needs Facebook has at this time?"

Within minutes I'm terrified of her. We haven't even made it past dissecting my opening four words. Marne is someone who really knows how to ask questions and does it relentlessly. I flounder. She stares into me with those hazel eyes, never seeming to blink. We actually cover a lot of my pitch but on her terms. She picks it apart, clinically.

"When I was at the United Nations, countries came together to figure out how to agree rules on the global movement of genetically modified organisms," I say. "This was a new technology that was scary and challenging at the time. The same thing is going to happen as governments figure out rules on data and content and all the other things Facebook is built on. A rulebook is going to be written. Facebook needs to decide where it stands on all these things. It needs to help write it."

"Why?" She's like a human metal detector scanning my words for something of value.

"Because Facebook is this global political force that is going to change the internet and the world, and these things matter."

"Matter to who?"

She is not buying this.

"To the people who'll decide on rules that might stop Facebook from growing."

This gets her attention. I realize that's the sweet spot. I'm focused on Facebook the global political force; she's focused on Facebook the global business force. The main thing that's interesting to Marne about other countries is whether they'll help Facebook prosper or try to stop it. I'd believed all the stuff Mark Zuckerberg had said about Facebook not being created to be a company, that it was built to accomplish a social mission to "make the world more open and connected." I hadn't grasped that Marne would see it differently.

As I lay out my case that it's important for the world that Facebook engage politically, how, like a diplomat serves a country, I saw the need to protect, promote, and defend Facebook, I sense how innocent and unnecessary this sounds to her. Especially coming from a young New Zealander with United Nations all over her résumé, which sits limply between us. Facebook has not yet experienced any real regulatory consequences or engaged with governments from outside the US. And it's doing fine. With so much to do in the US to establish the company, why worry about something that hasn't impacted the company at all?

I speak faster and faster, knowing that at any moment she's going to end our meeting and render her verdict, and I'll find myself ejected back out on the street. This speed, my New Zealand accent, and nerves combine into something that may not be entirely comprehensible. I'm not surprised when she cuts me off.

"Look," she says. "This has been fascinating. I've learned a lot and you have some really interesting ideas but"—and here she pauses, takes a deep breath, and her tone changes from brisk politeness to that of a person who's had to sit through a timeshare presentation on a property they were never going to buy—"this team is underwater right now on every type of issue you can imagine. I've only been here a few months and I've had Mark in DC with the Senate Republican High-Tech Taskforce and others on the Hill, I've had our new chief security officer Joe Sullivan making the rounds on the Hill. I've got letters from Franken, Bennet, Rockefeller, and Schumer and questions from Markey and Barton. The team is working around the clock and I need a lot of things right now, but let me tell you, a New Zealand Facebook diplomat is not one of them."

It's clear from the exasperated way she says "Facebook diplomat" that I need to drop that description of the role immediately, and I try to interrupt to say so, but she continues: "We're a tiny team right now—just a handful of people. And I need every single one of them focused on the Hill, focused on what's happening here. You're right that we need more people, and hopefully we're going to do that over time, but what I need are people who are expert in the US regulatory process, who know the FTC or the Hill or any of the bodies that can actually regulate us. We are an American company, we are regulated by Americans. I know you know this. What you're saying is fascinating but it's just not our focus. Thank you for your time. It was great. Have you got plans for New Year's Eve? Let's stay in touch."

Before I know what's happening, I'm back out in the biting cold wind on Connecticut Avenue. I stand on the sidewalk purposefully trying not to feel the wave of crushing defeat that I can sense is about to roll over me. But it doesn't come. As I start to walk the few blocks to my apartment, past groups of people heading out for an early lunch, I feel strangely at peace. Like, I lost. But I learned some new things there was no way of knowing from the outside. I confirmed that no one is thinking about this stuff inside Facebook. They're not thinking about any of the issues they're going to be facing around the world. And I learned that the way to get them to think about it is to make it all about growing their business. That's the kind of pitch they might respond to.

The brutal rejection only makes me more certain of the need to double down and convince them to create this job.

So I'm surprised and thrilled when Marne randomly calls weeks later and throws me a lifeline—by asking me more questions.

"Look—some of the things you suggested might happen in the Middle East are actually starting to happen and people are bringing up Facebook and we're wondering whether we should say something. We're seeing calls for Mark to take some credit and we're try-ing to figure out if he should."

"So you're asking whether I think Mark should take credit for the Arab Spring?"

At that point in January 2011, uprisings and street protests organized on Facebook had started in Tunisia and spread to Libya, Yemen, Syria, and Egypt. When we'd met a month before, I'd mentioned how people were using Facebook to organize in authoritarian states in the Middle East. I'd told her this would eventually lead to conflict with governments that would try to shut down communication, and put Facebook in a challenging position.

"Yes, well, it's just something that has come up; the media are quite interested."

"Well, I guess we need to talk about China."

There's an awkward silence, then a brisk, barely polite, clearly insincere offer to talk about China at a later date, and she tries to end the call, reminding me that all she needed to know is whether Mark should take credit for the Arab Spring.

"Yes," I say. "How you answer this question about the Arab Spring depends on what your strategy is for China. If you take credit for the Arab Spring, if you take credit for a people's revolu-tion, China will be less likely to allow Facebook back into China."

"I think we're just looking at this from the media interest here in the US."

I seize the moment to push again for her to create a role looking at global strategy across all the regions that assesses geopolitical risk so Facebook doesn't make these types of decisions in isolation. She quickly dismisses the idea but, almost as an afterthought, throws me a bone by saying they've opened a communications role in Australia that will do some policy work, as Facebook's under a lot of political pressure there because "somehow the worst of the internet ends up on Facebook Australia." I tell her I'm not surprised.

She makes it clear that this is very different from what I'm pitching.

Also, unpromisingly: "We already know who we want for the role and it's an Australian and I think we'll manage to hire them, but if you like, I'm happy to throw your résumé into the mix. Just as long as we understand each other so you're not disappointed. I wouldn't want you to get your hopes up."

Of course, my hopes are sky high. I hear nothing. Nothing happens. It's devastating.

In February, to try to break me out of the Facebook funk I have fallen into, my boyfriend, Tom, suggests that I accompany him on a work trip he's taking to Atlanta. I've been seeing Tom for less than a year. To this day, he says we met at a bar. I say we met at a party. What struck me when we met at a party held in a bar was that he was this person who seemed to be thinking the exact same thing that I was thinking. And saying the exact thing I wanted to say. Only somehow he would do it in a witty, charming way that I never mastered. By now, he has a key to my apartment and pretty much never goes home to his. He's a Brit, dark hair, green eyes, a reporter for the *Financial Times*.

We're sprinting through the Atlanta airport to try to make our flight back when my phone rings. It's a New Zealand number but not one I recognize. I answer the call while running, surprised to hear my sister's voice.

"I think I'm going to die."

"Wait, what? I'm in Atlanta!" I stop running and Tom slows down ahead of me and mimes his confusion, not wanting to shout at me across the concourse.

"I can't get through to Mum or Dad or anyone, I've borrowed a phone . . ."

"What are you talking about?"

"Just tell everyone I love them," she says. "I don't think we're going to get out and . . ." The call drops.

Tom hustles me to the gate—we barely manage to board the flight before it closes. I make my way to my seat and try to call my sister back. Nothing—I don't even recognize the busy tone at the other end of the line.

"What was that all about?" Tom asks.

"It was Ruthie."

Tom looks at me expectantly.

"Um, she actually said she thought she was going to die and she couldn't reach Mum and something about not being able to get out . . . and it wasn't her number and the whole thing was really strange."

It takes less than two hours to fly between Atlanta and Washington, DC, but it feels interminable. Ruthie's voice keeps running through my head. I can feel waves of panic rising through my body. Why hadn't I called our parents? Why did I just get on the flight?

As we descend into Dulles International Airport, notifications start hitting my phone and I see texts and messages from friends and family. "Has anyone been able to get through to Ruthie?" "Can't get hold of Ruth." "Is your family ok?"

Tom's googling.

"There's been an earthquake in Christchurch. It looks bad, Sarah, like 6.3 or 6.5 or higher. I keep seeing different numbers."

My hometown. Where Ruthie and my parents still live. Again, I try the number she rang me on. Nothing. I try her mobile. Straight to voicemail. I try both of my parents. I can't get through.

Tom leads me off the plane.

The initial reports out of Christchurch are hard to believe. Familiar buildings have collapsed, some with people trapped inside. It's clear there are fatalities but it's difficult to grasp the scale. Phone lines are down or overloaded. My sister's a TV reporter for TVNZ in Christchurch, but her station and nearly all the other news outlets in Christchurch have been damaged. So Facebook seems to be the best place for getting information—people are sharing reports, photos, personal updates, videos. I go through all of my sister's friends and focus on her colleagues and closest friends to see if anyone has any updates. All I find are people checking to see if she is okay, with no response. Eventually I manage to get through to my parents. They're unharmed but neither of them has heard from my sister.

After midnight I instruct Tom to go to sleep and I settle in on the couch, obsessively checking Facebook and New Zealand news sites. Facebook plugs me into the disaster in a way that was previously impossible.

Finally, as dawn breaks in Washington, DC, a message pops up, on Facebook of course: "Love you, lost everything . . . nearly died in that building . . . am so scared and have no idea where i will sleep tonight. I am tired . . . and living by the minute, but thankful I have a job to do. Escaping from that building was terrifying . . . cant explain it to you . . . There was dust and stuff falling everywhere . . . huge cracks. I am so lucky to be alive . . . and that sounds like such a small cliche . . . but I am . . . One of the workers just told me of pulling a man out without his head . . . and I have seen body after body . . . there is a morgue beside our live truck. Its scary here . . . as I write an aftershock is shaking the truck. Better go . . . I love and miss you."

I watch the aftermath of the earthquake play out on Facebook. People use the platform to let friends and family know they are safe, share information on road closures, coordinate sharing supplies, post warnings about drinking water, offer tips for managing liquefaction—a new concept to me that is basically the ground melting—offer up spare rooms, and support those who had experienced the unthinkable. The community whose physical infrastructure was damaged found a new infrastructure online.

Facebook was operating at every level, friend to friend, neighborhood to neighborhood. It was a way for the government to get messages to citizens and for communities to come together. But it all happened organically.

This is it. Seeing all this in action gives me a whole new sense of Facebook and what it can do. The meeting place Facebook had created online could be used as a practical political tool in the most old-fashioned sense. A digital political tool. New Zealanders had come together on the platform to figure out what had to happen next, to distribute resources and information, and to connect people to what they needed. This is new and so important.

It fits into this broader sense of discovery. How technology's opening the world to new, important possibilities that are going to help people, citizen journalists are bringing the news to us in real time through Twitter, the introduction of the Apple App store makes it simple to create mobile apps and get them into the hands of smartphone users without needing to go through telecommunications companies, and innovation is happening with mobile payment technology like M-PESA spreading through Kenya. Making the world a better place. It's not just me; it seems that everyone is thinking like this these days. There is a force field of optimism around Facebook.

As I scroll from page to page on Facebook, I know I have to tell Marne. I want to share this understanding, so I put together a script for the call. I want to show her how powerful Facebook is. How Facebook could work with governments after disasters to communicate essential information. How the connection Facebook provides feels like a lifeline after a disaster.

And more than I care to admit, having Ruthie vanish from sight, I'm also reminded how short life is, how you don't want to die with regret. Even though I'm sure Marne doesn't want to hear from me again and has no intention of hiring me at Facebook, what's the worst that can happen? She can continue to ignore me and I'll be in the same position I am now.

Getting no response on email, I decide just to call her on her mobile without trying to set up an appointment. She's definitely surprised and not in a good way when she hears my voice. Her irritation is softened by politeness and curiosity when I explain that the reason I'm calling is the Christchurch earthquake.

I know I have to pitch quickly. But where I'd previously struggled to articulate the power I saw in Facebook, now it flows, raw and personal. Almost too personal. I burn with embarrassment when my voice cracks as I describe how I searched for my sister. I explain how terrified I was for my family and the lifeline Facebook provided.

By the end of that call, I think she can finally see Facebook through my eyes. How it's going to change the world.

When I confess to Tom that I called Marne again to pitch working at Facebook, I'm ashamed. He's mortified. He'd argued strongly against it and he's convinced I've humiliated myself. Tom's British, and thus especially attuned to—and appalled by—any interpersonal awkwardness.

I don't hear back from Marne. Tom sits me down and tells me it's time to give up on Facebook and move on. I turn to my best friend for solace, and to complain about Tom, only to learn that she agrees with him and his aversion. She gently reminds me that after more than a year of trying to get my dream job, it still doesn't exist.

One week after the earthquake, I get an email from a recruiter about the position in Australia. It's a communications job I have no interest in, not a policy position, but I go for it, hoping to use the interviews to talk them into the job I think they should create for me. Getting each person I interview with to see the problem, the potential, and the solution: me. In each interview, I pitch that global policy job with a fervor Facebook employees seem to find surprising. Long story short, many interviews and three months later, Marne calls out of the blue.

"I'd like to offer you the job."

"Which one?"

"Well, which one do you want? The one you interviewed for or the one you pitched?" There's more than a hint of recrimination in her voice.

"The one I pitched," I respond without hesitation.

"I'm not sure that's how this should work, but the job's yours."

I can't believe I have the opportunity to work on the greatest political tool of my lifetime. I can't believe my luck that I'm going to be part of Facebook and the positive changes it's sure to bring. The biggest adventure I can imagine is about to begin and there's nothing on earth I'd rather be doing.

My title will be Manager of Global Public Policy.

"But you know," Marne adds, "I'm still not even sure this is a job."

I'm stunned and just sit on the other end of the phone in silence.

"I mean, it's great, you're great, and I'm sure you're going to find ways to add value. I'm just not sure that there's enough work to do on this stuff, I mean the stuff you're interested in, to make it a real job, but we'll figure it out."

I had no idea what I was getting myself into.

3

This Is Going to Be Fun

My first day at Facebook: July 5, 2011. The Washington, DC, Facebook office has moved downtown since my last interview and I'm incredibly nervous as I walk into the utilitarian reception area the next week. Like Facebook's offices in California, the DC office pipes and air ducts are exposed; it's all raw concrete and garish paint. Fake graffiti on the walls. If this seemed odd in Silicon Valley, it's ridiculous in this DC office building, which is so fancy that all the offices have glass windows facing a huge atrium, so you can see into the plush surrounds of lobbying and law firms.

Marne's assistant Meredith McCollum—who handled logistics for my many interviews—is there to collect me, and I'm relieved to see a familiar face. After a quick tour, she shows me to a barren white desk in a room full of desks. I've arrived early and the office is empty aside from the two of us.

"Okay—if you want to give me your laptop, I can get you set up before everyone else gets in."

"My laptop?" I stare at Meredith, confused.

"Ah, yeah. They gave you a laptop at orientation in California, didn't they?"

It slowly dawns on me that I've made a terrible mistake.

"Yes, they did," I respond as neutrally as possible. "It's just that I thought that was like a home laptop."

"What's a home laptop?" Meredith looks baffled.

"Um, you know, a laptop to use, ah, um . . . at home." I stumble across words, trying to explain.

"Why would we give you a laptop for your house?"

"I don't know. I guess I was expecting there to be a computer here at my desk. I mean at a technology company . . ."

"Well there would be, if you had brought your laptop in."

I incoherently try to explain to her that at my previous job— for the New Zealand embassy—any work on a laptop happened on our personal laptops at home. In fact, the embassy was so slow to adopt technology that staff didn't even have access to the internet at work, other than one "internet computer" we all shared. Security concerns, we were told. Incompetence, we suspected.

During the crazy, cultish Facebook orientation program, everyone kept talking about how generous Facebook was as an employer, so I just guessed the laptop was for home use. I was wrong. Meredith tells me I should run back to get it.

"Marne's going to be here before too long and she will definitely be expecting to see you and your computer."

I jog in unseemly haste and heels past the reception area I'd entered so recently, and back out to the street and the Metro. As I near home, I bump into a friend who's setting off to work.

"First day didn't go well then?" he says with a smile.

When I return to the Facebook office, Marne's already at her desk. She welcomes me and (re)introduces me to Meredith, who winks at me the moment Marne goes to speak to other members of the team. It's clear that Marne has no idea I'd been in the office an hour earlier.

As soon as we're out of earshot, I beg Meredith, "Please don't tell anyone I came to work without a computer."

"This is going to be fun," she replies, before turning to follow Marne.

I know what I want this job to be. It's clear that in these next few years, Facebook and governments all over the world are going to be figuring out the rules of the road for these giant, globe-spanning internet companies. What they set in place will determine how social media is used for decades to come. It will affect elections, privacy, free speech, taxes, and so much else. I want to be part of that. The debating, the shaping, the deciding. I imagine the kinds of arguments we used to have at the UN. We'll be sitting down with governments to puzzle out what's best, the trade-offs, the competing interests, sharing the spoils, all of it. We need to get this right, for the hundreds of millions who are sure to be using these platforms every day, for years to come.

So. Where to begin? I sit down at my new desk and realize I have absolutely no idea what I should do next.

I begin writing a memo to my bosses, suggesting that we create a "global council"—fifteen to twenty experts around the world who can advise us on the political and strategic issues in their countries, as needed. I check with a friend at Goldman Sachs who confirms that they have something like this. Other international companies do too. This idea is rejected within days. "We make the decisions," I'm told. The bosses don't want a bunch of outsiders all up in our business that way.

That first day I also get an assignment. Marne tells me I'm going to be in charge of one of the first visits by a foreign head of state to Facebook at our headquarters in California. Coincidentally, it's the prime minister of New Zealand, John Key. The perfect collision of my old and new worlds! Facebook hasn't done many of these visits, and building relationships with heads of state had been part of my pitch when I proposed this job to Marne. Building relationships before Facebook needs them.

I ask if Mark Zuckerberg will host the prime minister. In my old job at the embassy, we'd just assume that was how it would go. Our top person would meet their top person. The prime minister is seeing President Obama on this visit, so it doesn't seem like a strange question to me.

People don't openly laugh, but they come close. It's made very clear to me that Mark has no interest in policy or politics—that's Sheryl's world—and specifically no interest in meeting the prime minister of New Zealand. His focus is engineering, and his disregard for politics is a point of pride.

This seems odd to me, given that he's created one of the world's all-time greatest political tools. How can he not be interested in politics? I'm also disappointed because the implications are obvious. I had hoped he just hadn't got around to it. But if the CEO genuinely isn't interested in policy or politics, it's going to be hard to make much of the job I dreamed up, which is about Facebook policy and politics.

It's gently suggested to me that Mark's such a political naif that it isn't in the company's interest to put him forward to meet heads of state.

Yet I know that all John Key cares about is getting a photo with Mark Zuckerberg. I inform the New Zealand team that this won't be possible, but that I'm hoping to find someone senior for the prime minister to meet. The prime minister has briefed the New Zealand press that he's meeting "top brass" at Facebook and I'm desperate to ensure that isn't me. I've heard through other New Zealanders at Facebook that Sheryl has plans to visit New Zealand on vacation at the end of the year. Desperate for any hook to get an executive to take the meeting, I use that as the basis of the pitch to have her meet the prime minister. She tentatively agrees but it's made clear that Elliot Schrage should be presented as the host, as she is a very busy person. I should simply mention that it's possible Sheryl will "drop by."

Elliot is Marne's boss. He reports to Sheryl, who, of course, reports to Mark. He's one of the people I talk to almost every day. I'd describe him as a bearlike intellectual. Charismatic. Fatherly. Tall. Ferociously clever. Messy hair and rumpled outfits and glasses. Elliot ran communications and public affairs at Google in its early days, before he came over to Facebook to do the same. A family man, married with three kids. I like him. He's got a warmth and affable charm. But there's a steely side to him too. When people fuck up, he's quick to drill down and take them apart, point by point. He seems to be taking measure of everyone, all the time, and he's good at it. You want him to like you.

The New Zealanders aren't thrilled with the idea of meeting Elliot—rather than Mark or Sheryl—but as I learned during my time in the New Zealand Foreign Service, we take what we can get. So the meeting is scheduled.

The next challenge is figuring out what actually happens next. There isn't a set of talking points for what Facebook wants to say to foreign governments or a strategy. There's nothing.

So I prepare a briefing for Sheryl and a handful of senior executives about the prime minister's visit, laying out some regulatory and policy issues I think it'll be helpful for them to discuss with him. Hoping this will trigger interest in a broader strategy.

The only problem I run into during this prep is the number of random Facebook employees from New Zealand who simply assume they'll be participating in the prime minister's visit in some way. Following the protocol I learned at the embassy, I dissuade them. Heads of state shouldn't meet with a haphazard group of people from various departments for no reason.

Then I receive a call from Marne, who tells me that all of these people are "friends of Sheryl" and I should be as accommodating as possible. Right, I think. It's the private sector. Government protocols don't mean anything. Sheryl's friends do.

I let Sheryl and other senior executives know that they should manage their expectations about formality, because New Zealanders are very informal. I share the example of what happened when New Zealand's former prime minister Helen Clark visited the United Nations. The State Department officer who wanted to know how many cars would be in her motorcade couldn't believe it when I explained that she would probably just take a cab or walk. Assuming I was thick, he repeated the question, kindly giving me examples of other countries—"For example, Norway will have two cars in their head of state delegation"—before finally accepting that New Zealand would have zero cars in our delegation.

There's much incredulity about this fact when I explain it to the Facebook executives. There's also some cynicism, especially from Facebook's director of global communications, Debbie Frost. Debbie becomes one of my closest friends at Facebook; we started down that path during my job interview when she cut me off as I was trying to explain the work I'd done at the UN on a treaty for genetically modified organisms. She reached over and touched my arm. "If you found those fucking seeds at the boring United Nations interesting," she said, "then you're really going to love working here, where things are actually interesting." I loved that. And I'd learn soon enough, this was typical. In one sentence, she simultaneously dissed my work history, told me I'd bored her, and winked at me. An Australian with dyed blond hair who was raised in Hong Kong and educated in the United Kingdom, she's one of the few foreigners in senior roles at Facebook.

"Should we expect this prime minister to show up on foot or maybe a bike?" Debbie asks, deadpan.

I insist that I know what I'm talking about, and given my years as a diplomat, the executives give me the benefit of the doubt.

The following day the prime minister arrives in a full motorcade, with multiple armored vans and many California Highway
Patrol motorbikes to clear traffic. They speed into the entrance of
Facebook's unassuming headquarters on University Avenue. As the
prime minister, his entourage, and a swarm of security step out of
large bulletproof black vehicles into the blinding California sunlight,
Debbie turns to me and says, "Maybe the prime minister left his bike
at home today."

The security detail is surprisingly aggressive, particularly given
the threat level attached to a New Zealand head of state. They push
Facebook employees out of the way to clear a path for the prime
minister to walk. Perhaps they're unused to leading a head of state
through a building where women in tiny shorts on rip sticks zoom
past bearded guys on motorized beer coolers.

The New Zealand delegation is at least thirty minutes early. Perhaps they had nothing else to do. Before we proceed to the designated
meeting room, the prime minister turns to me and asks, "You're
Ruthie's sister, aren't you? I heard you just got engaged; congrats."

"Thank you! I'm heading back to New Zealand to get married
but we've planned precisely nothing. Just under six months to figure
everything out."

"Yeah, Ruth was telling me that. I actually saw her last week.
She's a bridesmaid, isn't she?"

While we chat, a handful of Facebook communications team
executives arrive and belatedly join our conversation. One of them
gestures to the prime minister and says, "Seems it's true that everyone in New Zealand knows each other or their sister. Are you two
related?"

"Can I introduce the prime minister of New Zealand?" I say.

"Yeah, right," he responds.

"No, seriously," I say.

"Seriously," repeats the prime minister of New Zealand. He starts
to explain how he knows my sister because she's a TV reporter, how

we all share a hometown, and how he bonded with my sister when he was surveying earthquake damage. She reported on it while still traumatized from being trapped in her collapsed workplace only hours before.

The Facebook employees stand together mute and embarrassed.

While the prime minister and I are chatting, Mark Zuckerberg emerges from one of the nearby conference rooms. I'd never seen him in person. Until now, any interaction had been over videoconference. He's smaller, paler, and—at the moment—angrier than I anticipated. With his ill-fitting T-shirt and jeans and unruly hair, he looks like the other engineers milling around the building—though more agitated. To be fair, we're in the middle of a companywide lockdown—several weeks where everyone is encouraged to stay at work day and night—triggered by the launch of Google Plus, which is widely seen as a "Facebook killer."

Mark quickly identifies me as the person responsible for the ever-growing circus of security, consulate officials, prime minister's staff, and New Zealand Facebook employees whom I'd worked into the meet and greet. He marches toward me, ignoring the chaos between us. Everyone's now watching. I feel rather than see the New Zealand prime minister straighten himself beside me.

"Hi, Mark—did you want to meet the New Zealand prime minister?"

"No. I already said I definitely didn't want to do that," he says, looking me directly in the eyes.

"Uh, well, okay . . . um, well, since he's actually right here, John Key, prime minister of New Zealand, this is Mark Zuckerberg, Facebook's CEO."

I gesture for them to shake hands. Mark looks stricken and jumps back. Key seizes the moment and steps forward with an outstretched hand. An enterprising mandarin from the New Zealand delegation lifts a cumbersome iPad, in keeping with the New Zealand embassy's Amish technical capabilities, and snaps a photo as the prime minister grasps Mark's hand in his—the only thing Key had wanted from the visit to Facebook.

Mark smiles automatically for the camera and then returns to irritation and discomfort, which he doesn't try to hide. He disentangles himself from the prime minister's grip and turns to me.

"What's going on? Some of my engineers are getting pushed around"—and he gestures at the large security presence that is encircling the four of us. This is the culture of Facebook. The engineers get what they want. All of us on "Sheryl's side" are lesser mortals who do the things the engineers don't want to trouble themselves with. We're not to bother the engineers.

I step closer to Mark and say as quietly as possible, "I know you're really busy, but could you please perhaps have a quick word with the prime minister?" The begging tone in my voice is unmissable. Even to the prime minister. Mark shoots me a look I struggle to decipher and then turns to the prime minister, who beams as he scrolls through the photos on the iPad, discussing with his advisers which one to post.

Mark makes what could generously be called polite conversation with the prime minister if he weren't so transparently annoyed. The effort is felt by everyone. The prime minister, with his photo in hand, is affable and happy to engage in small talk before Mark skulks back into the room crammed with male engineers.

I whisk the prime minister and his security detail over to the meeting room to meet Elliot. When Sheryl arrives a few minutes into the meeting, the contrast with Mark is striking. She greets the prime minister like an old friend. The stern professional I'd briefed the day before has transformed into a celebrity. For all the times I've met Sheryl, it feels like this is the first time I am really seeing her. She turns on the charisma and it transforms her from a normal-looking fortysomething woman into someone genuinely glamorous. I swear—her hair, her eyes, her makeup, her skin—suddenly she positively glows. Sparkles. Like she's the star of her own show, radiating confidence and charm.

The prime minister, sensing a like-minded politician, quickly relaxes into what feels more like a catch-up coffee than a meeting with a head of state. Until this moment, it had never occurred to me to see Sheryl as a celebrity or be awestruck by her. I didn't really know who she was before I started researching Facebook. But now I can see how she's sprinkling some of her stardust, whatever that magical quality is that she has that makes you forget to focus on the substance of the meeting at hand and instead wonder what it is she's doing differently that makes her better than you. As I look around, I see all of us are agog, in a way that we weren't with Mark or Elliot.

The prime minister's office had released a statement suggesting that cooperation on technology and innovation issues would be discussed, but it's more of a friendly chat with IT help thrown in. Sheryl spends most of her time advising the prime minister on how to use his Facebook page, trying to assuage his irritation about the five-thousand-person friend limit, and addressing his desire to continue using his Facebook profile rather than his Facebook page to communicate. From there I expect the conversation to turn to regulation, potential cooperation, privacy, security, or any of the other issues I had diligently included in the briefing I prepared for the meeting. Instead talk turns to my upcoming wedding and Sheryl's plans to vacation in New Zealand at the end of the year. It becomes more surreal as the prime minister starts imploring us to find his friend Choppy in Queenstown, who manages a scenic helicopter business, and to tell Choppy that the prime minister sent us to "get the real tour." Before I know it, the visit is over and I'm waving off the ginormous motorcade, wondering what just happened.

I'm stunned at the complete and utter lack of substance.

This is not how I pictured things working.

4

Auf Wiedersehen to All That

I'm determined to do better with the next foreign visitor the following week, the German minister of consumer protection. Most countries like Facebook. Germany's an outlier. The Germans disapprove of everything Facebook stands for.

It wasn't very long ago that Germans lived with networks of spies and informants in their country—the Stasi in East Germany and the Gestapo before that. As a result, they have a fundamental suspicion of anyone who wants to gather lots of personal information—which of course is Facebook's business model. Where others see a website that's good for wasting time, Germans see a comprehensive surveillance tool that needs muscular oversight. This instinctive and deeply held wariness of a technology company centralizing and processing vast amounts of personal information raises questions that Facebook has never had to answer, certainly not to a government. Germany, prescient because of its history, can see around corners. It's on the verge of passing laws and starting investigations into Facebook—one of the first countries to do so.

Because of all this, prepping to meet with the German minister is the first time Marne seems worried about accountability. I'm surprised by how nervous she is, given her extensive government experience.

The meeting will be in our DC office, and I suggest starting with a tour.

The minister and delegation start frowning as soon as I showcase the open-plan office. I assume they're troubled by the graffiti or the mess or the many Nerf guns and toy weapons lying around.

"Is everything okay?" I politely inquire.

"This is not very practical," the minister says, pointing at the ceiling, which is crowded with exposed air ducts, pipes, hanging bald light fixtures, and rough concrete. "All this infrastructure. It is surely not up to code? You know—a code violation?"

The rest of the German officials nod in vigorous agreement. Some mutter "code violation" to reinforce her point.

"Umm . . . er . . . it's meant to embody the journey of Facebook. To show that we're only one percent finished. I mean, I understand that before we rented this space, it was finished like those law and lobbyist offices you can see through the window. And then they had to strip back all that luxurious finishing. The carpets and everything."

"You dismantled the furnishing of a proper office to make it look like this? Like it is under construction?" one of the officials inquired, incredulous.

"It's symbolic," I start to say. This all had sounded much more convincing in California when Sheryl explained it to the New Zealand prime minister. I start to realize that Facebook's office is reinforcing the idea that Facebook is reckless and feckless and nothing good is going to come from continuing the tour. As the members of the German delegation stare at me in disbelief, with some audibly tutting, I make the executive decision to get to the meeting room as quickly as possible. Better to hurry past all the posters that say things like THINK WRONG, MOVE FAST AND BREAK THINGS, and IS THIS A TECHNOLOGY COMPANY?

As soon as the German delegation is seated in the meeting room, we start formal introductions. Marne explains her background, that she's relatively new to Facebook, having most recently worked at the White House under Larry Summers. At the end of listing her Harvard and government credentials, she concludes with, "And I'm Jewish."

The room is silent.

"I mean, I don't bring that up because of the Holocaust."

Absolute silence. As if every living thing in the meeting room has been frozen. I'm trapped in some terrible parody of diplomacy.

"It's just I figured you already knew," she continues. "We can discuss it if you wish?"

The tension in the room is unbearable. I picture leaving and walking back home. Leaving this whole Facebook thing behind me.

"I think we could probably turn to the substantive part of the agenda we agreed on, now that we've covered introductions," I cut in, desperately.

We settle into the discussion. Very quickly the delegation brings up content moderation. They want Facebook to be more vigilant in pulling down hate speech. Marne explains that Facebook's built on the kinds of free speech rights embodied by the First Amendment in the United States, so we generally leave content untouched. She then segues into an example of cultural differences between the US and Germany. She says she doesn't care to sunbathe topless or to share topless images, but that Germans seem to. I don't think I'm the only one in the room struggling to avoid the mental image of Marne topless. And the overgeneralization that all Germans enjoy sharing topless images isn't helping either. The minister physically bristles. I flash Marne a "What are you doing?" look.

It's downhill from there. The discussion on regulation doesn't go much better.

After the delegation is escorted out of our offices, I'm despondent. This was horrible at every level. We failed when it mattered. With the country we most needed to win over. I hadn't contemplated failing at this. For the first time, I think this might not work.

Marne, sensing my displeasure, says to me, "Not quite the foreign service? Regretting pitching this?"

I don't answer. One thing you learn as a diplomat, or maybe just as an adult: there are times to keep your thoughts and feelings to yourself.

No one's surprised when the German government opens an investigation into Facebook a few weeks later.

5

The Little Red Book

This place is completely different from anywhere I've ever worked. And it's not just technology that makes it different. There's also money.

One of the upsides of the immediately punishing workload that started as soon as I joined Facebook is that Marne's assistant Meredith is assigned to help me as well. She's the heart and soul of the DC office, and in addition to being caring and funny, she's incredibly stylish. One night she's staying late to help me and I notice that she's wearing shoes I've been admiring for weeks.

"I love those. That red sole is incredible. I've never seen that before. Where'd you get them?" I ask.

Meredith comes over to my desk and places her hands on my shoulders. I'm not expecting this kind of physical contact from our assistant, but Facebook is more informal than my other workplaces and I kind of enjoy the intimate gesture, hoping it's the prelude to her divulging where I can get these phenomenal heels.

"Sweetie, you'll never be able to afford a pair like these," she says, softly but kindly.

After I google "red sole shoes" and discover Christian Louboutin, it's clear she's right. I'm mortified.

I learn soon enough that I have no reference points for the obscene wealth that flows through Facebook. What makes it so strange is that it's based on tenure, rather than title. So assistants and junior staff are often worth vastly more than their bosses, based on when they were hired. Like people who bought a house in a neighborhood that instantly gentrified. All employees receive stock options, starting a year after they join. The company hasn't gone public yet—it's 2011—so there's no Facebook stock, but there's a thriving market of private investors who pay gobs of money to buy those stock options.

At work I get distracted in meetings by women's engagement rings that are so large it looks like it's hard for them to type, and diamond bracelets that cast small rainbows on the wall and clatter against laptops. I've learned my lesson and refrain from asking about all the matching handbags; turns out they're Louis Vuitton and cost thousands of dollars. Facebook offices are glutted with female status symbols and I'm ashamed at how many are completely lost on me. I'm not even at the starting line in this subtle arms race of assets and armor.

Another sign of the wealth at Facebook? The weird things people say. One day, Sam Lessin, a director of product, refers to himself as both "price insensitive" and "economically insensitive." I have to ask Marne what he means. The answer? He has so much money that he doesn't care what things cost.

When Debbie refers to herself as an "economic volunteer like most of the ex-Googlers at Facebook," I have no idea what she's saying. Over coffee she explains to me that she made so much money from the Google IPO that the salary she earns at Facebook is basically meaningless to her overall wealth. She's at Facebook waiting for Facebook's IPO.

My situation is different. Money's tight. I didn't negotiate for anything when I joined Facebook, feeling grateful that they would give me the job. They simply matched my (very much nontech) salary. Most of this goes to rent, because Tom and I have apartments in two expensive cities (he's recently taken a job in New York). A life where you aren't concerned about money is unfathomable to me, and that dividing line is a constant presence.

The other currency that flows through Facebook is stamina. Marne, Elliot, and Sheryl ruthlessly manage their own labor, extracting as much work out of each day as humanly possible. They expect their teams to do the same. Effort, productivity, and the sacrifice of everything else in life are valorized and fetishized.

Marne's work ethic sets the rhythm of my life, and it's unlike anything I've experienced before—even in the corporate law firms I worked at. Unlike senior diplomats who, in my experience, were often more grandees wanting to bless the work done by the team beneath them, Marne is a true Facebook Stakhanovite. Her ferocious work ethic and endurance are astounding. To me it seems her emotions, instincts, and physical needs are all sublimated into her job. A numb efficiency ruled by all-consuming self-discipline and self-denial. After a full day's work without break, Marne will regularly continue at home until the small hours of the morning, rising before 5:00 A.M. to begin work again before exercising. I rarely see her eat. From her toned frame, I assume every calorie is ruthlessly tracked, calculated, assessed, and efficiently eliminated. It's left her with a body that looks like hard work.

As her employee, I feel I have no choice but to adapt to her routine, working with crushing intensity and sleeping only for the few hours between 1:00 A.M. and 5:00 A.M. that she's asleep, to ensure I'm available to respond to her emails when she sends them. Sometimes I like to remind her—in the small hours of the morning—that she'd declared just a few months ago that she wasn't sure there was enough work to make my job a job.

One day I ask her about all we're sacrificing for our jobs—family, hobbies, friends, anything that's not work. She seems surprised.

"But this is it. This is what I do," she says. "I'm not going to learn the piano or run marathons or speak new languages. I'm not looking for hobbies."

"But what about friends?" I counter, instinctively knowing that the family question is off-limits.

"My heart is full, Sarah. I have wonderful friends. But they're in the thick of it too. I'm not looking to make new friends. I'm good."

Years later, after a few wines at Davos, Sheryl tells me that the punishing scale of work is by design. A choice Facebook's leaders had made. That staffers should be given too much to do because it's best if no one has spare time. That's where the trouble and territoriality start. The fewer employees, the harder they work. The answer to work is more work.

To encourage this, the Facebook offices are overflowing with "perks." I think this part of Silicon Valley work life is something everyone's heard about by now. It's parodied on TV shows. The offices are like a never-ending kid's birthday party. All meals are provided, endless free snacks, game arcades. Bring your laundry to work and someone will do it for you. They'll pay for transport if you can't access Facebook's free transportation. I feel deeply conflicted about these perks, simultaneously eye-rolly and loving it.

But the quid pro quo is clear. This stuff isn't free. As Mark declares in the Little Red Book every employee is handed when they're hired,

> Our philosophy on perks is that we want to provide services that are utilitarian and help people with things they need in order to help them focus on our long-term goals. Everyone needs to eat. Everyone needs to do laundry. Everyone needs health services. Everyone needs to get to work. If we can make these parts of our lives easier, then it helps us focus on what we're trying to accomplish at work and it makes us all more productive.

Like Chairman Mao's original, Facebook's Little Red Book is filled with quotes, images, and core principles from its supreme leader, although in this case of course that's Mark rather than Mao. Another MZ channeling his own peculiar form of Maoist zeal. The first page reads, "Facebook was built to accomplish a social mission—to make the world more open and connected."

Employees are encouraged to believe they're changing the world, not working for a corporation. "Changing how people communicate will always change the world," it declares. "We expect you to change the world."

The truth is, of course, that Facebook *is* changing the world—that's what attracted me to the company in the first place. But it's also a corporation. The Little Red Book says that what we're doing is more than capitalism; it's social justice. Facebook is social change, humanitarian change. And we are a family. The Facebook Family.

Most people seem to take it seriously. Both the idea of the Facebook Family and Facebook's mission. Maybe because we're mostly in our twenties and early thirties, we're particularly susceptible to the moral and social messages that leadership is indoctrinating us with. Or at least I am. I buy it. Working at Facebook isn't a job; it's your life. I don't quibble. I love the work. I feel privileged to be part of it.

And I like Marne. I like Sheryl. I like Elliot. This is so basic, but it's nice working with people who are so smart. And the work feels important. Like Facebook is a force for good in the world. It's a mission-focused company, and I share that sense of mission. I feel so lucky to be part of helping Facebook make the world more open and connected.

And within weeks after I arrive at the company, we do begin setting up some first rules of the road for how social media should operate, just like I'd hoped. It's exciting. I work with other teams to create the first public Community Guidelines for Facebook, detailing for users what you can and can't post on the site. We put out Facebook's first transparency report, which Marne pushed for. It's a count of all the requests that governments around the world make for us to take down content. We come up with Facebook's rules for dealing with law enforcement. What personal information will we give law enforcement access to? Under what circumstances?

When one of the few older women on the team tells me I'm spending too much time at work and this is just a job, I honestly think she's the one who doesn't get it.

6

What Do We Stand For?

Each day in Facebook's policy team brings fresh chaos. A contractor in Vietnam sends a casual email mentioning that he met with the leadership of the Vietnamese government and made a bunch of promises that aren't fully explained or doable. A Facebook consultant tells a government committee in Australia that Facebook removes twenty thousand underage users per day, which is simply incorrect. The Mexican president is hit by a poop emoji storm on his page and petitions us for its immediate removal. Sheryl asks if she should support a viral campaign to arrest Joseph Kony, the Ugandan militant responsible for abducting thousands of children for his army. ISIS posts a beheading video on the site. A group of mothers stage a breastfeeding sit-in to protest Facebook's policy on nipples. A rabbi posts that he's having coffee and a muffin in Israel, but Facebook's maps say he's in Palestine. The problems are relentless and varied. Figuring out how to solve them feels like connecting the pieces of a jigsaw puzzle without knowing the picture you're trying to build, but it feels important, working out how to do this stuff responsibly, if we're going to be a force for good in the world.

And Marne and I are a good team. I trust her judgment, and she listens to me. We're making steady progress, shaping this new future.

By early 2012, some of the men in the office start chafing at how we're lurching from one crisis to the next. These are guys we hired mainly to service Congress and state governments. They're creatures of Washington, DC, pugnacious and opinionated. They've formed a little cabal, and they want to understand what the company stands for. It's not an unreasonable request. This is the Obama era, a time when Mark and Sheryl are on the covers of magazines, giving interviews with flashy headlines about how they're changing the world. The boys corner Marne, demanding to know how we're meant to change the world. They're shocked when the answer is . . . nothing really.

Marne, meanwhile, is baffled by their questions. For her and her bosses Mark and Sheryl, it's obvious. We run a website that connects people. That's what we believe in. We want more. We want it to be profitable and to grow. What else is there to say?

There is no grand ideology here. No theory about what Facebook should be in the world. The company is just responding to stuff as it happens. We're managers, not world-builders. Marne just wants to get through her inbox, not create a new global constitution.

There is no bridging this gap in perspective. From the boys' perspective, they want something to believe in. Principles. Vision. Leadership. From Marne's point of view, there's nothing wrong with plugging along as we do, managing each crisis as it comes. That's business.

Nevertheless, something has to be done to quiet the troops. And that's how we end up planning a summit at headquarters in California for everyone who works on policy and political issues. To decide what we stand for.

I'm sympathetic to what the boys are saying. From the moment we met, Marne treated my "Facebook is a revolution," "Facebook is a political force" speeches as vaguely embarrassing. She politely ignored that part of my pitch and since then has consistently communicated that this isn't what we do here, we're not even sure there's a job doing the stuff I'm interested in, and please stop talking that way. I get that this is where she's coming from, but I'm also quietly confident that as Facebook grows, the company will find itself embroiled in conflicts and controversies overseas that will prove my point. My belief in Facebook and its historic importance overrides any fleeting concerns about Marne's attitude. The company will need to develop a theory of how to be in the world. And I'll help them shape it. Marne, Mark, and everyone else will come around to my way of thinking.

And this summit is a first step toward that. I'm excited for it.

This will be the first time we'll all be in a room together. The first time we will talk about how we can use Facebook as a force for good in the world. This could be the start of something important. A new beginning.

My first clue that this might not be everything I hoped for comes as the whole policy team gathers together at Facebook's newly minted headquarters in Menlo Park, California. We're still a small enough team, around a dozen people, that we fit around one table in a regular conference room. Instead of diving straight into the many critical issues we need to solve, we play icebreaker games and are assigned personality quizzes. It's not until late in the day that we turn to the reason we all flew in: finding an issue that Facebook can lead on. We agree that it has to be something where we'll be collaborating with governments around the world, to build trust. People on the team put forward various initiatives that they're passionate about: promoting Facebook as a way to connect abandoned pets with new homes, or showcasing Peace.Facebook.com, a crude dashboard that maps Facebook friendship connections made "just yesterday" between people across three conflict zones: Israel/Palestine, Russia/Ukraine, and India/Pakistan.

To my surprise, support coalesces quickly around Joel Kaplan's suggestion of a Facebook initiative to support the military. Joel joined Facebook around the same time I did. He's a Harvard grad and ex-marine who clerked after law school for Antonin Scalia and served as deputy chief of staff for George W. Bush. But as with Marne, I suspect the real qualification that ensured his hire was his relationship with Sheryl. The two met at the first night of Harvard orientation, they dated, she thanked him in her Harvard thesis, and they remained close over the years. His transition to the tech world from his role as a political operative and lobbyist has been bumpy. For weeks he turned up for work at Facebook in the DC uniform of chinos and blue blazer with gold buttons before realizing this was out of step with the guys in the office, who wore jeans, T-shirts, and hoodies. He gradually downshifted to a series of dad jeans and blazers before relenting to just dad jeans and a button-down shirt. He's a man of routine. Every day his assistant orders the same salad and every day he sits in meetings picking the olives out of the salad. When I ask why he doesn't just order it without olives, he gives me a look like "You'll never understand" and says nothing.

The team starts to map out specifics around what an initiative to support the military would consist of, and how much it would cost.

"Errrr—this is a US-only initiative, right?" I ask tentatively.

I'm the only non-American in the DC policy team and it feels lonely. So many of Facebook's day-to-day policy decisions are underpinned by a subterranean value system that I'm still learning.

"Nope—global," Marne responds.

"Well, um—it's just people and governments are still trying to figure out what Facebook is about, and I don't think we want to immediately align with the military."

"Wrong," Joel responds. "Military and veteran issues are sure winners. Here and everywhere."

"The first political action Facebook takes globally is military? State force? Maybe that makes sense in America, but there are countries that have a more complex relationship with state force. Countries where there have been military dictatorships, for example. . . ."

"Don't you love our troops, Sarah?" Joel interrupts.

"You're asking me, personally? Umm, yes. Of course. My point has nothing to do with me. I'm saying—even if you leave out countries whose military propped up dictators, if you just take the US military, not all countries feel great about the US military. Especially in some of the regions I'm responsible for, like Latin America and Asia. Vietnam, for example. Do you need me to explain why the Vietnamese do not love the US military?"

Without clear agreement, the whole initiative is abandoned. That is, until weeks later when Marne casually drops into conversation that Facebook's first proactive initiative to build relationships with governments around the world will be organ donation.

Body parts and personal decisions about what to do with them after death wouldn't have been the issue that I would have led with— any more than the military—if I wanted to show leadership and forge relationships with foreign governments, but there wasn't any discussion about this. Like many things at Facebook, it didn't matter what the policy team debated or decided; it mattered what Sheryl thought. In this case she had run into one of her Harvard friends, a surgical director of liver transplantation, at a Harvard reunion and offered to help him source donors.

I'm instructed to work with engineers to set it up. I don't know how to set up a global organ donation initiative. And the obstacles pile up quickly. Organ donation is not a universal practice. It's discouraged by some religions, some countries don't do it at all, and some make it impossible to distinguish legitimate organ donation from the sale of human organs. In others there are even darker issues of organ theft and trafficking.

In one of the first meetings with Sheryl to update her on the project, it becomes clear that we have different visions about the scope of the initiative and the regulatory framework around organ donation more generally.

The team of ten people working on the organ donation initiative are gathered in her meeting room at Facebook's headquarters. I'm nervous. I know my push for having Facebook stand for something in the world and what I bring to Facebook are both about to be tested by Sheryl. I walk her through what we've come up with, explaining that it's more like a "registration drive" to push people to their local donation sites, and that Facebook wouldn't be matching donors with patients or transporting organs around the world. We won't build our own organ or patient registries or gather detailed health information. In fact, we'll try to limit the information Facebook collects and holds. Sheryl seems baffled by this and fixates on why we haven't designed the initiative in a way that would allow Facebook to play a bigger role in the collection of data, marketplace of organs, and more. I start to explain the legal, cultural, and religious complexity around organ donation globally, and the sensitivity of the information that organ registries hold. She looks at me as if I am a complete idiot and have missed the obvious, which I suppose I have. I wasn't looking at this as a business opportunity, a way to start collecting health data from users. Sensing danger, I pivot to the risk of organ trafficking. I explain that countries have put a lot of thought into safeguarding organ donation information and guarding against cross-border transportation of organs.

She turns to me, indignant. The edge in her voice is unmistakable.

"Do you mean to tell me that if my four-year-old was dying and the only thing that would save her was a new kidney, that I couldn't fly to Mexico and get one and put it in my handbag?"

I look around the meeting room for support, not sure whether she is clueless or confused. Usually she's so savvy. But it strikes me she's serious and she's someone who's used to getting what she wants. Everyone in the room avoids eye contact with both of us, even Marne and

Debbie, my usual protectors. I realize that in delivering bad news, I'm the prey that's been separated from the herd.

"Ah, that's right," I say, with as much solicitousness as I can muster. "Countries generally have strict regulations in place to prevent black-market sales or theft or illegal harvesting of organs or body parts more generally. It's usually something determined by government policy rather than who can pay the most."

Sheryl glowers at me. I can feel her estimation of me drop as her indignation rises. There's a long, tense moment of silence.

Marne jumps in to save me. "Usually when Facebook releases new features, once the code is pushed, there's not a lot of thought to the real-world consequences. But organ donation requires us to think through all the relevant rules and laws in every country, plus we'll have to create partnerships with organ registries everywhere. We don't have the resources to do that sort of work for every country in the world."

In fact, the natural instincts of the Facebook team—collect data, use a uniform approach in every country and refuse to deviate from it—aren't going to work with organ donation. Marne points all this out to Sheryl, who reluctantly agrees to scale back the global launch to just four countries.

She is not pleased.

But she's undeterred. She wants to do everything possible to make this a success, this first project to spotlight Facebook's values. So, a few weeks later, she directs the company's engineers to add "registered as an organ donor" to the list of "life events" in people's Facebook profiles, alongside other, more traditional life events like "got married" and "expecting a baby." Sheryl also directs me and the organ donation team to include a megaphone—a pop-up that will dominate the screen for anyone who logs on to Facebook—telling them about the organ donation tool. The engineers aren't sold on this idea.

They don't think Facebook should be using the platform to push people to do anything—donate their organs, vote, eat more vegetables, floss, adopt stray puppies, anything. I agree with them. If we get into the business of advocacy, we'll have to make all sorts of choices about what causes Facebook does and does not support. We'll very quickly find ourselves in a world of impossible choices. This whole organ donation thing feels cursed. And a strange place to choose to confront these questions. When we gathered to decide what Facebook stood for, this definitely was not what I was hoping for.

And everyone in this conversation knows the stakes here. We know that when Facebook encourages people to do things, it seems to work. During the 2010 midterm elections in the United States, Facebook did an experiment in driving voter turnout. We put a message at the top of the newsfeed encouraging people to vote, with a link to polling places, and an "I voted" button they could click, as part of a gigantic, randomized trial (with a control group). A study later published in *Nature* showed that 61 million people saw the button, and it actually changed people's behavior: it led an additional 340,000 people to vote.

Sheryl hopes the same thing will happen with organ donation. But the engineers have made their concerns known to Mark and they say he agrees with them. Given the hierarchy at Facebook, where engineers always get their way—they're much more important than Sheryl's teams—I assume this pretty much kills the organ donation project, which Mark always seemed lukewarm on. Now that the engineers have pulled him in, he'll kill it.

And so now, for the first time, I'm leading a project that includes both Mark and Sheryl. It's the first time Mark's been involved in any policy project and it's not going well. I'm anxious about all of it. Facebook, like any company, is a web of relationships, and I really want to develop strong relationships with both Mark and Sheryl. I want them to like me. I want to become one of their trusted advisers. But this isn't the way to do it. This whole project was a bad idea from the start. So I'm relieved the project is dying.

But things take a turn for the worse. Sheryl really wants the megaphone. Even though she knows Mark doesn't. And she has a solution. She directs me to send an email to the whole team, including Mark, announcing that we're moving forward with the megaphone, and explaining Sheryl's point of view as if it's my own. I try and fail to convince her that it's not a good idea. She's having none of it. This is my job. If I can't write this email, what use am I to her?

It all comes to a head while Sheryl is on a private jet crossing the country. She steps onto the plane early one morning. As instructed, I send my email dutifully setting out arguments I do not agree with that valiantly champion the use of the megaphone for organ donation. Mark responds with a series of withering attacks, underpinned by his strong belief that Facebook must be a "neutral platform" and we should never use "Facebook's voice" to interrupt people's experience on the platform. I defend Sheryl's position, against my better judgment. Mark is brutal, and will hear none of it. Sheryl is silent. Later she'll tell me she missed the exchange because she didn't have Wi-Fi.

I'll never know whether she did—some of those traveling with her told me that of course the private jet had Wi-Fi—or whether she told me to send the email that morning knowing that she'd have a plausible reason to sit out on the exchange with Mark.

All I know is that I received my very first direct email from Mark Zuckerberg that day, one sent only to me. It was four words long and simply said:

"I am overruling you."

7

Show Him a Good Time

As we approach April 2012, I get an assignment from Elliot: to take Javier Olivan to Cartagena to show him a good time. I'm expected to do this at a venue that's not really known as a rollicking party: the Summit of the Americas, a gathering of presidents and prime ministers. I'd pitched that Mark go, to meet heads of state and start establishing relationships with them. Elliot nixes that and tells me to take Javi instead. The IPO is going to happen next month. Lots of Facebook employees will make millions. Many have already announced that they're leaving. (I'm oversimplifying only a little to say they divide into two camps: those who want to create their own start-ups and those who want to become DJs.) When you're a company that doesn't make or own something tangible, the threat that the most valuable thing you have—your talented employees—might just up and leave is a pretty big deal. Leadership is freaking out that certain key people might decide to go, and first among them is probably Javi.

I pitch my policy strategy for the summit to Elliot. He barely listens; a smile plays on his lips the whole time. "Just make sure Javi has a good time. Make sure he comes back from Cartagena wanting to stay at Facebook." It's not clear what exactly he wants me to do with Javi to make him so happy. It's just the two of us traveling to

Colombia. There's definitely a weird vibe to the whole thing. But I choose to ignore that.

Javi's one of the most important people at Facebook—one of Mark's top lieutenants, almost as powerful as Sheryl—but he has no public profile. People don't know him.

He's really like no one else in senior management. For starters, he's not American. In his late thirties, he's got close-cropped hair and a pronounced Spanish accent. An avid surfer, he developed a competitor to Facebook in his native Spain in his spare time. It was good enough for Mark to hire him rather than deal with the competition. A forceful, no-bullshit guy, but with a sense of humor.

And he's got a big job. He's in charge of Facebook's global growth. His growth team is the capitalist engine of the whole enterprise. Facebook's business model depends on it conquering new territories. Expanding exponentially.

The growth team is in charge of forging those new frontiers, and like most frontiersmen, Javi and his team play fast and loose. They're aggressive and quick to stake their claim, always looking for opportunities in the gray area created by the lack of regulation.

Javi's team is the group that came up with the idea of importing your contacts into Facebook—so Facebook could press nonusers to join the service. In the beginning, they didn't ask permission to do this. You could tell Facebook "don't take my contacts" but then when you opened Messenger, they'd take them by default. And his team is instrumental in the development of the "People You May Know" tool, which is described by Mashable as Facebook's "creepy as hell tool" for its ability to make uncomfortable friend recommendations, such as when a sperm donor was recommended a biological child he had never met.

It's a growth-at-all-costs approach. To me, it seems like a very American thing. When Alexis de Tocqueville visited the US in the nineteenth century, he was on a rickety steamboat that hit a sandbar and capsized, and he nearly drowned. Afterward he found the manufacturers and asked them why they didn't make the vessels safer. They explained that technological innovation in America happened so quickly there was no point; by the time they made the necessary changes, the boats would be obsolete anyway. Better just to take a chance on what you have. If some drown, no need to dwell, safe in the knowledge that something better is just around the corner. That cheerful recklessness combined with passivity, that forward motion without introspection, that's what Javi's team has.

When we start to run into politicians who put up roadblocks to our expansion, the growth team is quick to suggest that we "juice" the algorithm to help them bolster their Facebook presence. The way they put that? "Let's dial up the algorithm to give politicians some love." When they say that to me, I always say no, believing it's best for us in the long run to stay scrupulously neutral. I don't know what the other people on the policy team tell them. But that's the growth team's mentality. Like the posters all over the office say: move fast and break things.

Before I started working at Facebook, I didn't know enough to imagine the truth about the place, that this is the beating heart of the company, the growth team. Their values are the company's values. Their priorities are the company's. Those boys in the office who wanted to know what we stand for? This is what we stand for. Growth. More.

Obviously, I understand that in the history of the world, this conquering mentality has generally not worked out so well for everyone. And I know Javi's team is perfectly happy to bend the rules, to the extent that rules exist. But I figure, we're new, that'll work itself out. Excesses will be curbed. And the product Javi's promoting so aggressively—Facebook—seems benevolent. We're helping people connect, not selling missiles or nerve gas.

Javi's street smart in a way that Mark isn't. He's the guy who first alerts Mark to a new app called Snapchat. The way Javi tells it, he shows it to Mark and asks him, "You know what people are gonna use this for?" thinking the answer is obvious. Mark has no idea. Javi has to explain it: sexting.

So. This is the man my bosses want to stay at Facebook, and I'm supposed to make sure this trip to Colombia aids that cause.

Within weeks I'm walking down Cartagena's cobbled streets to collect Javi for the grand opening dinner with all the heads of state. It's being held in a breathtaking sixteenth-century fortress. Javi's tickled to be there. It feels important. He loves that they sent him, he loves the pomp and circumstance, he loves that everyone is speaking Spanish. He loves the whole thing.

Then we show up at the grand dinner, and no seats have been assigned to Facebook.

This kind of treatment isn't unusual. During this period, wherever we go, most government officials don't know what Facebook is or don't really use it or don't care. They don't want to meet. Facebook is not a big deal. Still adjusting to nondiplomatic life, I've mistakenly prepared as if Facebook will be treated as a government. It is not.

So we spend the evening standing near where the food is being prepared, watching the politicians eat, milling about with assistants, handlers, and security. Desperate to succeed in my mission to keep Javi happy, I occasionally break from milling around to stalk down people who have mild to no interest in speaking with anyone from Facebook. The awkward conversations that follow definitely do not help. Javi, to his credit, is relaxed. He's never been to a head of state dinner before and is eager to soak it all in. Once I find some beers, we spend most of the evening catching up, pausing only when we spot famous politicians or celebrities.

The next day, on a bike ride I organize in the spirit of showing Javi a good time, Javi—with no prompting from me—starts to talk about his future. As Elliot suspected, the IPO is weighing on him. He, like me, sees the possibility of what Facebook could become and is genuinely excited by that. But people he respects at Facebook are leaving. Given his entrepreneurial bent, he's itching to prove himself on his own terms. To go and start something. He wants to do both—to stay and to leave. But leaving seems more likely. That's not good news for me, with my assignment to keep him at Facebook.

It's a pleasant day of cycling to beaches and cafés, except for my growing fear that there's nothing I can do to convince Javi not to quit. Soon enough, it's back to work. I secured the slot for Javi's keynote right before the highest-profile session, which features the heads of state of Colombia, Brazil, Canada, and the United States, President Obama. This felt like a real coup. Javi was excited too. Unlike Mark, he enjoys the buzz of being in front of a crowd. But as he's about to take the stage, the audience surges from our auditorium to the one next door, in order to secure their seats for the session with the heads of state. Javi is left to address an almost empty auditorium containing the small handful of people who are interested in this strange thing called Facebook.

After the speech is over I apologize. It's clear to both of us that I messed up by booking him into the session before the heads of state. But he's not a dick about it. He's mainly relieved that his keynote is done. He shrugs and suggests we blow off being ignored at another official dinner, inviting me to come out with his friends.

I meet up with them at a restaurant a few hours later. It takes a bit to piece together everyone who's there—mainly CEOs from some of the region's tech companies. Then a striking, tall man with dark features sits beside me and starts to play the role of host. This is Juan del Mar. The balmy sea air, cold beers, delicious food, and animated conversation fade to the background when Juan takes the stage now and then to croon jazz with the band. This is a surprise given that I thought the host was a tech CEO, but Javi explains that he owns this restaurant. That's when I notice—"Juan del Mar" is emblazoned across the restaurant and the menus.

"Actually, he's a bullfighter," Javi says, scanning my face for a reaction. "And he's dabbled in a few other things."

"He's kind of built for it," one of the CEOs says cryptically. I'm the only woman there except for one of the CEO's wives, who seems to be in on the joke.

"I think he was hoping to show you," someone else pipes up, and everyone laughs. Except me.

As they continue drinking into the night, with Juan occasionally taking the stage to sing, the men keep coming back to this in-joke that I'm not understanding. They ask if I'm really engaged, because my engagement ring is "so small it was very hard to tell." Which is about the ring and also somehow about sex, money, power, and availability, but I couldn't exactly say how. The men enjoy my confusion and switch into Spanish whenever they want to say something about me. One of the things they definitely seem to be saying to Javi: nice job you have there, that they send this girl to hang out with you here in Cartagena.

Meanwhile, my mind is still racing, trying to figure out if any of this is going to make Javi stay at Facebook. Is this what I signed up for? Is this mission even possible? How can I get this done?

After midnight, someone suggests we head to a salsa club. Seemingly out of nowhere, large, dark executive vehicles, ones I'm used to seeing for heads of state, pull up. We're bundled in and quickly skirting the back alleys of Cartagena in the dark night. We speed into increasingly gritty neighborhoods. After all the drinks, things start to blur a little.

We pull up to an unremarkable door. Stepping out into the warm air of the unlit backstreets of Colombia feels illicit. I vacillate between excitement and apprehension. We're swept by someone's security team into a hot, crowded room where salsa music blares. Some strong unidentifiable drink is thrust into my hand and I'm pulled onto the dance floor by one of the CEOs or a bullfighter, it's hard to know who. After a few songs, Javi makes his way toward me.

He leans in to say something in my ear that I think I've misunderstood because it sounds like, "Hillary Clinton is here."

"Oh, Javi." I smile. It's clear that some combination of the drinks and the excitement of the summit, being around all these heads of state, has gone to his head. "There's no Hillary Clinton here. We're in some random back-alley salsa club. It's way past midnight, the floor is sticky, there's a half-naked woman right over there, and I promise you there is no chance that the US secretary of state is here. She's somewhere fast asleep. . . ."

Javi cuts me off by taking my hand and pulling me over to the edge of the club.

And there she is. Hillary Clinton. Beer in hand, next to the band, dancing with a small group of her staff, security detail conspicuous with their earpieces in the steamy club.

Javi looks at me, triumphant. "Hillary Clinton!"

It is undeniably Hillary Clinton. She's completely caught up in the music, right in the front, clapping and swinging her hips. I take in every strange detail of that sight and turn to look at Javi. The delight in his face at having bested me is contagious, and I take a slug of whatever sticky drink I'm holding.

"You're right and I apologize and will forever defer to your superior knowledge of foreign policy. I should never have doubted you."

He's beaming.

"Now you have to tell me the real deal about Juan del Mar," I shout over the dance floor.

"Okay," he says slowly. "He's a bullfighter, he owns bars and restaurants, and he's kind of an actor. He's what every man here wants to be."

"I still don't get it."

"Well, he's a special type of actor."

I turn my head from Hillary Clinton to look closer at Juan del Mar. "You mean he's an adult actor?"

At that moment Juan raises his glass in toast to us. Hillary Clinton dances behind him, just a few feet away.

"Yeah, I guess he's a porn star," Javi says.

"Are you going to quit?" I hadn't dared ask outright the entire time we'd been in Colombia but decide in the moment to rip the bandage off. I need to know if I've failed or succeeded. I don't even know if Javi knows the real reason he's here in Colombia.

"I don't know," he says, looking over at Hillary Clinton, seeming to weigh her presence in his head.

The music rolls over us and the dance floor pulses. Javi drains his drink, pulls me into the fray, and gestures for Juan to join us. We edge as close as we can get to Hillary Clinton.

"Just want to be sure," I say, leaning toward his ear. "Are you going to stay at Facebook?"

"I think I'll stay for now," he says, speaking more to himself than to me.

As I write this, it's more than a decade later. He's still there. Running the place with Mark, now as Facebook's chief operating officer.

8

Running Out of Road

Before long—October 2012—we're celebrating one billion people using Facebook. The festivities are really targeted at the lower-level employees. They get parties. Shiny silver and blue balloons—Bs and ones and zeros—float all around the office.

But for top management, one billion users is a crisis.

I'm in meeting after meeting where my bosses agonize about how we're "running out of road." That's the phrase they use. Facebook's stock has dropped by half in just five months, from thirty-eight dollars a share at the IPO—when shares were first offered to the public—to nineteen dollars now. They believe that the only way the stock price will rise is if we show growth, dramatic growth. But as Javi explains, the first billion users are the easy billion. He says it like everyone knows that. After that, you get into issues like how to reach children, how to reach parts of the world where there's no internet, how to get into places like China that are hostile to any social media site like Facebook.

Now, with our stock price falling, Facebook's survival depends on growth. As a result, countries outside the US become of vital importance. Before this, my work wasn't seen as something that would impact the share price. But now, getting past foreign regulators and opening up markets is the most important thing. Suddenly I matter.

And I've been busy. In the six months since Cartagena, I've been flying into countries to be the first person from Facebook that the government meets. I hand over a business card to the most senior member of the government I can wrangle a meeting with. Mexico, Vietnam, Brazil, Argentina, Colombia, Singapore, Canada, and probably a dozen other places. I let them know that if they've got a problem, I'm the person to call. If there's a problem already, I try to find the person behind the problem and solve it. I show them how the part of Facebook they're worried about works or how they could prepare rules or guidelines for it.

Sometimes, my bosses and I don't agree on the solution. We tussle over the issue of educating politicians and regulators who don't understand the complexities of our technology. When the Canadian privacy commissioner asks for information about the "People You May Know" tool on Facebook, wondering if it violates Canadian privacy rules, I'm ready to explain. I want to help. Marne and Elliot thought I was mad. "Why do you want to break into jail?" Marne asked.

As the teams start to look around the world at where they can pick up significant numbers of new users, Myanmar comes into focus. The way Javi and the growth team see it, there are more than sixty million potential new Facebook users there, largely untapped. But just as they start to hone in on it, the military junta that runs Myanmar blocks Facebook. We have no idea why. Maybe it's because on Facebook the junta is finally facing criticism, something it's never tolerated before. But at the same time, Myanmar's in the process of democratizing. It's headed toward its first democratic elections in over a decade. Why ban us now?

In the past, this would have been met at Facebook with the same indifference as the blocks in Iran, Cuba, Bangladesh, and North Korea. But with the pressure for more "road" and the lure of sixty million potential new users, this quickly escalates into something for top managers to address.

Javi explains his agitation to the small group of policy executives on a call. "It's the network effect," he says, meaning that increasing use will improve Facebook in Myanmar. As people are first getting the internet, getting them on Facebook from the start leads to exponential growth. If we're not available some other service will capture the value of the network effect. "Being blocked right now is a disaster. How quickly can we get this fixed?"

"They shut us down, we're completely in the dark, and it's hard to tell what's going on from here," I reply. "Military juntas usually want to control communications. I'm not sure we can convince this one to just be cool with Facebook. I don't think there's a quick fix."

"Nope—that doesn't work," Javi responds. "Someone needs to get on the ground and figure out what's going on."

"And fix this law," Marne says, referring to a law that had recently been drafted giving the junta formal power to shut down Facebook. "Otherwise this is going to become the new normal."

There's silence and I let it hang in the air. No one from Facebook has ever been there. The junta is still in charge. The country is barely online.

"Oh, you mean *I* should go to Myanmar?" I say eventually. "Should I stop off in North Korea on the way home?"

"Yeah," said Javi, not rising to my bait. "But more importantly, don't come back until you've sorted it out."

I really don't want to do this.

Days later I'm heading toward the center of the capital Nay Pyi Taw, on a desolate twenty-lane highway that's completely empty of cars. There's no way the average citizen in Myanmar can afford one, and there's speculation that the highway can double as a runway if junta leaders ever need to escape. Like an ornate castle from a fairy tale, the Presidential Palace in Nay Pyi Taw shimmers in the heat of the day, looming above the deserted road.

Nay Pyi Taw is a planned city, and it's a lot like this highway:

nice on paper but weirdly empty. Occasionally, I catch glimpses of women with chalked faces carrying children in their arms or on their backs, workers sweeping the empty roads with long straw brushes, men cycling on bikes loaded with wood or produce. They all look like actors who've strayed onto an empty set.

My hotel is extremely basic. Miles out of the city down a rugged dirt track, surrounded by scrubby fields. The hotel lobby is also the owner's living room. No electricity, hot water, or food available, and absolutely no internet or cell service. That makes setting up meetings basically impossible.

But the World Economic Forum (WEF) is holding a regional meeting in Myanmar. I've registered in the hope that I can connect with someone there who can provide a link to the junta. Despite coming from a country of fewer than four million people, I've found there usually is at least one New Zealander in even the most unlikely of places, and they're usually friendly and sometimes helpful. So I set out to find one, scanning the list of participants, which usefully includes everyone's home country. Bingo. The Kiwi I latch onto gets me into WEF events, including a party that feels like a portal to another time and place. A sumptuous feast in a giant tent in what feels like the middle of nowhere. There are tables groaning with exquisite food, limitless champagne, and musicians in flowing silks on stilts. It's grotesque in its excess, and the WEF guests seem oblivious to the abject poverty that's just outside.

It turns out that WEF would be a great place to meet an overconfident European corporate man in his late fifties. It's no place to meet members of the junta. And when I broach the idea of setting up meetings between Facebook and the junta, these men laugh, stare blankly, or warn me against the idea.

"You're in their bad books," a human rights lawyer says to me. "And you don't want to meet with the junta when you're in their bad books."

I use WEF's Wi-Fi to arrange a different hotel and message Tom—

who I've not contacted yet—to tell him, "My phone does not work in Myanmar. No coverage. No data. Will call as soon as you might be waking up. Sorry for any concern, I didn't expect this. Love you. Sarah x."

I also start trying to connect with Aung San Suu Kyi. The Nobel Prize winner is leading the opposition party that secured significant victories in recent by-elections. I want to find out if she and her team have thought about the role Facebook could play in helping Myanmar open up and transform into a democracy. But reaching her is about as easy as connecting with the junta.

After her assistant politely informs me that I will not be getting a meeting now or ever, I learn that she'll be attending a WEF luncheon in her honor. I get there early, walking in while the catering staff sets up, before WEF starts policing the guest list. My diplomatic training helps me locate the seating plan. Then it's simply a matter of plonking myself down at her table and waiting to see if anyone will remove me.

When Aung San Suu Kyi arrives hours later, she's elegant and more feminine than I expected. She sits with poise among the circle of men now assembled at her table, with a large fresh flower in her hair. Among the CEOs and politicians there's an unspoken competition to command Aung San Suu Kyi's attention. I am ignored. Meanwhile, I'm using all my limited energy, which is rapidly flagging due to jet lag, to act like I belong at that table, worried that at any moment someone will realize I'm not even on the guest list.

I'm so tired I can't even see straight, and as things slowly come into focus I see Aung San Suu Kyi looking at me. She gestures and I look beside me to see who she's granted an audience to, before realizing that it's me. She says across the table, "Come."

The heads of the gray men rapidly swivel and I meekly get up and walk around to assume a half crouch beside her.

"I noticed you," she says warmly.

"I'm Sarah. I'm from New Zealand," I say reflexively, still groggy from jet lag, and then am overcome with embarrassment. "I mean,

I'm from Facebook, but I'm also from New Zealand. . . ." Aung San Suu Kyi looks confused. ". . . But I live in the US." This is not going well.

She gracefully taps the person beside her in a gray tunic. "I want to introduce you to Shwe Mann, who is soon to be the Speaker in Parliament."

"Hi, I'm Sarah. I'm here on behalf of Facebook," I say quickly, determined to make a better impression.

"I'm sorry, I do not speak English," he says. As I look closer at his well-pressed clothes, short-cropped hair, and impeccable posture, I realize that he may be the first person I've encountered from the junta. In the silence, he assumes I haven't understood and repeats, "My English it is not very good."

"Oh, no, it's great," I reassure him, "and I'm sorry, I do not speak Burmese." He smiles politely. "And in fact some people think I don't speak English very well because of my New Zealand accent."

"I apologize," Aung San Suu Kyi cuts in. "You have a beautiful New Zealand accent, and I apologize for not speaking Maori."

Maori's the indigenous language of New Zealand.

"I'm actually here to talk about communicating," I say, smiling. "The way people and politicians are starting to communicate on the internet. Facebook, do you know what that is?"

"Yes," Aung San Suu Kyi interrupts. "Did you know Shwe Mann is very important in our country? We're from different parties but we have forged a wonderful working relationship."

She's trying to warn me. Whatever you say to me, you're saying to the junta. I try to carry on but she continues.

"His party and ours. We're trying to find ways we can work together. There's so much to do. And he is the right man to do it. Very clever."

Shwe Mann beams.

"I am conscious of how much you have to do. I think Facebook is going to play a role in Myanmar's future. I think it's important that we figure out some of the issues that are coming up, especially with the blocking, the new telecommunications law, and the upcoming election." I pause, fearing I've overreached.

"You really from Facebook?" Shwe Mann interrupts. I nod vigorously to ensure no misunderstanding on that basic point.

"Wow," he says, touching my face gently just to make sure I'm real.

When I return to my new hotel that night, there's a written message in my room letting me know that I have a meeting at the Ministry of Communications set for the next morning.

I'd picked the new hotel I transferred to because it advertised access to internet. In reality, there's no Wi-Fi, though for some reason there is a book next to the bed titled *How to Use the Internet*. The next morning I discover a rotary phone; strangely, you can't dial out, people have to call you. But these are far from my biggest problems. I have a 10:00 A.M. meeting starting soon with the deputy minister and no idea how I'm going to get there.

Overwhelmed by WEF chaos, the hotel staff are unable to help with transport. With little other choice, I walk alone down the road in full business attire and ponder whether the traditional hitchhiking thumbs-out sign will work in Myanmar, or whether I'd be better off waving money to try to incentivize a ride. Not that I have local currency. And there are no cars on the road. Those barren highways are still empty.

Then a car comes barreling toward me and I stand, one arm outstretched, dangling an American twenty-dollar bill, the other arm in an enthusiastic thumbs-up. The driver doesn't even slow down. Completely ignores my friendly New Zealand smile. In the long silence that follows, I think about the damage it'll do to Facebook's relationship with the junta if I fail to show up to this meeting that I was lucky to get in the first place. And how I'll explain to my bosses why I failed to fix Facebook's situation. Javi was clear that I shouldn't come back until this is solved. Saying I couldn't get a cab won't cut it.

I keep checking the time on my otherwise useless phone. Eventually I see a speck in the distance coming closer. It's an old car. I decide to take drastic action and step out onto the highway to stop the car.

The middle-aged Burmese driver is confused and winds down his window. I lean in, waving my American money, and hit my next stumbling block: he doesn't speak English and I don't speak Burmese.

With no alternative, I mime driving and attempt to pass the money to him, and when he doesn't take it I mime again, with more determination. He seems to get it this time and accepts the money. I get into the front seat and quickly fasten the seat belt before he can change his mind. He starts to drive and, with no other cars on the road, we make a quick pace. He's speaking to me rapidly in Burmese and I realize he's asking where I want to go. I try saying "Ministry of Transport and Communications" three times but it doesn't work. I take out paper and pen from my handbag and carefully write the name of the department before remembering that Burmese has a different script, so this is as worthless as my phone without internet. After repeating the name of the ministry hopelessly and seeing a cloud of confusion start to stretch across his earnest face, I return to miming. I'm at a complete loss for what else to do. I mime driving, then answering a telephone, and then draw a square box in the air, which is as close as I can get to "government ministry." When he still looks unsure, I do it again. Eventually, he nods and turns off the highway into a denser area with more buildings but still mostly devoid of people.

He slows as we approach a collection of shops and nods at me earnestly before pulling to a stop outside one of them. This is clearly not a government ministry. It looks like some kind of empty internet café. I have to hand it to him: given my mime, that's a pretty good guess. But it's not where I need to be. I shake my head no, but try to smile encouragingly. He responds with a worried look like, "Uh oh—how do I get this foreigner out of my car?" Meanwhile, I'm panicked that I'm going to have to leave his car in this random place and lose my only shot of making it to the ministry.

I belatedly remember that the government is a junta, and mime regimented marching and saluting before redoing the previous mime. Miraculously, he seems to get it and we set off. But while he may or may not understand where I want to go, it doesn't seem like he knows how to get there. I mean, he's not a taxi driver. He's just some punter whose car I stood in front of. We start to drive into a more remote area, and fear surges through my body. Not only because no one knows where I am, with no form of outside communication, alone in a car with a Burmese man who could drive off and take me wherever he wants without anyone knowing. But also because my meeting is supposed to have already started and I don't know what the consequences are if I don't show up.

We drive around what seems to be a circular business park, then turn another corner, and unexpectedly I see a spartan building that looks like a government ministry. A big concrete box that would look right at home in downtown Beijing or a lesser Soviet republic. I'm late but so grateful to be there. I thank my savior, who appears both relieved and genuinely excited we made it, and race inside.

When I announce that I'm from Facebook, the receptionist shakes his head in a way that makes me think I'm in trouble and not just for being late. He requests something that I don't understand. I hand over my business card but that's rejected, and then I realize he wants my passport. I hand it over and he takes it and puts it in a drawer that he locks. Oh no. I decide not to protest, but as he leads me upstairs and through a rabbit warren of sterile corridors—and I feel myself moving farther and farther away from my passport—I regret not taking a firmer stand on that one. He leads me into a grand hall. It's dark and somber like a Gothic cathedral. The scale of it is ridiculous.

I was expecting an office or conference room. There's a large, thick curtain, and the room is dominated by large, ornate chairs that look like medieval thrones carved from dark wood. They line each side of the room. Against the far wall, raised on a platform, are three even more ornate, larger thrones. I feel tiny and instinctively want to stick by the door. But the receptionist leads me over to a seat near the wooden thrones on the raised stage and then leaves. I sit.

I'm alone in a place that could not be further from Silicon Valley. It's like some dimly lit feudal court. I check my phone, interested to see whether the government department responsible for communications in Myanmar has Wi-Fi or any form of cell phone reception.

Of course not.

Time passes slowly in the silence of the throne room. Suddenly, there's movement behind the curtains and a bright, blinding light bursts through. I can't see anything but this light pointed straight in my eyes. As it moves toward me, I start to make out shapes and realize that a group of men are approaching, one of them holding what looks like a large video camera, another the large light, followed by more men in tunics. I am petrified. I'm reminded of videos of ISIS captives that we'd debated removing from Facebook, in comfortable, well-lit meeting rooms back in Silicon Valley. The videos never included the moments before someone becomes a hostage, but I guess this might be how they start.

As the camera moves steadily toward me, my mind starts replaying the things people in Myanmar had said about how angry the junta is about Facebook, and the trouble it was causing in Myanmar. I know that this junta is vicious, committing human rights abuses with executions, torture, gang rape, forced labor, and human trafficking. Not long before I arrived in Myanmar, the possession and use of telephones, fax machines, computers, modems, and software was a criminal offense. They've arrested people for as little as listening to a foreign radio station.

I try to calmly and rationally calculate a safe route out. But

beyond the name of the ministry, I don't know where I am. I'm out-
numbered by these men and I don't know if I could wedge open the
heavy ornate doors that seal the throne room shut, much less navigate my way through a maze of identical corridors to retrieve my
passport. I'm now absolutely terrified. No one knows where I am.
No one is coming to help me. I think of how angry Tom will be if I
become a hostage in Myanmar. He'd told me it was crazy to come
here.

Two men in frog-collar tunics peel off from the group and move
toward the raised thrones. The camera crew comes and stands beside me—wordlessly—their light pointing directly in my face and
their camera drilling into me. I feel my heart pounding. I start to
detect some kind of mechanical grinding movement from within
my chair and fear that some handcuffs or footcuffs will emerge, but
no—it's a microphone that slowly extends from somewhere noisily.
In the half darkness I have no idea who's controlling it. I gulp down
air and consciously direct my face away from the camera and toward
the two men in tunics. I make eye contact with the closest one, who
looks down at me from his raised throne. I can't read his expression.

He and the other man introduce themselves, and I strain to understand their heavily accented English. They both have short dark
hair, and one has very bushy eyebrows. At least one of the men is the
deputy minister of information, though it's possible that they both
are. Their thrones are of equal height. I introduce myself, speaking
deliberately, conscious that it's all on film and may possibly be the
introduction for a hostage video.

I'm surprised when the men respond in humorous disbelief. As if
I'd just crawled out of some hidden computer monitor.

"You are from the Facebook? You are from the internet?" one
says.

I assure them I really am from Facebook and there really are people
who work there. When I sense at least one of them is unconvinced,
I fish around in my handbag and pull out a business card, which I

hand to one of the camera crew to walk over to the deputy ministers. Somehow it feels like I should not leave my throne. The deputy
ministers pore over it.

In truth, I don't really know what to do next. This isn't like a
meeting I'd prep for Sheryl or Marne to do, where I'd have scripted
out a plan.

The men look at me expectantly.

My adrenaline-fueled fear starts to ebb away. Their looks of genuine astonishment—their amusement—signal that maybe they aren't
going to hold me against my will or do anything to me, at least not
at first.

So I start with the basics. I ask them why they were blocking
Facebook. What were they worried about?

In halting English, they outline a scenario they'd never expected
to face.

The junta had controlled the internet until recently, and they
priced it so very few people could afford to go online (it was $300
for a SIM card, if you could find one). The infrastructure they'd built
also let them do all the surveillance and censorship they wanted. But
now the country is opening up—transitioning from military dictatorship to electoral democracy—and the internet is moving to everyone's
phones. (This is new, for a country to go online without a desktop
phase.) They're deciding whether to allow foreign phone companies
to come in and—in a broader way—they're figuring out how to handle the internet in this new semidemocratic Myanmar.

The men tell me that only 1 percent of the population has access
to the internet right now, but nearly all of them are on Facebook.
With poor connectivity and challenges navigating to other sites,
it's become the default home page for the country. So Myanmar is
discovering the internet in a completely idiosyncratic way; it's as if
Facebook were the entire internet.

They explain their concern: that some people are intentionally
fueling ethnic tensions and sowing discord between Muslims and

Buddhists by posting things that are false on Facebook. Also, they're worried people are saying nasty things about the junta. The junta's natural instinct—like that of any authoritarian military dictatorship—is to control information at all costs. Facebook and the internet are a profound challenge to this. So they do what comes naturally. When there's a problem on Facebook, they simply switch it off.

No one on Facebook's side has been tracking this closely, but the sense I get from the deputy ministers of information is that they have been switching Facebook on and off for years and basically Facebook hasn't cared, until the whole "running out of road" thing became an issue. The transition to a pseudo civilian government and the growing access to the internet and Facebook, to say nothing of Facebook's growth ambitions, mean this isn't tenable in the long term, but they don't have any other solutions.

The deputy ministers make the arguments for banning Facebook permanently, and I try to convince them that that won't solve the fundamental problems in Myanmar, arguing that their country has a lot to gain from freer flows of information, outside state control. They know the internet is coming to Myanmar. The political changes in their country mean they won't be able to keep it out forever. All we can agree on between us is . . . to talk.

I ask that before they switch off Facebook again, they at least reach out and explain the problem. But even that is complicated. They don't know how we could communicate. They don't have working government email addresses.

"But how would we do this?" they ask. "Could we call you on the telephone?"

I joke that my phone isn't working in Myanmar so it wouldn't be a good system. I wave my useless phone at them but they do not find this funny. It's like a curtain falls. I suddenly remember that I'm at the Ministry of Communications. We'd been getting along—a little—and now it's clear I've offended them. One of the deputy ministers seems a little embarrassed; the other is stern.

And with that, the meeting is over.

We agree to stay in touch, but don't specify how. I leave thinking that, for the moment at least, these two deputy ministers will support switching Facebook back on. Unfortunately, they're not the only ones that have to be convinced.

I'm sent to meet other men in different locations—some spartan, some that look like bunkers, some that are like Bond villains' lairs, with too much carpet and portraits of generals whose frames are encrusted with sparkling rubies and garnets. I'm too nervous to ask if they're real.

Many of the men are in traditional dress. Others are in full military uniforms adorned with medals. All of them act like they're used to being obeyed and rapport is not part of their job description. The raw power they project is clear and not obfuscated in the way you often get with officials around the world. But somehow, we reach a tentative agreement to unblock Facebook and to talk the next time before they decide to block it. Because there will be a next time.

By the end of the day, I'm overwhelmed with a sense of absolute exhaustion. It's unlike anything I've ever felt before—like every molecule in my body is heavy and yet I feel empty, dimly aware of a gnawing hunger, hollow and unable to bring my brain into focus. It can't just be jet lag, can it? I limp toward my hotel room, feet blistering from the heels after walking across unpaved roads and paths.

I'm writing up notes from the meetings when my rotary phone rings. It's a sound I haven't heard in years. Like 1982's calling. The receiver's cumbersome and heavy. I assume it's the front desk calling about transport to the airport the next day, and I'm surprised to hear Tom's voice.

"I've been calling since I woke up. I haven't heard from you since you left for the airport days ago, apart from your email about the hotel saying you would call me." His anger's palpable. Had he somehow found out I'd been deep inside a government building with the junta and no one at Facebook knew my whereabouts? That was impossible. Had he somehow learned of the whole hostage confusion? Surely not.

"I'm sorry, I had no way to contact you. I can't dial out on this phone. I know that sounds crazy but it's true. It only takes incoming calls. My mobile doesn't work in Myanmar, but I guess you know that, and it says there's internet here, but I haven't been able to figure it out and I've barely been in my room anyway."

He cuts me off and his words tumble out in a flood of concern, anger, and hurt. He's telling me that the situation is ridiculous and untenable and when am I coming home and he's worried about me and why am I there, and everything he says seems to blur together. But it's unlike any conversation we've had before. This time his anger has a new, insistent edge.

Because I'm pregnant.

I was too scared to tell my bosses. I felt like I was still on trial for this job they never wanted to create in the first place. I was sure it would count against me if I told them. And I was certain they'd tell me to go anyway. Marne is someone for whom work always comes first. I felt utterly powerless.

And I didn't want to be a whiner. I didn't want to ask for special treatment. I felt like I had a job to do and I had to get it done. That's how I was raised. You tough it out. Mind over matter, stop your hyperventilating.

Tom thought it was a terrible idea for me to do this trip, and when I vanished for two days, well, of course that was hell for him.

I hang up and, in a daze, climb straight into the shower feeling an unfamiliar mix of lonely, chastened, desperately unhappy, irresponsible, and ashamed, knowing that the water will wash away the tears that are already streaming down my face. I'm so used to trusting my instincts. Suddenly my center of gravity is shifting. I don't know if I've done anything right for Tom or the junta or Facebook or my bosses at Facebook or Aung San Suu Kyi or the people of Myanmar. I don't know if Facebook is the right thing or at least I don't know if it's the thing I thought it was. I'm hoping I'm wrong. I'm at a bit of a loss because none of this feels right.

Of course there's no hot water at the hotel. Crouched on the floor of the tub, the cold water against my skin brings me out of my mind and back to my body. I sit cross-legged under the cold water, sobbing, unable to stop. Tom's not being unreasonable. I get it. He was right and I was wrong.

Instinctively, I move my hand to my stomach, gently prodding and feeling for signs of life from the baby that's slowly growing inside me.

9

Lady McNugget

Lean In marks a new era in Facebook. When her book is published in March 2013, Sheryl goes from COO to celebrity and everything is about *the book*.

The line between Facebook work and Sheryl's personal benefit had always been blurry. Like the time I had to help her get tourist visas to Australia for one of her nannies through my embassy connections. But the book blasted this to a new level.

There's a carefully orchestrated media campaign attached to the launch. The women in the Washington, DC, office—there aren't many of us—are expected to help by doing menial tasks that suspiciously resemble the "office housework" (administrative tasks that help your bosses but don't pay) that Sheryl rails against in her talks and a *New York Times* op-ed. Some women grumble about having to give up our evenings to do free labor for her book. It's not like we're short of work—in fact quite the opposite. We're fielding regular crises at all hours, in countries around the world. No one ever explains why we have to help with the book. I guess it's too crude to tell us it's because we share a gender.

My job is passing out name tags, a crushing exercise as I have to ask the names of DC types who, mortally offended, look at me with a "don't you know who I am" face. Which I obviously don't. When I'm released from that task, I have to shadow Sheryl, holding her business cards so that she can work the room unencumbered. My presence is acknowledged only when she wants to do someone the honor of giving them her contact information.

I make a point of catching Meredith's eye every time I'm called over, like a dog, to perform the trick of handing over Sheryl's card. But I also know that Sheryl thinks she's doing me a favor, having me ride shotgun with her through this power broker cocktail party. And it is kind of cool. I'm glad to be there. It's exciting whenever she's around. We don't have women like Sheryl in New Zealand, and I like it whenever she breezes into DC.

Watching her work is like a study in female success. How she comes to decisions, her relationships with men—both the ones she works for and the ones who work for her—what she wears, how she's groomed, how she speaks. She can drop into a soft girlish voice, like you're sharing an intimate secret with her, and yet still command a room. Sheryl's amazing.

Lean In is based on eleven principles that basically boil down to: if a woman works hard enough, she can thrive at home and at work. These include:

Sit at the table: Sheryl admits to feeling "imposter syndrome" but encourages women to "fake it till you make it." She says that women keep themselves from advancing because they don't have the self-confidence and drive that men do. "We lower our own expectations of what we can achieve."

Don't leave before you leave: This is Sheryl's belief that many women tend to "quietly lean back" way before they have children, worrying how they'll manage family and work commitments.

And my favorites—they're both about cultivating and nurturing honesty in the workplace:

Seek and speak your truth: Sheryl explains how she's tried to make Facebook a nonhierarchical organization where everyone is free to speak their thoughts and criticism.

Let's start talking about it: Sheryl outlines barriers women still face in the workplace, including "blatant and subtle sexism, discrimination and sexual harassment," and encourages women to start talking about sexism in the workplace.

Over the coming years at Facebook, I'll see both of those tested, chewed up, and thrown aside. But at this point, they seem very real to me.

Around the office there's a divide. Some of the older women think *Lean In* is bullshit, a way to get more out of us for nothing. The younger staff are uniformly starstruck by Sheryl's celebrity. I'm somewhere in between the two groups, closer to the younger staff. One of the lobbyists, a woman in her forties, pulls me aside to say, "Don't take the book seriously. It's just a way to make you feel bad about yourself. Which is what Sheryl does." She thinks I have stars in my eyes. I'm embarrassed to admit that maybe I do, so I just nod.

At a *Lean In* roundtable for the dozen female DC staffers the day after the book launch, we're told we should be grateful for the opportunity to sit with Sheryl. Which is true for some of us—the interns raise their hands to volunteer how the book changed them and how they love her dress.

"Narciso," she coos in response. Which, not knowing the designer, I hear as "narcissism" and am very confused given the broader chat in the office.

"Why a book and not something else like another TED talk or

speech or video?" one intern softballs from around the conference table, sidestepping the fact that before Sheryl arrived, we'd all been discussing why she didn't post any of this stuff on Facebook.

"What a great question, an absolutely fantastic, insightful question," Sheryl responds, sparking a wave of thinly veiled jealousy around the room among the interns. "Because I wanted to start a national conversation and the best way to do that is a book. It's the starting point for not just a conversation, but a movement."

Of course, Facebook claims proudly that it's instrumental in starting movements and conversations, in digital disruption, and she's the COO. But it seems clear to me that she hates using the platform personally. Like most of Facebook's senior staff, Sheryl hardly ever posts.

Eventually, the women in the room stray from the book talking points and start asking about Facebook. One of the younger women asks what the biggest risk for Facebook is.

"Us," Sheryl says. "The greatest threat to Facebook is us, it's all of us."

She sits back, taking in the shocked silence around the table. Then she says, "I've seen this happen before. We, the company, get too confident, too complacent. We think we know everything, that we have it all figured out.

"I worry about this for everyone, even me. I worry about the day when people won't tell me the truth straight. When they won't have the hard conversation with me. When I sit in a meeting and everyone will agree with me. They won't give me the bad news. They won't challenge me. We are our own greatest risk. All of us."

I hang on every word. This seems like such impressive self-knowledge and insight that I want to bottle it. I write it down thinking that we can add it to her speeches elsewhere.

It's unthinkable that we wouldn't speak honestly with Sheryl or share bad news. We say what needs to be said. She's the champion of these "hard conversations" telling people what they need to hear even if it feels difficult to do so.

I underline "it's all of us" three times.

Funny thing about *Lean In*: If you happen to be a youngish, pregnant-looking woman who is the perfect visual accompaniment to some of the book's maxims—for example, "Don't leave before you leave," Sheryl's thesis that you should scale back at work only after a child arrives, not before—you might find that your book duties extend beyond the launch party. You may soon find yourself winging your way abroad as part of Sheryl's international book tour. I'm told I'm going to Japan.

Japan has always been a difficult country for Facebook. Our growth rates there have never matched those in the rest of the world. The most compelling theory is that Japan has a culture that doesn't like sharing personal information online. Facebook's lack of popularity in Japan and the fact that Sheryl is not CEO (visiting a country that is very conscious of status and gender) meant that I was flummoxed when Sheryl announced she wanted to meet Prime Minister Shinzo Abe as part of her book tour. How do you casually set up a meeting with a head of state from a G7 country for a tech company that is not even popular in that country, not to mention that the meeting might also be a Trojan horse for book promotion? The answer, I learn from trial and error, is that it's a lot like getting my job at Facebook. Basically I ask over and over until someone says they might be able to help. I tell Abe's office that *Lean In* will be helpful for his "womenomics" agenda, which is trying to encourage Japanese women to stay in the workforce, and trying to boost the percentage of women in leadership.

They buy it. Abe says yes.

We land in Tokyo and arrive at the flashiest hotel I've ever stayed at. It's humbling. Sheryl's room at the Ritz-Carlton Japan is several times larger than my apartment. She's decided to bring her children and parents on this trip. I'm excited to meet them until she requests that her parents accompany us to meet Prime Minister Abe. So now I have two delightful retirees looking forward to meeting the prime minister of Japan after they finish their tea ceremony or whatever. In my time in the foreign service, I'd never seen a head of state show up with their mom and dad, and I don't really know how to handle this ridiculous request. I call up my best friend, Bec, who used to work at the International Court of Justice. Bec assures me she's seen heads of state take meetings with their families alongside them and I could just sneak Adele and Joel Sandberg in. I ask where she's seen this, who, and how.

"Robert Mugabe. I think he routinely takes meetings with members of his family," she says, laughing, before I hang up despondent, sure this will be a disaster.

Fortunately, Abe's office is categorical and says no parents can attend the meeting with the prime minister of Japan. Sheryl begrudgingly accepts this.

I may have already been looking for evidence to confirm my sense of foreboding but when I arrive at Sheryl's suite at the Ritz-Carlton the morning of the meeting, I see a stunningly beautiful Japanese woman, perfectly made up and stylishly dressed, quietly crying outside it.

"Are you okay?" I ask tentatively.

She nods. The tears streaming down her cheeks somehow make her even more impossibly lovely.

At that moment Debbie comes bundling out of Sheryl's suite and pulls me close.

"I wouldn't go in there."

"Why?"

"You were going to go in there, weren't you?"

"Um, yeah—what's happening?"

"Major issue with the makeup and hair."

"Is that who's crying outside the door? The makeup artist?"

"Ah, yeah. The makeup was a disaster and let's not mention the hair. I mean, I think it was basically fine, but Sheryl hated it and some of her instructions were lost in translation and it's all come to a head."

"Or on her head?" I try to pun. Debbie ignores it.

"Oh god. Is it a cultural thing?" I ask. "Like was the makeup artist doing what she thinks Western women want? Quite eighties? It's still really early. Can you get someone else?"

"Ah, that was the someone else. She already fired the first makeup artist."

"Ouch. She made her cry too? Okay, so I'm guessing a third makeup artist isn't going to happen."

"No, I think she's going to do it herself, but this does not bode well for the day ahead."

This is a side of Sheryl I have not seen before. Debbie lets me know I'd better get used to it.

I take her warning and go back to my room to continue prepping for the meeting with Prime Minister Abe. Sheryl's approach is very different from Mark's. He wants briefings no longer than a text he can read on the screen of his phone without scrolling. Sheryl wants as much detail as possible.

More than anything, what she really wants is a photo of Prime Minister Abe holding her book. And that's the one thing that the Japanese prime minister's office has very politely but firmly insisted could not be done. Sheryl decides she'll simply hijack the prime minister with a presentation of the book at the end of the meeting. I'm carrying the book. I've added an inscription to the prime minister and his wife. It feels like smuggling illicit contraband. I hate myself for being part of this.

Arriving at the prime minister's sleek office, I'm surprised by the crowds of photographers and self-conscious about my pregnant body. I'm not enjoying my role as the designated *Lean In* visual aid. Sheryl and the prime minister mug for the cameras, doing the Facebook thumbs-up sign. Then the press is dismissed and they sit and talk. It's the two of them, each with a couple of advisers and interpreters, whom we don't use. Abe does the whole meeting in perfect English.

It goes better than I ever imagined. Sheryl hits every single talking point. There's actual policy discussion about data centers, consumer protection and privacy. The *Lean In* connection to womenomics works—he's interested, and it doesn't seem out of place. It's proper diplomacy. His team used everything we gave them and Abe came prepared to respond to all the issues we'd raised. Sheryl pitches changing Japanese law to allow politicians to use Facebook for elections. We tell him about the disaster response tool we're developing in the wake of the tsunami, which interests him. By the time they're done talking, it feels like we have a real relationship with him and his key advisers. It's our first successful meeting with a head of state. The whole thing is like a symphony I orchestrated.

Sheryl and the prime minister stand up. This is the moment I've been dreading. I have my hand firmly on the gift copy of *Lean In* and thrust it toward the prime minister like it's a bomb about to detonate. I then leap out in front of the two of them with my phone, quickly snapping off three photos before his team can stop me. Or maybe they're just reluctant to wrestle away a pregnant lady.

We return to our van outside his office, ignoring the questions the media are shouting, and Sheryl asks me to sit beside her. Unexpectedly, she wraps herself around me and gives me a deep, long hug.

"That was amazing, Sarah. I don't know how you pulled it off, but it was phenomenal."

I'm trying not to blush. "It was a team effort. Really, everyone here in this van, it couldn't have happened without them."

Her tone changes. "Learn how to take a compliment," she snaps. "This was all you and it was wonderful." I feel like I'm being told off.

After a day of media events and Sheryl's *Lean In* town hall, Debbie and the others urge me to come with them for a drink, but I'm tired and pregnant and opt to go back in the van in a group that includes Sheryl and her parents. I sit in the back seat trying to be as inconspicuous as possible, letting the warm glow of the day wash over me. The others are talking through the events of the day.

I'm not really listening until I hear Sheryl's voice change sharply at the mention of her children having had lunch at McDonald's. She's furious that her children have eaten at the fast food restaurant; she would never let them eat "that sort of food."

We all stare out of the van at the lights of Tokyo flashing past. It is gently suggested that this was a thoughtful decision. Informed not just by the children wanting some comfort in an unfamiliar place with unfamiliar food, but by a photo she posted on Facebook. Taken at McDonald's corporate headquarters, Sheryl beaming as she's eating Chicken McNuggets and burgers. She barks back that "of course she wasn't really eating." That was just a photo. She doesn't eat McDonald's and neither should her children. What if they were seen eating that crap?

Everyone in the car slips into painful silence. I'm scared that Sheryl will remember I'm there in the back seat. I focus on folding my pregnant self into the smallest space possible, barely daring to breathe.

My mind involuntarily keeps repeating the John Updike quote "Celebrity is a mask that eats into the face." The glow from the day's success is now completely gone and I just feel sad. Sad because every person there is trying to do the right thing. Sad because Sheryl can't see the good intentions of everyone in that van. Sad because it's so understandable to take a photo at face value. To believe it is real. How was anyone supposed to know those publicity photos were just the mask Sheryl chose? And, finally, I feel a deep sadness for Sheryl, who let the mask eat into her face.

We all fly out the next morning—them on United to San Francisco, me on Asiana to New York—and spirits are low. As soon as I land in the US and switch on my phone, a bunch of messages pop up, checking to make sure I'm okay. Weird. Googling, I learn that an Asiana plane, one that departed a little earlier than mine, had crash-landed at San Francisco International Airport, killing three people and injuring over two hundred. I flip through the news and see reports that Sheryl, Debbie, and others on our team were supposed to be on that flight. They apparently got this from Sheryl, who (for a change) posted on Facebook that she and our colleagues "were originally going to take the Asiana flight that just crash-landed. We switched to United so we could use miles for my family's tickets." This of course unleashes a storm of concerned comments.

Immediately I stop scrolling and call Debbie.

"Are you okay?"

"Yeah, I'm tired and my neck . . ."

"No," I cut in. "I saw you guys were supposed to be on the Asiana flight. Did something change?"

"You mean Sheryl's Facebook post about being booked on that flight? It's totally weird."

"You weren't on that flight. I mean you guys were giving me shit for flying Asiana, calling it a budget airline."

"I know, it's so strange. Sheryl always flies United. That's who she has status with. We never considered Asiana. I don't know why she posted it. I don't know why she tagged all of us. Now I've got to deal with incoming media queries about it, though apparently she's just emailing reporters herself."

"I don't get it," I said. "I know I'm jet lagged but this doesn't make any sense."

"I know. It's fucked up. You should get some rest."

I hang up, but I'm unnerved and the feeling of disquiet never really leaves. A friend who has seen the reports and knows I'm traveling with Sheryl messages to check that everything's okay. Initially I repeat what is in the press, thinking that's what I'm supposed to do, before calling her back to tell her the truth. People don't lie about narrowly missing plane crashes, do they? Why would she? It's not like she needs attention.

I never see Sheryl the same way after that.

10

Only Good News

It's not like I didn't know about Sheryl's temper before the Japan trip. I'd seen her blow up many times, at lots of people, berating them, humiliating them, including Marne, one of her best friends. But after Japan, what hits me, over and over, is how arbitrary it is. I never can predict what will trigger an outburst, which makes it especially unnerving.

One memorable example, nine of us are in Sheryl's conference room. The name she's given this room is as ominous as you could get, given her anger-management issues: Only Good News. We're waiting for a meeting to begin. The start time comes and goes and we all sit there, eight of us, looking at her expectantly.

"Where's Debbie?" she demands. I'm confused. Debbie's been involved in the issue we're discussing to provide comms advice, but she's not leading the meeting. Someone reassures Sheryl that she'll be here soon but we can get things started.

"Call her," Sheryl commands.

Someone punches Debbie's number into the Polycom in the middle of the table and gently asks her where she is.

"I'm nearly there," she assures the gathered group. "Start without me. I'll be with you shortly."

"Where are you?" Sheryl demands.

"I'm just turning into campus," Debbie assures her. "At the traffic lights."

We all look at Sheryl, ready for her to start the meeting. But she just sits there and waits. And so do we. It's just awkward silence. Minutes pass. Eventually we're past any reasonable amount of time it could take to get from the traffic lights to Sheryl's conference room.

It probably wasn't much more than ten minutes.

Finally Debbie enters the room in a bluster of apologies. Sheryl looks at her accusingly and says, "You weren't at the traffic lights."

"Sorry, traffic was a nightmare. I'd just come off the highway . . ."

Sheryl cuts her off and, in front of her colleagues, gives her a dressing down about blaming the traffic rather than accepting responsibility for not anticipating traffic. She asks how many times she's driven this particular road, why she hadn't considered the needs of her coworkers in deciding when to leave her house, what time might have been more appropriate to set off from San Francisco to reach Menlo Park. She vents that Debbie has wasted her coworkers' time (making no mention of her own decision to waste our time with this performance).

By now I know there's probably no specific reason for this outburst. Debbie's not in the habit of being late. I'd be shocked if she had been underperforming in the days or weeks before this. It's just Sheryl, in an arbitrary flex of power. That seems to be how she operates, unpredictable, keeping us all on edge. Never quite knowing when she'll strike, so we're never tempted to push any boundaries, even the simplest ones. Strict rules, selectively enforced and the baseline of ever-present fear. It ensures we obey in advance. Why does someone need to be so mean to the people helping her? I've been at Facebook for a few years now, and I've hit a point like the phase of a romance where you still see everything great that attracted you to the person in the first place. You're still excited by the future you're building together. But you've spent enough time together that you also see their flaws. And wonder how deep they run. I don't know if Sheryl's outbursts are an occasional thing—which I can cope with—or if that's who she is. And I'm nervous it's the latter.

I feel this way about the job in general. I'm the person Facebook flies in to deal with governments around the world. It still feels exciting and important to spread this tool around the world to improve people's lives. But at the same time, there's the disturbing things we're starting to hear about bad experiences users have on the platform, like kids being bullied, privacy violations, harassment and crime triggered by Facebook posts. And there are moments like this.

I'm worried that I'm getting used to these things.

We all sit there and witness Debbie's humiliation. This is someone who normally owns the room. Sassy. Now flustered and small and apologizing over and over: "I'm so sorry," "You're right," "I should've left earlier," "So sorry, Sheryl."

I feel terrible for her, but none of us leap to her defense. There'd be no point.

Or there is the time at the World Economic Forum in Davos, Switzerland, in 2013, when there's a badge missing for one of Sheryl's assistants. The guilty party is back home in Silicon Valley, so Sheryl lets loose on the people who happen to be standing in front of her, me and her best friend, Marne.

We're standing in the registration tent. Lots of people are milling around and witness her tirade. "Why did no one think about this? Do I have to do all these things myself? Why do I have a team that doesn't think through the most basic requirements? What is the point of having you . . ." I start to respond that our jobs are in policy, neither of us is responsible for the badges, but Marne stops me. "Take it," she says to me quietly. "Just take responsibility." So I do, kowtowing to Sheryl as Marne grovels alongside me. Then she and I march into a WEF workroom and literally stand over a staffer, refusing to leave until they print a badge.

Other times, of course, Sheryl is charming, charismatic, whip-smart. She's all these things at once. There's talk of her running for office, or taking a job in the Obama administration. There's an influx of people to Facebook who want to work for her. They're drawn to her like moths to a flame. There's a growing class of people looking to align themselves with a billionaire on the up, but people are drawn to Sheryl in particular. It's a running joke in the DC office, where we know they've only seen one side of her: "Incoming moth number twenty-seven. Prepare for impact."

Sometimes, of course, you can predict that something will upset Sheryl. When I learn that Angela Merkel—the German chancellor—has declined Sheryl's request for a meeting, Marne tells me not to tell her. "We never can let her know," she says. "Just say it's a scheduling issue." We both know how angry Sheryl would be if she found out that Merkel doesn't think Sheryl's important enough to talk to.

So that's what I do. I lie to Sheryl. This doesn't feel right. Weeks later, Marne cracks and tells her. I don't know why. Exactly as she predicted, Sheryl's hurt and furious. Not at us for lying (although she probably should be worried about that). She's mad at Merkel and at us for not overcoming any reservations Merkel had about meeting. For months after that, anytime her name comes up, Sheryl bitterly reminds everyone how Merkel wouldn't meet with her. It gets to a point where we all try to avoid mentioning Germany at all.

In January 2014, I'm in a meeting with an all-male lineup of Facebook law enforcement experts when my water breaks. I Uber to the hospital and things get underway pretty fast. I get a message. Sheryl's about to unexpectedly go into a meeting with the president of Brazil at Davos and she wants talking points. I'm in the delivery room, my feet in stirrups, in labor. I put down my phone and reach for my laptop. I start drafting.

"What are you doing?" Tom asks.

"Just getting Sheryl some talking points."

"Sarah, no."

I continue typing. He appeals to my doctor, a person he knows I deeply respect: "Dr. Veca, make this stop."

"Two more minutes," I say, between contractions. Trying not to think of *Lean In*'s direction: *don't leave before you leave.*

Dr. Veca reaches over and gently closes my laptop. She says, "It's a very special thing to give birth to your first child. I don't think you should be working through it. Sheryl will understand."

"She won't," I say. "Please let me push Send."

"You should be pushing," she says. "But not send."

Despite the disapproval in the room, I quickly reopen the laptop. I send the email. I know how this looks, and I can't defend it. Looking back, I still can't quite believe it. I'm ashamed. And I can't blame this entirely on Facebook. I've been this kind of driven person my whole life. I don't like to let people down. But it's also true that at Facebook, I didn't feel like I had a choice.

Not long after, our daughter Sasha is born.

Compared with New Zealand, where there's six months' paid leave and many people take a year, maternity leave is short in the US, and I feel pressure to return to work even before I use it up. I'm not really sure how to combine this job with motherhood. Especially since this job never stops. When I have to travel to work in the Silicon Valley office, I take the baby and pay coworkers' nannies to watch her. For the part of my job that falls outside traditional work hours, Sasha comes with me. To a rally in Madison Square Garden for India's newly elected prime minister Narendra Modi. To Canada, where Facebook has been ordered to testify in Parliament, and where I'm detained at the border, until a phone call to Tom satisfies border officials that I am not absconding to Ottawa after kidnapping a tiny baby.

I thought I was doing a good job in a difficult situation. But my first performance review after maternity leave is problematic. While it's positive, the only negative feedback relates to my baby. The fact that people can hear her in the background on calls—mostly because West Coast time means I'm often taking the calls on the East Coast in the evening, at home, where my baby lives. Travel is more complicated. I'd relocated to New York, and that meant I now had to travel to Washington, DC, regularly. Where I'm from it's more usual for a baby to be with its mother or family for the first six months of life if not longer. My family is trying to come up with creative ways to make that happen with my mother, grandmother, and sister all traveling to New York to help.

A few weeks after the review, Marne and I are at Facebook's headquarters when Sheryl pulls me aside.

"Marne told me about your childcare situation," she says breezily. I'm mortified this is something that has been discussed with the COO. But I understand this is her way of caring. She's trying to be nice. She's saying this because she likes me.

"Hire a nanny," she instructs. "Be smart and hire a Filipina nanny."

She mistakes my look of horror for skepticism.

"Sarah, I'm telling you, they're English speaking, sunny disposition, and *service orientated*." Marne echoes this sentiment. Both have at least one Filipina nanny in their retinue of staff.

I call Tom and tell him about these conversations, telling him the COO of Facebook is now involved in our childcare.

"This is appalling," he says. "How can employers say such things?"

"I guess this is the real *Lean In*. The stuff Sheryl really believes about work and womanhood but doesn't put in the book."

I don't want it to be an issue for my performance reviews in the future, so Tom and I follow their instructions.

The day our new Filipina nanny starts, I'm in Mexico with Mark, meeting with the Mexican president. He was completely against this meeting, and I don't feel like I can opt out, after browbeating him into it as part of my push to have Mark engage at the presidential level to understand how Facebook is impacting other countries. It's my first time leaving Sasha and I cry the whole way to the airport.

Tom is a vigilant father in ordinary times. The first day the baby's alone with the nanny he's extreme. Obsessively checking the baby monitor, which streams video. He's set it up on his mobile and the desktop at his office. During one of these checks, he sees the baby alone in her playpen, the nanny conspicuously absent. At first, he's curious. But the longer he watches, with no nanny in sight, the more alarmed he becomes. He tries to call our new nanny. She doesn't pick up. Panicked, he continues to obsessively check the monitor and call the nanny and then everyone we know in the neighborhood. Nobody's home. Eventually in the background he sees a firefighter in full fire gear walking through our small apartment. He immediately abandons his desk and calls 911 demanding to know why emergency services are in our home. They can't help. He calls me in Mexico City.

"The baby," he says as soon as I pick up. "The baby is alone and there's a firefighter in our apartment."

Panic doesn't begin to capture the terror I feel as he relays what's happening.

I'm in a car with Elliot and Javi, speeding from the Mexican president's house to a Carlos Slim event. As Tom speeds through the streets of Manhattan as fast as the taxi agrees to drive him, I don't think I've ever heard him more scared.

Ultimately, Sasha's fine. Our small New York third-floor walk-up has some cupboards outside the front door. Our nanny went to get something from the cupboard and found herself locked out, with her phone inside the apartment. Eventually, she used a stranger's phone to call emergency services, who broke in through the roof.

With everyone safe and accounted for, we eventually forget about it, until my next performance review when Marne raises it:

"You shouldn't tell stories like that, about your baby and nanny."

My heart sinks. She wasn't even in Mexico.

"It wasn't a story. My baby was trapped by herself and the fire department was called. We didn't know if something terrible had happened."

"That's not the point. These are personal issues. I'm trying to help. To give you honest feedback. When you're with the most senior members on the team, Mark, Elliot, Javi, you need to be professional and focused on them."

Seriously? My baby's alone in an apartment with emergency services breaking in through the roof and I'm not supposed to mention it because it's personal? And they all discussed this situation afterward and found me lacking?

The expectation at Facebook is that mothering is invisible, and the more skilled you are, the more invisible it is. Months later when the baby's rushed to the hospital in an ambulance, I don't mention it at the office for days. Then I only mention it in passing, assuring Marne that it won't affect my work in any way.

This "don't mention the children" ethos is of course the opposite of the cheery slogans at Facebook to "bring your authentic self to work." All Sheryl's *Lean In* stories about leaving work at 5:30 P.M. and telling her coworkers she needed to be home with her children. Because the reality is that there is a big difference between what people at Facebook say and what they do, especially in relation to children. For example, Facebook had planned to launch a Facebook for children codenamed "Project Family," and Sheryl would occasionally remind the policy team of their "failure to do this while we had the opportunity," blaming the policy team for missing the chance to get kids on Facebook but she, like most of the leaders at Facebook with younger children, severely limits her kids' access to screens, let alone social media accounts. And she never shares images of her children on social media. Silicon Valley is awash in wooden Montessori toys and shrouded in total screen bans. Parents at work talk about how they don't allow their teens to have mobile phones, which only underscores how well these executives understand the real damage their product inflicts on young minds.

This year, like every year, Sheryl hosts Women's Day, an offsite conference for all the women who work for Facebook. At that point, it's hundreds of women, whom she flies in to stay at a hotel in San Francisco. We're asked to share hotel rooms, an odd professional situation for grown women, forcing us to navigate sleeping, sharing bathrooms, and wearing pajamas with our colleagues.

Women's Day is part evangelical church event, part multilevel marketing summit, part Tony Robbins seminar, part yoga retreat, part *Oprah* episode. Sheryl presides, dressed in Lululemon yoga pants and Ugg boots. There's a lot of talk about motherhood. Sheryl's favored lieutenants, in shiny uniformity, provide relatable stories of how they balance parenting and demanding careers. The head of HR mock-confides in a scandalously humorous tone that she sometimes gives her children cereal for dinner. Sheryl tells a story from *Lean In* about bringing her four-year-old daughter on a friend's corporate jet, the eBay Gulfstream, where her daughter announces, "Mommy, my head itches!" Sheryl checks. Her daughter has lice. "I was the only person bringing young children on this corporate plane," she says. "I spent the rest of the flight in a complete panic, trying to keep her isolated, her voice down." This is offered as a story any mom can connect to. As if we all have friends with Gulfstreams. There are videos of women from Sheryl's inner circle—all white, beautifully lit and shot—working out in their palatial home gyms, playing with their photogenic children, and relaxing with their mutely supportive husbands. All of these mothering fables are careful to edit out the role played by the phalanx of nannies and other help who usually do the bulk of the actual labor of raising children.

Mothering in form, not function.

They don't discuss the real secret behind maintaining their work-life balance, mothering as if they don't have children: it's under-girded by their multimillion-dollar paychecks.

There's usually some trauma porn, heroic tales of less high-profile employees working through cancer or some other tragedy, but with a video montage they always triumph and return to Facebook working harder and better than they did before. The point, I suppose, is to measure your life against theirs, and inspire you to work harder.

Sheryl pushes the same kinds of messages in weekly updates she sends to senior executives called HPM (Highlights, People, Me). Stories like the time Sheryl and her family went on holiday with Marne and her family in Europe:

> Due to work issues and the time change, I wound up missing most/all breakfasts and dinners as I was on the phone. . . . During one of the last dinners, my kids came to find me—I was sitting in a staircase outside the restaurant on the phone. They looked upset and started to tell me that they thought I should be at the dinner but I had to tell them that I had to finish the call and then talk. When I was off I came to find them, expecting them to be upset. Instead, they gave me a big hug and said, "we just want to thank you for working so hard to help billions of people!" I looked at Marne, who was on vacation with us and another family, and asked what happened. Marne had seen them upset and explained that she knew I did not want to miss meals and I was upset too but I had a job I needed to do and they should be proud of me. . . . It was a brilliant reframe that I know I will try again when I need it. And might help some of you when you need it for professional or personal reasons one day too.

Sheryl's messages weren't subtle.

11

Road Trip

Lots of moms have issues combining breastfeeding and working. My issue is the expectation from my bosses that breasts can be turned on and off like a faucet and I can breastfeed anywhere, anytime. And I really mean anywhere.

In summer 2014, Colombia's minister of information technology and communication invites Javi to Colombia 3.0, a tech conference in Bogotá. I think Javi can handle this one on his own, and I have a five-month-old at home. My bosses think differently. I'm ordered to go. I reconcile myself to this. It's three days. I can't bring the baby but I can bring a breast pump. I can handle it.

We're in Colombia because of something called Internet.org. Mark launched it nearly a year ago, in August 2013, with a paper grandly titled "Is Connectivity a Human Right?" In his opening paragraph, he lays out what he calls "one of the greatest challenges of our generation":

Today we connect more than 1.15 billion people each month. But as we started thinking about connecting the next 5 billion, we realized something important: the vast majority of people in the world don't have access to the internet.

Mark then presents his vision for how to give free internet to all those people. He explains that we could radically reduce the cost of building the infrastructure and delivering data, if we start them off with very basic service. The key is that it would be all text. No movies, no high-resolution photos, no music—those all use too much data. He says the priority should be tools to get people the information they need. For Mark that means search, some version of Wikipedia, weather, messaging, and—of course—social media. Websites would be modified into text-only versions. Already, Facebook has an app like this called Facebook Zero, with lots of users across Africa and Asia.

Who'll bear the cost of all these free services? The mobile operators—telecom companies around the world. They're the ones who'll invest. Mark argues that this scheme makes smart business sense for them because it delivers hundreds of millions of new customers who eventually will want to upgrade and buy data plans for their phones. One of his big talking points is that once people get a taste of what's on the internet, they'll want to pay for more data and more access. In Africa, Facebook users are already making the switch to broadband, so they can get pictures and everything else you don't get on the text-only product. The "org" in "Internet.org" is a way of suggesting there is an altruistic mission at the heart of this.

So that's the vision.

A few months later, Mark announces partnerships that Facebook's Connectivity Lab has established, "to build drones, satellites and lasers to deliver the internet" to the billions of people who don't have it.

I'll admit, I and the rest of the policy team don't pay much attention to all this. Internet.org is in such a nascent stage, and just one of the projects Facebook has going at the time. Facebook buys both WhatsApp and the virtual reality company Oculus within a

month of Mark's announcement to build a fleet of low-flying internet drones. But from the little I know it sounds like a good thing.

Then, in May 2014, Chile's telecommunications regulator makes
it illegal to give away the kinds of free services Internet.org plans to
offer, effectively banning the venture before it's even launched. I hear
about this from Javi, who's alarmed. "Chile is small but if this starts
spreading to other countries," he says, "we will have a problem." We
decide we need a quick win, some Latin American government saying yes to Internet.org. To help convince them, I suggest to Javi that
we add free e-government services to the Internet.org apps, things
like paying your taxes or signing up for social services. That will give
each government skin in the game.

And we're here in Colombia to try to convince its president Juan
Manuel Santos to be our partner. I need some big name to stand
on a stage with us to tell the world—especially other presidents and
prime ministers—they love Internet.org and make the Chileans re-
consider their decision.

The way I get President Santos is first to court his minister of
information technology and communication. Javi signs us up to
see firsthand the challenges of connectivity in the jungle. The
minister describes it to Javi as getting to know the "real Colombia"
through a road trip. We fly to Bucaramanga in the north. When
we land, we're led to a line of armored vehicles occupied by lots
of military men with large guns and dark green uniforms. Turns
out, the area is a stronghold for the militia of the Revolutionary
Armed Forces of Colombia (FARC), revolutionary guerrillas who
are still fighting and kidnapping foreigners, despite ongoing peace
negotiations.

My sense of alarm rises when it's explained that the minister will
not be riding in the big black ministerial jeep, or the decoy big black
ministerial jeep, which we're told to ride in, but instead in one of the
many security vehicles accompanying them, perched among a group
of soldiers with automatic weapons. I ask Javi if it's such a good idea

to get in a car that's too dangerous for the government official to ride in. He's like, let's just roll with it. We get in.

We drive for hours into the jungle, off-road. I mean, there are no roads. And obviously no electricity. No privacy. It's hard to imagine a worse place to try to use a bulky electric breast pump that needs to be plugged into a wall. Four or five hours into this, I'm in physical pain. But I don't dwell on that because I'm so afraid we'll be attacked. We seem like a ridiculously conspicuous target, churning our way through the wilderness. I think, if we're kidnapped, pumping will be out of the question. And ultimately it is for this trip. Despite the excruciating pain, I don't pump until I'm safely back in Bogotá that night.

But this wasn't even my worst experience. Two months later, September 2014, I go to Turkey. After my experience in Colombia, I'm nervous about pumping. I'm right to be. The pump needs to be plugged in, and once our Turkish Airlines flight hits cruising altitude, I discover that neither the bathroom nor the seat has any outlets. Over the next ten hours my anxiety rises as my breasts swell and harden with milk. I'm in a black cardigan and white T-shirt, and by the time I make it through customs and immigration the white T-shirt is soaked and I'm in agony. Predictably the cab line is long and the traffic in central Istanbul is terrible. By the time we make it to the hotel I am beyond desperate to pump. There's a massive line to check in and I find myself tapping my foot and squeezing my palms, ready to burst.

As soon as I'm safely in my room I simply drop the suitcase, grab the pump as fast as I can, and plug it in—not even bothering to remove my T-shirt, which is now a translucent rag. I just use the V-neck. I attach the arcane pieces of equipment and flip the switch to start the pump. It turns over.

Click. . . . Click. . . . Click.

I check that the room key is in the slot for electricity just in case that's the issue, but no. Nothing. I navigate my way back to reception, where there's still a long line. When I get to the front and try to explain the problem, the woman at the desk looks confused and apologizes, saying that her English isn't very good. I switch to hand gestures, lots of circular motions and squeezing my hands. I'm so close to tears of frustration and pain, and at a certain point I just gesture at my breasts and sopping T-shirt and make a squeezing motion. She finally smiles knowingly, gives me a wink, and assures me she'll have it sorted in no time. I head back to my room.

As soon as I hear the knock at my door I race to open it. There's a man in overalls, dark shaggy hair, stubble, gray eyes. I give him the most welcoming smile and hurry him into my room, closing the door. I bring him over to the pump by the bed and explain the clicking noise. It becomes clear that he does not speak English at all. But what's weird is that he seems uninterested in the pump. I've perched beside him on the bed trying to explain the issue, and at a certain point I realize he's gently guiding me *into* the bed and has something else entirely on his mind.

I shake my head no. And point back at the pump.

He looks confused, gestures at my wet T-shirt and my breasts popping out of the V-neck, and lifts his hands. He does the same air-pumping motions I'd performed in the lobby earlier.

I suddenly realize the kind of pumping he has in mind. And it's not going to help me.

I point to my wedding ring and shake my head no.

He musters some English: "No problem. No problem. It's no problem for me."

"Yes—but it's a problem for me. There's been some kind of mis-understanding. This is not what I need."

I walk to the other side of the room. Open the door. And walk out.

At a nearby pharmacy, I buy what I surmise is a hand pump. Finally, relief. Roughly half a day after I first needed it.

12

The Body

We're about to travel to the one country in the world where there's an open arrest warrant for Mark Zuckerberg. And Mark thinks this is the time to show us his fake gangsta handshakes.

Debbie and I are trying to teach him the respectful bow one's supposed to do when meeting the leader of South Korea. Sheryl of course diligently absorbed all our advice on bows, greetings, gifts, and other protocol issues that arise when meeting with a head of state, but Mark treats it like a weird goofing-off session. Debbie and I demonstrate where to put your hands when you bow to a president, how to arrange your face, how deep the bow goes. He crosses his arms like the Kangol-hat-era LL Cool J and rocks his body from side to side hip-hop-style, before moving to a series of fist bumps, high fives, and backward low fives.

Let's not even get into how odd the moves look, coming from this slim, pale-to-the-point-of-translucent man with a square haircut and very rigid posture. It's troubling because this matters. When Bill Gates greeted the South Korean president with one hand in his pocket, it was considered so disrespectful it made headlines as "the handshake that bruised a nation." It undermined anything else that came out of those meetings, and my Korean friends still talk about it. Mark doesn't care.

Of course, this is the same man who's shown absolutely no interest in policy issues or countries outside the US since I arrived at Facebook. Or almost no interest. The first time Mark traveled to a country to meet with a foreign head of state since I arrived was in 2012 when he flew to Russia. He met Prime Minister Dmitry Medvedev, and then in 2013 he had a perfunctory meeting with the Korean president, both of which Marne handled. Mark was nervous and sweaty in both.

The few policy meetings that Mark agrees to do after that harden his belief that meeting with foreign leaders is not a good use of his time. Midway through this protocol session, I realize I'm one of the few people who work with him on something he's scared of. His discomfort and fear are visible and can be measured in sweat.

This trip—in October 2014—is the first time I'm going to be working so closely with Mark. Up until now most of our interaction has been over email, or filtered through Sheryl, Elliot, or Marne. It's been functional exchanges, the occasional meeting, not weeks together on the road. Four years after I had pitched Mark on engaging with heads of state, we're now trying to secure meetings with a bunch of them in one trip, including those of Indonesia, Japan, and Korea.

This does not go down well with Sheryl. Meeting with world leaders is her terrain. She instructs Elliot that Mark should not be doing "other stuff" beyond business meetings outside the US. Elliot rolls his eyes at this. Of course the company's CEO should be meeting with presidents and prime ministers. He tells me he'll take care of it and he does.

Mark is bringing the Mteam—the top managers of the company (M for "management")—on this trip. It's the first time they're traveling together outside the US. The full-court press is because the company's growth is increasingly in Asia. This trip will open up a new front in Facebook's slowly expanding war with Google. Despite the fact that, or maybe because, so many of our top managers worked at Google, there's a profound mistrust of the search giant and a discomfort about the way Facebook relies on Google for the company's future success.

Right now, most of our users access Facebook on their Android phones or iPhones. Android's made by Google, so this gives Google and Apple very meaningful control over Facebook. Either could potentially remove Facebook from their app stores and devices, or restrict the way things like notifications work with Facebook. Google—very aware of its power over Facebook—is increasing pressure in a variety of ways, like requesting payment or data in return for Facebook's use of Google Maps. (Years later, when Apple allows iPhone users to opt out of the tracking Facebook does for advertisers, Facebook's market value drops $10 billion.)

At one point, Facebook tried to take more control of its destiny by creating its own phone ("Project Buffy"—named semi-ironically for *Buffy the Vampire Slayer* and "social layer"). It launches in 2013, a collaboration with a Chinese company called HTC, and is a massive flop. *Time* magazine calls it one of the biggest tech failures of the year.

In fact, the trip to Korea is framed to Mteam as a trip to Samsung. The goal for the trip is to deepen trust and build goodwill with a company that isn't Apple or Google. Maybe Samsung will agree to preload Facebook on all Samsung phones.

Unfortunately, Korea is the one country that has an open criminal investigation into Facebook executives. There are arrest warrants for Mark and Sheryl and other Mteam members.

The reason for this is unclear, but it appears that the body that oversees gaming in Korea wrote to us warning that Korean law required Facebook to submit the games on our platform to be rated by the government. It's not clear exactly what happened after the letter was received, but the Koreans say that Facebook ignored it. It's shocking that there was no reply. But it's plausible. The company is still very "move fast and break things" and "ask for forgiveness, not permission."

Now the situation has escalated. The Cybercrime Branch of the Seoul Police has gotten involved. And you don't mess around with Korean police. When they started investigating Google, Google's head of Korea had to flee the country.

Still, Facebook appears to stonewall, claiming that basically no one in Korea—not the Korean government, not the Korean police—has any power over them. This seems to be Facebook's preferred position with all countries outside the US and Ireland (where it has its international headquarters). The company disputes their power to regulate Facebook at all, unless they've enacted specific laws targeting our business and legislating jurisdiction. So, I believe, if a local government notices false advertising on Facebook and asks us to take it down, unless they have a law giving them power or prohibiting misleading ads that specifically applies to social media companies, Facebook won't act. Brazil smartly passed a law saying that everything in all its other laws now applies to all internet companies, but other countries haven't been so farsighted. Facebook's American leadership believes the "values" it defines can trump national laws when they conflict.

That's what seems so outrageous to me about how Korea is being handled. The government there *does* have a law demanding that we get our games rated and approved, and it seems we're refusing to even acknowledge it.

It's a hard argument to make, rejecting the authority of a government or police agency in a country where you operate.

And Korea isn't alone in cracking down on Facebook. Other countries have opened investigations for all sorts of reasons. Our international offices have had "visits" and "raids"—armed and unarmed—in Brazil, Korea, India, and France. I usually hear about these when a phone call or email arrives from our local head of office. ("Hiii! There's a man with a gun here wanting to know when we'll be paying taxes in Brazil.")

By now it happens with enough regularity that we've set up emergency procedures for raids. They include shutting down access to Facebook's network. Because of course the real difference between a "virtual state" like Facebook and a "real state" like Brazil or Korea is they have real police with real arms.

In India the situation's so bad, Facebook's leadership hires an ex–police captain who's been given some boring, official-sounding title but is understood by the policy team to be someone who "would be able to handle an arrest situation well"—that is, go to jail in a clash between Facebook and the Indian government.

In August, just a few weeks before our trip, a Korea crisis meeting is called. Elliot is part of Mteam and going on the trip, so he is suddenly very focused on the potential for him, Mark, and Sheryl to end up in a jail cell. Our lawyers have sent an email that includes the line, "The threat of jail and criminal liability is very real."

I set out various solutions, based on the possibility that Facebook is guilty as charged. Like, we could cooperate with Korea's Cybercrime Police. Or we could shift Facebook's whole approach and review how we obey the laws of the countries in which we're operating.

"Would this apply everywhere?" Marne asks.

"Yes, we can't just make a change for Korea, or other countries will see why that happened and issue arrest warrants for Mark," I say to a dissatisfied room. "I think it's a change we need to make everywhere anyway."

This gets no traction. So I decide not to speak any further, ceding the floor to those more senior than me.

"We need a body to arrest."

"To call their bluff."

"See how serious they are."

It's breathtaking to me, how casually leadership speaks of employees being jailed. As if it's a fact of life like taxes (though of course that's something they try to avoid). Everyone starts calling this a "mitigation strategy"—even though the mitigation in this case is to find a "body" to be arrested.

I lose track of the conversation and get lost in thought about how their language removes the moral questions. "A body to arrest" is more like chattel you own, rather than somebody's son or daughter. Such an odd phrase to hear in corporate America.

This is what we're talking about. Rather than whether our actions in Korea are right or not.

"We need to get someone to test the appetite of the Korean authorities for arresting someone from headquarters. It can't be someone located there. They need to fly in before Mark and Sheryl do. You know, a body," Elliot states matter-of-factly.

The room falls silent. It's a weird thing to realize that the tech world, this most modern of industries, has cannon fodder.

"I can't go," one of the senior security guys in the room quickly says, followed quickly by others. But they didn't need to. Everyone in this room is too senior to be "the body."

Eventually, the silence becomes awkward. I slowly realize everyone is looking at me. The least senior person in the room.

"Me?" I ask, as if there's been a terrible case of mistaken identity.

Elliot nods.

I'm the body.

13

Stockholm Syndrome

I don't think this says anything good about me, but I would've gone and gotten arrested. Somehow, it didn't seem like I had a say in the matter. This was my job. I started to prepare. It took Tom to point out, no, you have a seven-month-old baby at home. Doing jail time in a foreign country is not a reasonable ask from your bosses.

It honestly had not occurred to me that I could say no. I have this thing, which sometimes I think is related to being an eldest daughter, that someone has to take responsibility and do the hard thing and I guess that's going to be me. Also, I had survived a near-deadly shark attack once. So how bad could it be? Somehow, I convinced myself it would be like Myanmar or Colombia, bad with the potential of being awful, but whatever was thrown at me or wherever I was confined, I would figure it out.

Tom's suggestion that I can just refuse to go seems revolutionary. I envy his clarity of thought and, honestly, am filled with relief—and grateful to Tom—for this paradigm-shifting notion that I could tell them no. But I don't say that. I'm too annoyed because he also suggests that I have Stockholm syndrome. That I'm a victim who has come to regard my "captors," Sheryl, Elliot, and Marne, with trust and affection they don't deserve. Something about that comment stings but makes clear what I have to do.

I begin a back-and-forth with Elliot, with Marne, and with the legal and security teams, trying to extract myself from that Korean jail cell that's started to feel very real. I throw out different arguments hoping desperately that one will work: that with a tiny breastfeeding baby at home it isn't really feasible for me to be indefinitely detained in an Asian prison. That there are other crises around the world that need my attention. At times, it feels like it would be easier negotiating with the Korean authorities for my freedom.

Finally, the thing that clinches it appears to be that they need me to be at work, not in jail, in order to make Mark's Asia trip a success.

That's what gets them. Not concern for me and my family.

I take this in. This is the first time I've refused to do something they've asked, and it's a clarifying lesson. I can see my bosses a little more clearly. And now I understand more about how they see me. It's an uncomfortable realization of how little they care, these people I'm with for sixty, seventy, eighty hours a week. Facebook's leaders aren't the people I hoped they were. And in retrospect, I should have thought a lot harder about this fact than I did. But for the first time, I think maybe this place shouldn't be my home, not forever. Of course, I talk myself out of any drastic action like quitting and finding a job somewhere else. The logistics of doing that with a new baby seem daunting.

Predictably, one of the only other female directors on our team is sent instead of me. She's new to the team and looking to prove herself. Or maybe she didn't feel like she had a choice either.

She meets with Korean authorities and doesn't get arrested. So—presumably—the coast is clear for Mark and Sheryl and Elliot. We prepare for the trip.

14

Five Settlers and
One Billionaire in Catan

As I understand it, the first time you ride on a private jet you're supposed to act like you always ride on private jets. Or at least that's what everyone else did.

Long before we make it to this point, I've unintentionally made it obvious that I am a random person from New Zealand, not a seasoned executive used to private jet travel, by earnestly explaining to Mark—in one of our trip preparation meetings—the different options for layovers en route to Asia, and the amenities in various airports. I tried to convince him we should stop in Singapore's airport between flights, as it has a great swimming pool.

Not one of the many coworkers in that meeting, including those I consider friends, corrected me. Nor did Mark.

When I'm told I'll be traveling on the private jet with Mark and the Mteam, my first thought is all the frequent-flier miles I was hoping to rack up on the trip. I'd been saving them, hoping to upgrade my grandmother when she flies to New York to meet her great-grandchild. I broach this with Debbie, who's also going with Mark on the trip.

"Do you think anyone would mind too much if I just take a normal flight?"

"Are you an idiot?" Debbie says, assuming that's the end of the conversation.

"Why would you say that?" It seemed a reasonable question. Facebook has a generous travel policy.

"Do you know how valuable those seats are?" she asks, as if speaking to a small child.

"I know literally nothing about private jets. I don't even know if I've ever seen one."

"Don't you understand that people would give anything to spend hours jetting around the world with Mark Zuckerberg?"

This definitely had not factored into my thinking.

"There's competition about who gets to be on those flights," she continues. "And it's cutthroat."

"Okay, okay, okay," I interrupt. "Forget I asked."

Once I'm onboard, I'm surprised by so many things on the private jet. Like how difficult it is to figure out where the toilet is in the bathroom. The whole bathroom is so refined that I push and pull on lots of levers and handles in its leathery expanse. These reveal cupboards and drawers, but no toilet appears. I can't reemerge from the bathroom to ask without looking like an imbecile, and the flight is long enough that there's no choice but to persevere and figure it out. Eventually I prod or lift something I thought was a bench and miraculously a silver bowl appears from discreet surrounds.

I'm also surprised by how beige and tan everything is. Not just the bathroom, everything. Like an eighties boardroom. It's boring. And devoid of the things I usually rely on to get through flights: solid in-flight entertainment, lots of food, and a little alcohol. There's only one screen and the only thing on it is a flight map. No one seems to request anything else. Mark doesn't have a working TV at home and seems completely uninterested in anything like watching a movie. In terms of food, it's Mark's favorite foods, which at this moment are fried chicken and McDonald's (which I feel sure would horrify

Sheryl) or other fast-food options, the type of fatty, salty food you eat when drinking. Although there's no chance of that here.

There's also the fraught decision of where to sit. There's obviously an internal hierarchy within the team but I have no idea how this maps to the geography of the plane. So as everybody boards and starts to settle in, I stand around in the center of the jet like an idiot, hoping everyone will take a place and through the process of elimination it will become clear which seat is mine. When I end up sitting beside Mark, I can't tell if this strategy has worked or backfired but I suspect the latter.

Traveling with Mark's inner circle makes me feel like an outsider. These are people who are there to look after him, they're used to spending day after day together, and they're used to a different kind of luxury. All of this becomes very clear once we land in Indonesia. The place we're staying—the Amanjiwo resort—is spectacular. Mark doesn't have the best room in the place; he basically has an entire compound. To me it looks more like a citadel than a suite. Large stone pillars support an expansive rotunda with an excessively large daybed at its center, commanding gorgeous views of lush rainforest on all sides. Steps cascade down the hill from the daybed to an enormous private swimming pool, which looks like a public swimming pool from my world.

When I arrive there for a senior staff get-together, Mark's stretched out on the daybed in his swimsuit, his white body propped up on some cushions. It feels like I've stumbled into ancient Greece, though a toga and laurel wreath would match the room better than his swimsuit. I half expect someone to appear to feed him grapes, but instead we all make do with an exotic fruit platter.

Mark announces that we should all go for a swim. I'm immediately self-conscious about the whole swimming-with-my-bosses situation.

I had packed a bikini, which led Tom to ask why I need a bikini on a business trip, but I guess my hope was that there'd be an opportunity to swim at some of the hotels by myself. With work and the baby, I couldn't remember the last time I'd been able to go for a swim or do anything indulgent, just for me. My life is entirely in service of the baby, my bosses, or basic survival. Everything else is disappearing through disuse. Rightly or wrongly I'd fixated on this swim, a few minutes by myself submerged and unavailable, as the highlight of the trip. I hadn't planned to climb into my bikini and dive in next to Mark Zuckerberg.

It's one thing to travel with your bosses. It's another thing to get into your bikini while doing so, especially when your stomach has visible shark jaw marks and other very large, unmissable scars all over it from doctors who weren't thinking about your bikini body when they hacked you open. I almost never tell anyone about the shark attack. I don't want to be known as the girl who got bit by a shark. I had that experience already, in high school.

Another issue: I'm still breastfeeding and pumping, and my bikini top hasn't really accounted for that whole situation. It's fitting on me like a pair of pasties. This wasn't a problem when it was just going to be me swimming by myself. Panic sets in, and I look around for another woman to get guidance on whether to swim. Should I just watch everyone else get in the water? Is there a nonswimming activity I could pivot everyone to?

But there are only two other women on this trip. Everyone at the citadel is male, and they're all sitting around talking about computer games. I start to message Debbie, begging her to get here as fast as she can because I have a breast bikini situation, but before I can hit Send I realize Mark is looking over my shoulder.

"What's that?"

My stomach drops, thinking Mark's read my SOS bikini message—which may or may not have included references to him and his swimming trunks.

"It looks like Home. Is that like an ancient version of Chat Heads?" he says, clearly disapproving. I can't tell if it's because Home was a failed product—part of Facebook's disastrous attempt at a Facebook phone—or because he disapproves of my lax approach to updating my phone, or because he'd managed to read my message.

"Ah, yeah. I'm not good about updating any tech. I'm more of a policy person. Do you want to go over any of the briefings, preparation, protocol?" I say, trying to distract from the swimsuit texts clearly visible on my screen.

"Now?" he says, surprised.

"Well, you know, always good to be prepared," I say uneasily, aware this is perhaps the world's most unenticing offer. Let's not swim and relax in stunning surroundings. Let's talk about policy and protocol.

"It's the weekend. We've got plenty of time to prep. I'm going for a swim now. You're coming, right?"

"Ah, yes. I will. I just forgot something in my room, so I'm just going to get that."

"What?"

Panic doesn't serve me well. "Just a thing I forgot."

I turn and head toward the hotel lobby and find the gift shop. Predictably, everything is doll sized to suit the bodies of the 1 percent—or what look like tiny sizes to me and my breastfeeding breasts—but I manage to find a one-piece and a cover-up that provide a modicum of modesty and thankfully cover my shark bite–scarred stomach. The price is astronomical and I blanch when the sales assistant tells me the total, but hand over my credit card because we're in a remote part of the backwaters of Java and I don't see any alternative other than baring my shark scars to my bosses.

I return to the pool to find Debbie posing for Instagram photos in a fantastic skimpy bikini and feel suddenly overdressed in my one-piece and cover-up.

Everyone swims and lazes about. Picks at the fruit platter. Mark sits in his little rotunda, shooting the shit with the guys. I join them and I'm surprised they're talking about babies. I'm thrilled for an opportunity to speak about what is actually preoccupying me, missing my baby. But that's not the direction the conversation goes in. Mark's expecting his first child, and he tells us he might not be present for the birth. As the only person there who's birthed a baby, I'm stunned. And genuinely curious. "What would you be doing instead?" I asked him. Like, what in the world could possibly be more meaningful to him than the birth of his first child? He had no idea. Just "something more important might come up."

He told us he'd discussed this with Priscilla and I was fascinated by her response. Apparently she told Mark that *she* would be totally fine with him skipping the delivery but that he might come to regret missing the birth of his first child.

Well played.

At some point in the afternoon, Mark decides that we should all play board games, but they've been left on the private jet, which is many miles away. I assume that'll be the end of it and we'll come up with some other activity, but hours later one of Mark's security detail returns with the games. After a dinner that, in keeping with the surroundings, felt more like a sumptuous feast of ancient times with rose petals scattered everywhere and more courses than I could count, we retire to one of the rooms in Mark's complex and start to play Settlers of Catan. It's me, Debbie, Mark's assistant Andrea, Mark, and two of the guys from the communications team, Dex Torricke-Barton and Derick Mains.

Everyone's really into it despite the blatant nerdiness of it all, building their little empires and strategically negotiating. But as the night wears on, it becomes more and more obvious that people are letting Mark win.

Initially, it's just small things, people not building near his settlements or going soft when they negotiate with him. As the game continues, things become more explicit, with people "stealing" from everyone but him and never placing the "robber" on Mark's empires. After a particularly egregious move by Dex in which he uses the robber to block Debbie, who's closest to catching Mark on victory points, I cry out.

"You're letting him win, Dex and Derick. You're enabling it."

I know it's nerdy and I'm ashamed of myself for caring, but I can't choke it down anymore. Everyone looks suitably shocked by the accusation. Dex and Debbie flash me looks of "don't say this in front of Mark."

"What do you mean?" Dex asks brazenly.

"You know exactly what I mean. You could have placed the robber anywhere but you never place it on any of Mark's hexes. You always place it on his closest competitor."

"That's ridiculous," Dex says.

"It's random," Derick chimes in, offering support.

"No, it's the parts that aren't random that you're swinging his way, the negotiations where you're saying no to everyone else and then yes whenever he needs a resource, the robber, anything."

They both look at me as if I'm crazy . . . for giving the game away.

"Can't you see what they're doing?" I appeal to Mark. "You don't want to win that way?"

"I'm not winning that way," he says. He genuinely doesn't see it. Seems perplexed by my outburst.

I retreat to silence but shake my head at Dex and Derick and everyone else who has agreed not to see what is really going on.

"You know what you're doing," I say quietly.

The accusation hangs in the air. Everyone pretends it doesn't. I feel the dynamics in the room shift and not in a good way.

The next morning we rise before dawn to climb Borobudur, an impressive Buddhist temple, now a UNESCO World Heritage Site. I visited it a few years ago. While we're hanging out at the top, I notice some tourists trying to take a photo and as I offer to take it, Mark cuts in and takes a quick snap. They have no idea who he is but are thrilled with the photo and the whole thing is very sweet. Mark is delighted. I can see he likes his newfound common touch. I take a picture of Mark shooting their picture, which we pass around and everyone showers Mark with love.

When later we tour the Hindu temple Prambanan—which the guys overwhelmingly prefer because it's just like in *Tomb Raider*—Mark marches up to another group of tourists, clearly wanting to build out his man-of-the-people vibe. They don't speak English, so he reaches for their phone to snap a photo. They rebuff him brusquely—like, What are you doing? Get away from us! Mark looks astounded and a little hurt. He's so used to people walking up and asking for selfies and photos with him, which he allows reluctantly, that he doesn't know how to handle this particular situation. His instant dejection is so comical that it's hard not to laugh, and I fail and laugh, which does not go over well. I pivot to comforting him.

"If they ever realize, Mark, I'm sure they'll be really sad," I say. He definitely doesn't see the funny side of it and tries to rationalize his way out of his embarrassment.

"Maybe they weren't actually wanting a photo there."

"Or maybe they thought you were trying to steal their phone?" I offer.

He looks crushed. He's so utterly unprepared for rejection like this. And I never see him offer to take another photo.

15

A Simple Request

This three-week-long Asia tour is going to be a real test for Mark. It's his first trip visiting multiple heads of state overseas, so I'm anticipating lots of questions and requests from him. I didn't anticipate the only request he makes: a riot.

To be precise, his exact request is for a riot or a peace rally.

At first, I think he's joking. Peace rallies are not my area of expertise, and—to be frank—I've never been asked to organize a riot before. Especially one for a tech CEO. I assume something has been lost in his communication—that it's some sort of mix-up. "Riot" and "peace rally" are such completely different things. Then Debbie emails to say that she ran into Mark and he told *her* that he wants a peace rally or a riot and we need to come up with some ideas that will enable him to be surrounded by people or be "gently mobbed." I don't really know what "gently mobbed" means, so I push back against this whole idea. Debbie and I use the one argument that might change his mind, and remind him of how badly starting a riot in Asia would be viewed by the Chinese government. This does no good. He's insistent. And I realize he is definitely not joking.

If anything, he's really hung up on the size of the crowd. That's what matters to him. A public rally of over one million people. That's what he wants more than anything. He never says why he wants this, and I don't feel I can ask. My guess is that he wants to test out how effective his product is in turning Facebook's online tools into offline power. Like, there are all these people on the platform. Can't we figure out a way to mobilize them? Put them on the streets?

But irrespective of why, my job is now to *start a riot*.

That's why I'm nervous when we land in Jakarta after our weekend playing tourists in Java. By the time we make it to the Four Seasons, the relaxed vacation atmosphere has definitely dissipated.

The tension gets ratcheted up further with some wardrobe issues. Somewhere in the back-and-forth with various government officials, an expectation was seeded that Mark would wear the traditional Indonesian batik shirt, as a sign of respect, for his meeting with President-Elect Joko Widodo. The shirt is wax-printed with bright colorful patterns and is basically the opposite of what Mark wears every day. Early in the morning, I deliver it to his suite at the Four Seasons. As soon as he sees it, he balks.

"There's no way I'm wearing that." Then he disappears back into his bathroom.

I try to make myself and the loud shirt inconspicuous in his suite, but we're at a wardrobe stalemate. I'd told Mark that when we're meeting heads of state, he should plan to wear a suit, and it appears the batik shirt is a bridge too far. I'm worried he's going to revert to his usual uniform and we're going to have yet another hoodie battle. Like when he wanted to wear his hoodie and T-shirt to meet the president of Mexico.

When he doesn't emerge from the bathroom, I'm apprehensive. Mark still hasn't prepped for this meeting with the president-elect of Indonesia. The only prep time is now. And yet our scheduled departure time comes and goes. It's nearly 9:00 A.M. and we're still at the hotel. We're going to be late and unprepared, especially as traffic in Jakarta is unforgiving. And yet we sit there, Mark's assistant Andrea and I, waiting for Mark to reemerge in whatever clothes he deigns to wear.

We trade tense smiles as we wait. She's a Chinese American former gymnast who uses busyness as a sword and shield. Not one for polite chitchat. Eventually, she slips into Mark's bathroom and I hear unexpected giggles.

Finally, Mark pops his head out of the bathroom.

"I split my pants."

This wasn't a problem I had foreseen. He usually wears jeans. While we have backup shirts to deal with the sweat issue, we don't have backup pants. But somehow Andrea has managed to mend the pants amid the giggles in the bathroom. The president's people are now calling me, wanting to know where we are and why it's not city hall, where we're supposed to be. I choose to blame traffic rather than pants to explain our delay. By the time we pull up at city hall we're seriously late. I push everyone out of the van as fast as possible.

I'm so focused on getting to the meeting as quickly as we can that it's not until I've reached the top of the stairs in front of city hall that I realize chaos has broken out. A swarm of people envelop us and it's rough. Some of it's press, some isn't, and they're shouting and jostling us, forcing themselves between us, separating the Facebook team. They catch sight of Mark and everything kicks up a notch. There's a frenzy to get to him. As we try to get through the doors of city hall, the crowd surges and I'm lifted out of my high heels and carried forward, my feet not touching the ground.

I find Elliot's hand and grab it as I'm buffeted from side to side. I scan the melee trying to spot Mark. We've had some intense pre-trip security briefings, delivered by buff Israelis whose qualifications for the role I try not to think too hard about. They've taken our fingerprints to identify us in hostage situations, giving me visions of my fingers being individually mailed to Facebook's headquarters. Now I start to worry that this mob scene could all be a setup. Like some Batman movie before someone gets taken hostage from city hall in the chaos.

I see Debbie and then Mark—who's with Todd, the head of our security detail. Todd is a huge guy, ex-military. He's holding an Indonesian man by the scruff of his neck, his muscular arm pulled back, fist balled, about to punch the guy square in the face.

We later learn that this guy he's about to punch is the head of the Indonesian president-elect's security detail, and apparently a two-star general. Which is funny, but only in retrospect. At the time, it's pure adrenaline and terror.

This isn't even the riot I organized.

The crowd continues to surge forward into the lobby and Elliot loses his grip on me. Now I can't see anything because I'm too short and someone stomps on my feet. In the shock of pain, I'm pushed around the crowd and then eventually emerge in the clear. The crowd moves on. I can't see anyone from our team. It dawns on me that they've already gone into the meeting room with the president-elect without me. I rush toward the door, which is guarded. But before I charge in, I spot my shoes, lonely and askew, in the lobby of the grand entrance. I go back for them, wipe the blood off my bruised feet, and put them on, knowing that it probably doesn't help me look any more professional, I'm so disheveled from the humid brawl.

Expecting some kind of pushback from the guards, I thrust my way into the meeting room and loudly disrupt what is clearly the quiet, polite protocol part of the meeting where Mark is asking the president-elect about his priorities. I awkwardly greet the president-elect in a studied Bahasa Indonesian phrase and sit down in the space Mark makes near him.

The room's crowded. I'd spent weeks negotiating the number of people who'd be here, to ensure we had similar numbers on both sides, but all those negotiations have obviously been ignored. This whole thing is a free-for-all. I can identify some of the ministers and officials in the room, but sitting beside the president-elect is a guy who is definitely not a government official. He has shaggy long hair, a short-sleeved shirt with sunglasses perched near his collar, and a large chain hanging between his jeans and back pocket. He looks like he's lost his way to a nightclub, and I'm completely confused to see him seated at the right hand of the president-elect.

The conversation restarts after I'm seated but as the president-elect starts to outline his priorities, the door swings wide open again and Debbie bounds into the room, interrupting him again. This disruption gives me the chance to quietly ask Elliot who the guy is who's seated beside the president.

"Apparently he's a famous Indonesian pop star," Elliot whispers.

"Riiiiight?" I say uncertainly, still waiting to understand what is happening. "Why's he here?"

"Big fan of Facebook."

"Aren't we all?"

Elliot shrugs and I start taking notes—ready to prompt Mark or the president-elect if we drift off the areas of discussion that we'd prenegotiated: tax issues, content issues in this predominantly Muslim country, and their demand for Facebook to store Indonesian user data in Indonesia.

This whole thing had been difficult for me to set up, because President-Elect Widodo has been keeping a low profile since winning the election, and he's acutely aware that meeting with Mark Zuckerberg would get incredible press scrutiny—which we'd just experienced in the flesh. It's also delicate politically for him and for us, because we're not meeting with the sitting president. And because Facebook's an American company. This is one of the first public things the president-elect has decided to do since winning the election. It's risky.

I couldn't understand why he agreed to do this, but watching him, I come to realize the debt he feels to Facebook for getting elected. He really believes it wouldn't have happened without us.

"I'm the Facebook president!" he says. He's so earnest and almost innocent in the way he speaks, it's hard not to be charmed and disarmed by him. "I wasn't supposed to win, I'm a carpenter after all, but I could talk directly to people through Facebook."

And it was true. Jokowi (that's what everyone calls him) is a relatively young outsider, a clean break from a line of presidents who were known for their corruption and cronyism. He'd used Facebook and the internet in interesting ways, like inviting people to vote on Facebook for which ministers they'd like to see in his cabinet. That's why I wanted Mark to meet with him right at the beginning of his administration. He's of the internet, a new type of head of state born of the new Facebook politics. At this moment, I'm still so convinced of the positive power of Facebook that it doesn't occur to me that Facebook could push things the other way, toward a different type of candidate. In different ways, Jokowi and Mark both have this youthful optimism and sense that they shouldn't quite be where they are. And that seems like a good thing.

16

Just Keep Driving

After the meeting ends, the question of the "riot" I organized hangs in the air. The president-elect is famous for *blusukan*, where he makes spontaneous visits to villages and city slums to walk around, connect with people, and understand what communities are worried about. These are popular, and researching it I learn that he gets what is described as "gently mobbed," which seems to me exactly what Mark ordered and the right balance between riot, rally, and million-person event. I'd convinced the president-elect's team to have Mark join him on a blusukan, despite some initial skepticism, especially from my team.

"This will end badly" is Debbie's response when I let her know about my small victory in winning over Jokowi.

Mark seems up for it when we arrive in Jakarta, but then the president-elect's security team raises the issue of a sniper. The risk of one being used during a blusukan in the lead-up to the inauguration, that is. Mark's assistant Andrea shuts the whole thing down before we even arrive at city hall.

So it's surprising, at the press conference after the meeting, when someone from the president-elect's office comes to chat with me about the blusukan that Mark will be doing with Jokowi. I let him know it's been canceled, and he corrects me. "No, the location has been moved for security reasons but it's going ahead."

After the city hall mayhem this morning, I'm scared.

Mark is standing next to the president-elect for the formal photo op and I pull him aside.

"The president wants to do the blusukan."

He beams. "Cool. Yeah. Let's do it."

I then tell Elliot.

"Absolutely no way. Not happening."

"Well, you better tell Mark because he just said he wanted to do it."

Elliot goes to Mark. The press and I watch him whispering in Mark's ear. One of the formal photos from our press conference with the president-elect shows Elliot doing a very theatrical whisper into Mark's ear. His lips are forming the "o" sound of the word "no."

We're then unexpectedly led into an ornate anteroom. The president-elect explains to Mark that his security people are out "sweeping the route." I'm behind them petrified because we've used up all the talking points in the briefing, and no one is prepped to just hang out indefinitely with a president-elect. I suspect this is well out of Mark's comfort zone, given that he barely does small talk at the best of times, with people he actually knows.

Out of the corner of my eye I see Elliot striding toward me purposefully.

"Have you told the president that the blusukan is off?" he asks.

I gesture helplessly at the president-elect and Mark chatting and drinking tea and say, "Is that my place? I mean, do I tell presidents what to do?" noting privately that Elliot's not offering to speak to the president-elect himself.

"You seem to have no problem telling them what to do before now."

I suspect he's joking but he probably isn't.

"They both seem to want to do it and there's a security sweep happening now. Whose decision is it?" I ask, genuinely unsure.

Elliot walks over to Mark and the president-elect and—as the two of them continue their conversation—leans in and whispers sternly in Mark's ear. Mark looks over at me. I shrug. And then he turns to Elliot and shakes his head. Elliot returns to my side.

"He still wants to do it. This is madness, after what we went through on the way in here. It's not safe. You need to speak to their side and shut it down."

I spend the next ten minutes ping-ponging between various officials in the president-elect's entourage, Mark, our security detail, Elliot, and back again before Mark stands and follows the president-elect to his vehicle, carefully avoiding Elliot like he's worried that Elliot might abduct him.

And then he's gone. With the president-elect.

Elliot and I catch sight of Todd, the head of the security detail, whose whole job is to stay close to Mark and protect him, now not with Mark. Todd is very stressed.

"Get in the van," he instructs firmly. "Now."

I can't tell if it's because of the snipers, the chaos earlier, the fact that Mark is separated from his security detail, or my worries about what in the world he'll be saying as he speeds along with the president-elect, but there's absolute silence in our van as we twist and turn through the Jakarta streets chasing the president-elect's motorcade.

I'm surprised when we come to a stop outside a shopping mall because the president-elect's team had said the blusukan would take place at a nearby slum. We all jump out to try to locate Jokowi and Mark. Within moments we're overtaken by people, tens of people at first, but soon it's hundreds—swarming, clawing, pushing, pulling, waves of people, nothing but bodies. I attach myself to Elliot again.

People are overcome. Bowing, clapping, weeping, outbursts of violent emotion as if this moment in this shopping mall in Jakarta is the second coming, but it's not for Mark. They're only interested in the president-elect.

I catch sight of Todd trying to make his way through the swarms of people and realize he's living a security professional's worst nightmare. As we're knocked around, our little team tries to anchor to each other, but our sweaty hands keep slipping and we have to push our way back toward Mark and the president-elect. They seem to be basking in the adulation, enjoying the rush of the crowd, the waves of emotion, and each other's company. As they move from stall to stall chatting with people, it's like a scene from a buddy movie, one with a large budget for extras. Eventually we're pushed toward the exit and Todd bundles Mark and the rest of us into the van before yelling at the driver to go as fast as we can to escape the crowds that are trying to climb in and on the van.

As we pull out I can see Elliot is incandescent with rage and it feels like 99 percent of that is being directed at me. I suspect this may be the last time I organize a head of state visit or a gentle riot.

Mark turns to us, pauses to make sure he has our attention before he renders his verdict, and I feel sick, like there are squirrels in my stomach. I'm anxious that he's also livid about the security risk I exposed him to, or possibly all the small talk he had to do with the president-elect. It honestly seems possible I'm about to be fired.

"That. Was. Awesome," Mark exclaims. His eyes are more alive than I've ever seen them, face flushed, beaming with pure joy.

"Not for Todd," someone pipes up from the back of the van.

"Did you see how much they love him? That crowd was crazy for him. I've never seen anything like it. I've never seen a crowd like it."

This from a man who is used to getting a lot of attention. For once, he's seen something and someone bigger than him, someone with more impact, someone who people are personally devoted to.

I can tell it's affected him deeply, as he relays everything that was said when he was hanging with the president-elect, adrenaline still pumping. But he keeps going back to that crowd, how big it was, how much they loved the president-elect. We speed through the crowded streets and onto the motorway, miles from the shopping mall, before someone realizes that in our haste we've left a member of our communications team behind, and they are lost and alone in the swarm of the Indonesian crowd.

"Just keep driving," Elliot instructs from the back of the van.

And we do.

17

Going Down in a Blaze of Glory

When we get to the South Korea portion of the Asia tour, Sheryl joins us. I've tried to get a meeting for Mark and Sheryl with the president of Korea, and the president's office didn't dismiss it out of hand. They politely inquired whether we have any announcements about any "investments" we'll be making in Korea—casually mentioning that Google had opened a campus in Seoul when they asked to meet the president. But Facebook's pretty cheap about that kind of thing. And I'm not surprised when our refusal to "pay to play"—combined with the open arrest warrants for Mark and Sheryl—means that the president is unavailable to see us.

Mark and the team meet with Samsung, but nothing big comes of it.

After a long dinner at Samsung's headquarters, there's a karaoke party just for the Facebook team staffed by Korean DJs. Mark gives it his all on the Backstreet Boys' "I Want It That Way" lyrics. The party spills over to the private jet flight from Seoul to Tokyo. There's a smaller group traveling on. Elliot and Sheryl have gone back to the US and it's mainly guys on the business and growth teams left. Everyone's drinking. Before long an in-flight karaoke system appears and the party on the plane kicks it up a notch. Without Sheryl or any senior women, things are crazier than on the ground in Seoul.

The guys are dancing and goofing off. Mark is back at it again with the Backstreet Boys, interspersed with Adele and Disney—"A Whole New World" from *Aladdin*—and I perch at the back of the plane just trying to make myself as invisible as possible, not sure what the etiquette of this situation requires. I suppose I could find this charming and vulnerable, Mark trying so earnestly to sound like a Disney cartoon character and the Backstreet Boys. But somehow it makes him seem so much smaller. Like a kid. Honestly it feels a little sad. *This* is what he does to cut loose? I'm exhausted and missing my baby. It's a physical thing, the absence of her, not having her on my body. Not being able to hold her and smell her. That baby is a whole world to me. I scroll through photos Tom has sent and feel alone.

About halfway through the flight we strike turbulence. I've flown a lot and am a very relaxed traveler, but this is a magnitude I've never experienced. Even the captain and flight attendant seem worried. The flight attendant belts herself into her seat and hugs herself with both arms. The captain comes over the PA several times urging everyone to sit down and belt up. Nobody listens but me. The plane lurches up and down violently. It shudders and rattles, like a flimsy toy being slapped around in the sky. Somehow this just makes the party more frenzied. Someone puts Bon Jovi on the karaoke system and the guys drunkenly belt out the line, "Going down in a blaze of glory." On the word "down" the plane drops again. They take turns on the verse and then boom out "Going down in a blaze of glory" together. In the back, the flight attendant and I catch each other's eye and share a look. Her eyes squeeze shut with each plunge.

Traveling is when you really get to know someone, and this is the trip where I start to really get to know Mark. I think he feels the same because during this trip, he friends me on Facebook.

As we hang out at temples and the Tokyo fish market, karaoke, and ridiculous Michelin-star restaurants that specialize in fried food of course, we talk about all kinds of things. I'm fascinated about how you think about life when you're one of the richest people in the world. What changes? What doesn't?

Being dropped into this world of luxury hotels, private jets, infinity pools, and personal concierge service, I feel as if the furniture in my home has all suddenly been massively upgraded but time and the fundamentals of what I do all day—eat, sleep, work—don't change at all. But what's it like for him?

Sheryl once explained the cycle of wealth to me as she saw it. I was complaining that someone I really admired had retired from Facebook at a very young age. I couldn't understand why they'd do that. What would they do instead that would be so interesting? She said matter-of-factly that they would probably follow the cycle of wealth she'd observed at Google and Facebook: exotic travel for a year or more before becoming bored of that, then transitioning to getting very fit or some other personal goal. After achieving that goal, buying a boat or some other extravagant hobby purchase, and then finally getting divorced or going through some other personal crisis. If they come back from that, maybe they attempt their own start-up or fund or, most likely, philanthropy.

None of this sounds very enticing.

Given the scale of Mark's affluence, what actually matters to him? It's unfathomable to me. This endless wealth. I try to explain that to him over dinner.

"I was actually talking about this with Masa the other day," Mark responds. Masayoshi Son is CEO of SoftBank, a Japanese conglomerate that invests heavily in technology companies, including many of the buzzy start-ups Mark's interested in. "And we both agree."

"Agree on what?"

"The most important thing."

"What is it?"

"Food," he says, lifting a chopstick toward his mouth. A dangling piece of fried deliciousness hangs in the air near his lips.

"Are you serious?"

"Yeah. I mean, he's even more serious about it than I am. Every day he has someone go to that fish market we went to this morning and buy the absolute best bluefin tuna in that market. He eats the best food in the world. He has the best chef in Japan."

During my time working on environmental issues, one of the things I'd been involved in was trying to protect southern bluefin tuna, which are critically endangered. I know that a single fish can sell for millions of dollars. I also know that efforts to regulate and save the fishery are seriously failing, and the reason those fish command such high prices is because they are rare and at risk of extinction. It's as if he's saying the best thing about being rich is eating fresh, tender, endangered baby elephants or munching on little imperiled panda bears.

"I didn't think you even liked tuna. You like McDonald's and fried chicken," I say, puzzled and also, if I'm honest, really hoping he's not about to tell me he wants to eat endangered species himself.

"True. As soon as I knew there was a three-star Michelin fried-food restaurant in Japan, I knew we all had to try it."

"Right—but that's because you like fried food. You don't need to be the richest guy in the world to have fried chicken and McDonald's every day."

"No, but if I want the best bluefin tuna . . ."

I cut him off. "You're going to have to fight Masa for it. But what else?"

"Well, Kevin introduced me to his wine dealer." I know Kevin is Kevin Systrom, cofounder of Instagram.

"You don't really drink wine, though."

"No, but I love Andrew Jackson."

There are a lot of downsides to being foreign, but an undisputed benefit is that you can ask dumb questions, simply because you want to hear how someone answers them. I know Mark doesn't particularly care for alcohol, but he now tells me he's collecting either sherry or port, I never know the difference, and what matters to him isn't the alcohol itself but that it's from when Andrew Jackson was president. So I ask him who Andrew Jackson is and why he likes him so much. Mark explains that Jackson's the greatest president America has ever had, that he was ruthless, a populist and an individualist, and that he "got stuff done." He also spilled a lot of blood expanding the territory of the United States, sent five Native tribes out onto the Trail of Tears, but Mark doesn't mention that.

"What about Lincoln or Roosevelt?" I ask, pushing my foreigner credentials. "Wouldn't you say they got stuff done? Couldn't one of them be the greatest?"

"No," Mark says firmly. "It's Jackson. It's not even close."

After his blusukan with the Indonesian president-elect, and his first experience of wild, politically fueled adoration, a switch seems like it's been flipped in Mark. As we prep for Prime Minister Abe, he asks searching questions in a way he never has before—How do elections work in Japan? Why did Prime Minister Abe resign and return? Who holds power in Japan, is it the emperor or the prime minister?

By the time we meet with Abe, it feels a little like coming home. We're really starting to build solid diplomatic relationships in several countries, and the relationship between Facebook and Japan is much better than most. It's the same staff I dealt with for Sheryl's visit a year before. Same venue. Similar format. I make a point to remember to wear a different dress.

When he walks in, Prime Minister Abe comes over to me immediately and smiles.

"Good to see you again. You just always look so young," he says to me, which given Japan's hierarchical and patriarchal society is probably not a compliment. Then he turns to Mark and says, "Wow, you also look so young."

Mark smiles gracefully and, defusing what could be an awkward moment, he responds, "I guess that's because I am."

Abe beams. The rest of the meeting feels like progress. Like what I'd imagined this tech diplomacy would be. Abe has followed through on things we'd discussed with Sheryl, like legalizing the use of social media in elections in Japan. And we'd followed through on things we'd offered, like the disaster response tool, a way for people to mark themselves "safe" notifying all their friends and family—which of course had been inspired by the 2011 earthquake and tsunami in Japan. This tool was personal for me after Christchurch; I'd had to wrangle engineers and design teams, and it's one of the first pieces of engineering that also feels like a policy project. An intersection between tech and the good things we can do to help people and countries.

While we're there, Abe announces the launch of the disaster response tool and praises it to the press, even though his office had told me several times before the meeting that the prime minister never endorses products and never makes exceptions.

When Abe promises to visit Facebook's headquarters, I know he'll follow through. We've established something that for so long felt impossible—an embryonic statecraft for Facebook—and Mark, as our founder and CEO, is the face of it.

But I didn't follow the team where they were going next on our tour. I knew it had the potential to make any progress we'd made come crashing down.

They were heading to China.

18

Red Flag

For Mark, it's hard to imagine a future for Facebook that doesn't include China. The country already has nearly 650 million people on the internet, more than twice the entire US population.

For most of 2014, he's been putting a lot of time and energy into getting Facebook into China. A few months before the trip, he sent an email to his closest advisers explaining why:

From: Mark Zuckerberg
Date: July 25, 2014, at 9:51:37 A.M. PDT
To: Sheryl Sandberg, Elliot Schrage, Vaughan Smith, Kevin
   Systrom
Subject: China 3-year plan

I've said recently that I'd be willing to take 3 trips to China per year and to engage more intensively in trying to help us operate there. I've also encouraged Kevin [Systrom] to engage more as well. Some of you have seemed surprised by this, so I wanted to provide some context on why I believe it is time to take this more seriously. In our mission to connect the world, there have always been a few difficult problems we've always said we'd get to eventually: connecting those who can't afford the internet, building satellites for those who don't have any connectivity in-fra, and connecting countries where we're blocked like China. We've now made progress on every single other major problem, and the last one on the list is China.

He says everyone needs to tackle this intensively right away, if Face-book's going to get into China anytime soon. Instagram is already in China—and I suspect that's one of the reasons it was such an attrac-tive acquisition target for him.

> If we don't, it's most likely we'll regress and all of our services—including Instagram—will be blocked. . . . I think we should view this as a 3-year plan to have Facebook fully operational there. In year one, we can aim to have key services like Instagram remain up and running, and we should try to get our sales of-fice running with a senior Chinese leader. By the end of year three, we should have hopefully built the relationships that would enable Facebook to operate in China as well. (In the best outcome, it may be the case that Instagram becomes the Facebook of China and the Facebook app's full success is not as necessary.)

He ends with one more bit of context on why we have to do this now:

> We've always needed to connect China, but there have always been other major projects we could take on to connect large pop-ulations instead. Now there are no other major projects left. It's time to really build these relationships and make this partnership with China work.

What's not in Mark's email is more telling than what is. There's no acknowledgment at all of the moral complexity of working in an authoritarian country that surveils its own citizens and doesn't allow free speech.

This is July 2014. Google has already withdrawn from China, years before, saying it was "no longer willing to continue censoring" Google products following the breach of human rights activists' accounts on its service. Mark, Sheryl, and Elliot all know this well. Both Sheryl and Elliot were senior executives at Google during that period. Elliot even testified before Congress about Google's China strategy, a bruising affair in which he and a Yahoo executive were condemned for colluding with the Chinese government. "While technologically and financially you are giants, morally you are pygmies," the chair of the House Foreign Affairs Committee told Yahoo.

But after all that, there's no question in Mark's email of "Should we operate in China?" or "How do we manage the inevitable moral dilemmas that are sure to come?" China is, in Mark's eyes, just the end of a to-do list, the last major project to tackle. Like he's playing a game of Risk and he needs to occupy every territory.

I don't believe Facebook is going to get into China. The mission of the company—making the world more open and connected—is the exact opposite of what the Chinese Communist Party wants, particularly under President Xi Jinping. I can't imagine they'd allow us in. And I don't want to help Facebook try. The way I see it, the only way in will be to collaborate with the CCP and make compromises we shouldn't. I tell Marne and I think she gets it. She takes on nearly all the China-related tasks herself.

Mark, meanwhile, is learning Mandarin. He tells people he's studying every day, and he gets together with Mandarin-speaking employees for conversational practice. Eventually, he's interviewed in Mandarin, onstage in a classroom full of Chinese students. The video of this is completely charming; he's loose and self-deprecating and funny. The students cheer and burst into applause when he first busts out his badly accented Mandarin. "I need some practice after all," he tells them, and they laugh. "My wife is Chinese"—more

laughter and applause. "We speak Mandarin to her grandmother."
When the footage is posted on YouTube, many people comment
that he has more personality—he seems more human, cooler, and
more relaxed—in Mandarin than he ever seems in English.

For the longest time, Marne had been leading the policy work on
China, with the Asia business team managing the day-to-day. But while
I am out on maternity leave in early 2014, Facebook announces a new
leader for the China team. Instead of bringing in someone with specific
experience in China, they tap Vaughan Smith from Facebook's corporate development team. He'd been working on mobile partnerships
at Facebook after previously working at eBay. This is consistent with
Facebook's approach to everything; they prioritize insiders over outsiders, business experience over policy expertise (China expertise, in this
case), which seems like madness to me. By coincidence, Vaughan's also
a Kiwi and attended the same high school my mother taught at and my
brother went to, plus university in Christchurch, my hometown.

Vaughan's an affable, enthusiastic guy who talks quickly and always seems to have pep in his step. I like him. It's hard not to. He's
wiry, maybe because of the cycling, waterskiing, and other sporty
leisure activities that he mysteriously seems to have ample time to
pursue—unlike his American coworkers, who seem to have no time
for leisure. His friendly features are complemented by sandy hair,
blue eyes, and a thick New Zealand accent. Several people tell me—
the only other Kiwi they know—stories in which Vaughan has insisted on "showing them his deck." The New Zealand accent turns
e's into i's, so it sounds like a lewd proposition rather than a business
invitation to review some slides. Javi apparently responded, "No,
man, no! I don't wanna see that." Vaughan's the sort of guy who
laughs that off, the misunderstanding being a feature, not a bug. He
seems immune to any kind of social mortification, and glows with a
kind of cheerful, locker-room bonhomie.

Vaughan often hosts people in his palatial Palo Alto home, where
his very good-looking family mingles with assorted Facebook staff

around their outdoor fire pit or swimming pool, depending on the season. Vaughan presents as—and I have no reason to doubt this—a man who has everything he wants.

Vaughan operates in a different way from me and most of the policy team. He decides to crack the China market with his golf clubs, sending updates about whom he has golfed with and how this might lead to opportunities to meet with key government officials. The actual work, preparing briefings, tracking regulations, or analyzing political developments, he delegates to interns, or the women who work for him.

Sometimes Vaughan seems oblivious to important facts. He schedules Mark's visit during the fourth plenum, arguably the busiest week of the year for China's top officials, who are all expected to attend the Communist Party's main policy-setting conference. Vaughan only seems to realize the plenum's happening a week or two before departure.

With Vaughan still settling into the role and only days after Mark sends his China email, we learn that Instagram, which is still operating in China, might be blocked. In fact, there are rumors the Chinese might go a step further and remove Instagram from both the Apple and Android stores in China.

The sudden threat to ban the service inconveniently highlights how little Facebook can control its fate in China, with no direct communication from the Chinese government before their announcement, and no ability to stop the block or even know when exactly it will happen.

While others panic, Vaughan, from the ninth hole, is the only person who shrugs it off.

"Bummer as China has been Instagram's fastest growing country for a while and could have passed the US as our #1 country in 2015 had the previous trajectory continued."

Instead he focuses on setting up a physical office for Facebook in China, and pursuing a partnership that'll help the platform enter China.

He's targeting venture capital firm Sequoia, private equity boss Stephen Schwarzman, and information technology company China Broadband, among others. Anyone who might be able to get Facebook in.

I still can't figure out what his strategy is. Until I get a glimpse of how the team is thinking about Hong Kong and China. I'm cc'd on an email from a junior staffer. It's about a letter Facebook promised the privacy commissioner in Hong Kong, responding to questions about the privacy of Facebook users there:

> Update: Rob and I spoke with Vaughan and Zhen on the China team yesterday, and they flagged a potential complication arising from the likely course of our negotiations with the Chinese government. In exchange for the ability to establish operations in China, FB will agree to grant the Chinese government access to Chinese users' data—including Hongkongese users' data.

Facebook will grant the Chinese government access to Chinese users' data—including Hong Kong users' data—in exchange for getting into China? This can't be true. It's one of those crazy ideas the other offices at Facebook are always floating that Marne and I beat back down before they go very far. This proposal, which would surely violate the consent order Facebook agreed to with the Federal Trade Commission in 2012 (and the earlier 2011 agreement with the Irish Data Protection Commission), doubtless is the work of juniors who haven't subjected it to any scrutiny by the actual decision makers at Facebook. This is so far-fetched I'm sure there's no danger of it becoming real anytime soon or ever. So I ignore it, even though the next sentence in the email explains exactly how Facebook would accomplish this:

> New users in China will agree to a modified DUP/SRR reflecting this practice, but we will have to re-TOS Hongkongese users.

Translation: new users in China will have a new Data Use Policy they'll agree to when they sign up for Facebook—a policy that discloses that the Chinese government will have access to their data—and existing users in Hong Kong will be forced to accept a new Terms of Service (the contract Facebook has with its users) that will also contain this stipulation.

Again, I don't buy it. It sounds so unlikely that the company would use the data of Hong Kong users as a bargaining chip to get Facebook into China, and then force Hong Kong users to accept it with a new Terms of Service that they must consent to or lose access to Facebook, that I assume the people on the email—who are US privacy experts and not especially senior—have simply misunderstood. Surely, there's no way that Facebook would leverage Hong Kong users' data as part of a deal to get into China?

Later—just a few months later—I'd learn no, no . . . this was how the head of the China project was thinking things would play out. But I'll get to that.

In the meantime, the rest of us are trying to figure out why China is threatening to block Instagram. Why this aggressive move now? We don't know for sure, but we suspect that it's Instagram's role in protests in Hong Kong. Tens of thousands of prodemocracy activists are taking to the streets in the Umbrella Revolution, and Instagram is one of their preferred ways to organize and get the message out, in part because it's not blocked in mainland China. The Chinese activist Ai Weiwei posts a selfie holding his own leg and aiming it like a rifle. It becomes an instant meme; Hong Kong protesters photograph themselves in the pose and post on Instagram to symbolize their own demands, along with the main protest hashtags.

Another possible reason for this potential block is that, back during the Hong Kong elections a few months before this, in March 2014, Facebook deployed a megaphone to encourage people to vote. China makes it clear that Facebook should not have run the megaphone or taken any actions to increase democratic engagement. In-house, it's seen as a mistake, a black mark against the policy team. I escape blame only because I was on maternity leave at the time.

As the protests in Hong Kong escalate over the summer months, in September China makes good on its threat and Instagram is blocked completely in China. Vaughan's cheery updates start to take a less optimistic tone. Less golfing, more gloom.

Before this China trip, we have to figure out what both Mark and Vaughan will say about Hong Kong's Umbrella Revolution both publicly and in private. In an email, Vaughan suggests:

"My pov is it's a good opportunity to talk about the rule of law and praise HK."

In other words, support China's violent suppression of the protests by parroting its claim that it was upholding the rule of law. Praise Hong Kong means praise for Beijing's puppets on the island who support the crackdown.

I'm shocked. Everyone else seems to be also. Debbie fires back an email in response to Vaughan's suggested talking points. She starts:

I think only very skilled people will be able to do this well.

Devastating. Then:

I feel we say something very bland
I do not want to talk about rule of law

"Like everyone around the world, we continue to watch with interest the events in HK and the peaceful demonstrations of the HK people."

Maybe fearing that Vaughan won't understand why Debbie's correct, Elliot chimes in:

Debbie is 100% right here.

Vaughan, you need to appreciate that "respecting the rule of law" only goes so far to explain or justify government behavior. To many people who follow human rights issues and international law, the foundation of international law is the rejection of the so-called Nuremberg defense—the claim by Nazi's that they "were just following orders" and respecting the laws and policies of the Nazi state.

Vaughan simply thanks Elliot for "the articulate background." I can't tell if he's being brazen or genuine. There is simply no putting this man off his putt.

Either way, I think the point at which you have to explain Nuremberg to the head of the team leading your China entry is probably a red flag.

19

PAC-Man

Not long after I return home from the Asia trip, Marne leaves the policy team to become the COO of Instagram. After years of being connected to her via email almost every waking moment, I feel an unexpected sense of loss.

She's replaced by Joel Kaplan. It isn't a complete surprise. Joe, the former Bush aide, is coming from the role of vice president for US policy. Plus, he's Sheryl's ex-boyfriend, and by now I've realized that Facebook's leadership includes a web of people all entangled as bridesmaids, best friends, neighbors, and exes. Their fealty is seemingly to each other, their tribe, ahead of any ideology or anything else. Their pasts, presents, and futures are all deeply intertwined in a way that mine are not. They hire each other for jobs with big salaries, responsible for each other's promotions and bonuses. A tiny enmeshed group of people increasingly responsible for shaping the attention of billions. Their preferences turned into policy. The challenge is that Joel doesn't seem to have any interest in the world outside the US or even outside Washington, DC. His career and passion is Republican politics. He didn't just serve two full terms in the George W. Bush administration (eventually rising to deputy chief of staff), he was part of the "Brooks Brothers riot" in 2000 that helped put Bush into office. This was the melee that shut down the Florida recount in 2000, ensuring that Florida went for Bush. During Joel's confirmation hearing, he claimed, "While I was there, I was not, to the best of my recollection, a participant," but his memory seemed way better by the time he was at Facebook, sharing stories over drinks after work about the craziness of participating in the riots.

At the White House, he was intimately involved in the response to the 2008 financial crisis, and he remained bitter about Andrew Ross Sorkin's account of his role in the book *Too Big to Fail*, where he felt the importance of his role was downplayed and he was portrayed as a confused frat boy, desperate for information to feed back to President Bush, who had given him the nickname "angular dude."

I'm surprised to learn, again over drinks, that he had initially been a Democrat. I would eventually see some irony in his stated reason for breaking with the party, but he's adamant that Bill Clinton's behavior with Monica Lewinsky turned him into a Republican.

At Sheryl's urging, he was offered the job of general counsel in Facebook's early days, but he found the suggestion that he leave the White House for a college website preposterous. Now he ruefully acknowledges a certain jealousy of Ted Ullyot—another Harvard grad, Scalia clerk, and Bush alum—who did take the job. I don't think that's just about the immense wealth he initially missed out on. He's openly bitter about how those who stayed until the very end of the Bush administration were treated. In Joel's telling, he's still surprised by the meager career offerings that were available to him. When he eventually joins Facebook, he makes clear that he'll only consider the job if he doesn't have to interview for it. His first position is running US policy. Because Facebook is so heavily aligned with the Democrats, it needs someone who can handle Republicans.

Now in his newest role, as vice president of public policy, Joel's a very different boss from Marne. Where Marne had been deliberative, thorough, ever questioning, Joel's her opposite, impetuous and dogmatic. Joel sees everything through the lens of US power. Facebook, like the US, is a superpower. When something goes wrong outside the US, he reflexively turns to the State Department to task them to solve it. Almost like he considers them an arm of Facebook. When the island nation of Nauru blocks Facebook out of the blue, Joel contacts the State Department to have the US government publicly condemn the block. Which they do. It changes nothing. I urge him, in this case and others, to reach out ourselves. Figure out why the government blocked us and contact them directly to resolve it.

Joel is surprised to learn Taiwan is an island. Often when we start to talk about pressing issues in some country in Latin America or Asia, he stops and asks me to explain where the country is. This happens so frequently that a few weeks into his tenure, I offer to buy him a world map. He turns that down, but days later, a large framed map shows up in his office.

Just a few weeks after he takes over Marne's job, Joel starts hiring a political sales team to push politicians—here and abroad—into becoming advertisers. The idea is, if politicians depend on Facebook to win elections, they'll be less likely to do anything that'll harm Facebook. If Facebook is the goose that lays the golden egg, no one wants to kill the goose. Get them hooked on those golden eggs. Also, unlike Marne, Joel wants the policy team to generate revenue. The way he sees it, Facebook is a business and the policy team should be contributing to the bottom line. He doesn't want to be viewed as a "cost center" internally. Political advertising is a way to change that. And elections are the biggest opportunity. Fresh-faced Harvard grads start moving into the Washington, DC, office to sell ads to politicians and political campaigns.

I find this all repugnant. I feel alienated from this new regime from the outset. As a foreigner, I have a very different perspective on money in elections. New Zealand, like so many other countries, has strict limits on electoral spending: under $20,000 per candidate. I'm astounded at the role money plays in elections in the US. It determines so much about whose voice gets heard on every issue from guns to abortion to much else. I'm also against exporting this value system. But Facebook is effectively bringing this in globally by stealth.

The result? In Brazil, Facebook's already facing fines of millions of dollars and court orders to block the platform for violating bans on electoral advertising. In Mexico, Facebook is being investigated for defying restrictions on political ads.

My disagreements with Joel come to a head when he tells me to establish PACs in other countries. Political action committees, of course, are an American invention that pull together donors to give money to political candidates. There are PACs for every possible cause: to elect more women to office and to elect candidates who are friendly to Realtors, or beer wholesalers, or teachers' unions. Home Depot runs its own giant PAC, as does AT&T.

"We were so late in establishing Facebook's PAC in the US; I don't want to make that mistake in other countries," Joel says insistently. "We need to get moving to establish PACs outside the US. We should have done this a long time—"

"So, this is awkward," I cut in. Joel looks puzzled.

"That's illegal. Only US citizens can contribute to elections here. That's true everywhere. Nobody wants foreigners bankrolling their elections."

"Really?" Joel looks shocked.

"Definitely. That's why even though you regularly invite me to contribute to the Facebook PAC you founded, for me to do so would be illegal as I'm not a citizen."

"Well, I was actually meaning the other way," he says defensively. "Contributions to politicians in other countries. We need to get moving on channeling money to our key allies offshore, you know, our most influential politicians in other countries."

"Ah, that would be considered bribery and corruption in most of the countries I'm responsible for," I say, careful to strike a neutral tone.

Joel looks crestfallen.

"Except the dictatorships," I offer. "They'll probably take your money."

For a minute I worry that he's seriously considering it.

20

Slouching Toward Autocracy

Joel isn't the only one starting to flex on foreign policy. So is Mark.

The first time I see it is Russia. An event page has been set up for a rally in support of the country's opposition leader Alexei Navalny, on the day he's going to be sentenced for trumped-up embezzlement charges: January 15, 2015. Over sixty thousand people are invited to the event and over twelve thousand respond. But Facebook staff block the event page in Russia the Friday before Christmas, after receiving a complaint from Russia's internet regulator, the wonderfully named Roskomnadzor.

Facebook gets a lot of criticism for this, including in the tech community and on sites like Techmeme, which Mark is particularly sensitive to. He's really annoyed the issue wasn't escalated to him.

Sheryl writes to him on Sunday, December 21, 2014, at 9:17 A.M., defending her policy team:

Mark—this is the right course of action to take to balance free expression with staying up in Russia—and it is consistent with how we deal with requests. This is certainly small compared to potential China requests and will be noted by them too.

BUT, if you were optimizing for free expression / tech community only, you would restore these pages quickly.

The team's actions here are consistent with the guidance they have from you. This could become bigger and be negative in the tech community—so if you want to restore pages, please let us know now. If not, we sit tight.

Hours later, at 1:34 P.M., Mark replies:

I spoke with Elliot about this yesterday.

My view is that for such a sensitive case, this should have been escalated to me (or at the very least Elliot) before we took it down in the first place. My guidance at that point would have been to try to push back on the request rather than immediately taking it down.

At the end of the day, however, since the request actually is fully compliant with Russian law, if we really came to believe not taking this down would cause the whole service (including this page) to be blocked, then I would have supported taking the page down. We aren't helping anyone if the whole service becomes unavailable.

From there, Mark lays out our options. He says we can't unblock the page now because at this point it probably will get Facebook shut down in Russia.

On the flip side, it will also look incredibly weak for us if we unblock the page and then block it again within a few days if the whole service is about to be blocked.

To make a complicated decision worse, the State Department gets in touch to relay its "concern" at Facebook's removing the event page for the Navalny rally. Joel has a surprisingly brief and unfriendly phone call with them. The State Department official tells him that if faced with the choice of removing an event page like this one or being shut down in some country, the US government position is that Facebook should be shut down.

And that's not all.

The kicker is that the government threatens to publicly criticize Facebook to pressure the company to take a principled approach.

Joel is shocked at this, that the government would prefer for a US company to shut down its operations rather than comply with another government's legal request. He fumes on email, "I reacted with astonishment and asked whether he was sure that was the official U.S. government position, because I had never heard that articulated before and found it extremely surprising. I told him that if it ever got to the point where he thought the U.S. government was going to suggest as much [say publicly that Facebook should let itself be blocked], then I'd want a heads up, because I knew that Mark or Sheryl would want to talk to Secretary Kerry directly."

Elliot responds, "Wow—these guys really don't understand how soft power works."

He and Joel start putting together plans to "tell them that this is not how we expect to work with our own government."

Joel rings me after he's had a bruising discussion with Mark, who wanted to understand "the facts" about how content is removed from Facebook. He's now thinking that instead of having the content operations team follow the same rules they've followed for years, all requests for removal of content from "sensitive countries" should be escalated, potentially to Mark. Certainly to Joel and Elliot.

What Mark's really mad about over that frenzied holiday weekend is that he sees the decision as his to make. Which is mystifying to the content operations and policy teams who've been applying the Community Standards and making difficult decisions like this for years. Until now, they'd escalate particularly hard decisions to Marne, occasionally to Elliot, and rarely to Sheryl. No one can remember ever escalating this type of decision to Mark. But now, two months after our Asia trip, Mark's interest in the politics of these decisions is growing. Now, for the first time, he wants to be the decider.

It's painful to see, given how much work went into putting those guidelines in place. The system we developed isn't perfect, but it has checks and balances, and isn't guided by just one man's whims. When I arrived at Facebook in 2011, the rules were extraordinarily crude and decisions were made by a team that reported to the vice president in charge of global sales. The team hated taking anything down. They pushed back nearly all requests. Then we had a series of troubling incidents. The office of Australian prime minister Tony Abbott asked us to remove a page called "Occupy Tony Abbott's Daughters' Vaginas." Someone at a consumer packaged goods company reached out to Sheryl to complain that their ads appeared on a page called "Riding her gently while she sleeps" and another with a name that was something like "She bites the pillow while I enter the backdoor." The content team used the same arguments they had for keeping beheading videos on the platform and fought ferociously against taking down any of these pages. After this, the content team was swiftly removed from the sales operation and put in the public policy team under Marne. She ordered a summit to develop a set of principles and processes for what can and cannot be posted on Facebook. After many philosophical and practical debates, and getting myself personally invested in way too many arguments with bearded guys about John Stuart Mill, we agree on Facebook's first public Community Standards. It felt like progress to have the policy and operations teams come together and develop a set of principles that would guide decision-making for all content on Facebook. I wanted to make these public, so users everywhere would know what the rules are. This would also make us more accountable, ensuring everyone at Facebook followed the same clear principles. And we do.

Navalny is the starting point for Mark wanting to overrule this imperfect but functional system. And as time wears on and weirder and more inconvenient facts present themselves, Mark steps in more and more.

Mark decides to block a video of the aftermath of a Mexican school shooting when the president of Mexico reaches out to him personally; he blocks some Indonesian political speech threatening a coup against his buddy President Jokowi; he blocks political speech that the South Korean National Election Commission wants removed.

Most of those decisions are contrary to the Community Standards. The ones we've made public. He's replacing the process we've developed over years with whatever he thinks is right. And there doesn't seem to be any form of accountability. It's also hard not to notice that in nearly every case, his decision happens to coincide with his business interests, mollifying governments so he can keep Facebook growing.

It starts to feel like all the guidelines we'd spent years endlessly haggling over and refining are irrelevant. The new test on difficult decisions about government requests is whether there's a risk that Facebook will be blocked if we don't comply. It's just a question of blunt power.

Around this time—while he's personally ordering us to take down posts that don't violate our Community Standards—Mark starts opining publicly about freedom of speech. The day after the Charlie Hebdo attack, where twelve people were murdered, he posts, "This is what we all need to reject—a group of extremists trying to silence the voices and opinions of everyone else around the world. I won't let that happen on Facebook. I'm committed to building a service where you can speak freely without fear of violence."

In our offices around the world, there's a sense of whiplash. The people I've hired are confused about these departures from policy. When we gather the entire policy and communications organization together for an annual offsite meeting at headquarters in February 2015, Joel outlines what he sees as Mark's new approach. When governments ask us to take down content that we believe should not come down, he says, it will only be taken down if one of two criteria is met:

1. There is a credible threat to block Facebook.
2. There is a risk to employees.

The team peppers me with questions. How can they possibly tell if the government is going to shut down Facebook in their country? How can they escalate to Mark? What if we guess wrong about the risk and then they're in jail and it's too late?

It's five dozen people at this meeting, in a big conference room on Facebook's campus—and the ones objecting the most are recent hires from South Korea, Brazil, and other places where governments have shown a willingness to arrest or use a show of force against employees:

"How can Mark understand the politics in my country?"

"How can he overrule it?"

"How can we defy the government making legal requests and then ask to work with them?"

"How can we say our rules are one thing but actually they are another?"

These are the very people most at risk from this decision. It's them, not Mark, who are most likely to be jailed if push comes to shove.

Joel's response? He's frustrated and can't understand their confusion, seething at what he sees as insolence and ignorance. The audacity of questioning authority. Basically, management issues the orders and employees outside the US are expected to comply. He lectures the team that Mark's been clear on the two principles. Everything stays up unless Facebook is going to be blocked or someone is arrested and sitting in a jail cell with no way out. How many times does he have to say it?

Everyone seems shocked that there's no discussion or input—just an edict from Mark, enforced by Joel. They struggle to understand why Mark's getting involved, why instead of the set of rules we tout to governments, decisions are made on his whim.

What Joel and Mark are doing, whether they realize it or not, is sending an unfortunate message to governments around the world. If the only thing that will make Facebook change its position is jailing its employees or blocking its service, they're effectively issuing an invitation to these governments to do just that.

After this, we escalate all difficult decisions to Sheryl and Mark for them to decide. Although in reality it's just Mark. Facebook is an autocracy of one.

21

Billionaire Time

Good news from Colombia. President Santos has agreed to be our knight in shining armor and get onstage with Mark Zuckerberg to show the leaders of Latin America that it's a great time to sign up for Internet.org. This will happen in January 2015.

There's only one snag: convincing Mark to do this in the morning, which is the only slot that's free in the president's schedule. Santos's staff is clear with us that they're squeezing Facebook in as a favor, while the president is in the middle of heated negotiations trying to get the FARC militant group to lay down their arms. However, Mark's assistant Andrea is firm that noon is too early for Mark. She insists on 12:30 P.M. or later. Mark has spent a lifetime staying up late into the night coding, and has a strict policy: no appointments before noon. Which works at home; there are few people in Silicon Valley who aren't going to accommodate him. He owns time. But presidents are different. Turns out, they're very busy, tightly scheduled people. It creates enormous issues all the time. It's hard not to feel like "Who does Mark think he is?" Like his time is more valuable than that of someone involved in a delicate peace process to end a brutal fifty-year-old conflict?

Back when he was a freshman in college, in an interview with the Harvard college paper the *Crimson* (about the brand-new

"TheFacebook.com"), Mark actually said, "Not having someone tell me what to do or a timeframe in which to do it is the luxury I am looking for in my life."

A week before the trip, this scheduling issue—Mark's refusal to meet in the morning—scuttles the whole thing. But this one's too important to miss. I'm called in to mediate between their palace and our palace. Andrea holds firm at 12:30 P.M., and after much coaxing the president's staff concede to 12:15 P.M. The plans are back on until a day before the event, when Andrea lets the palace know we'll be there at 12:30 P.M. They respond—confirming the meeting for 12:00 P.M., their original time. At this point both sides remove me from the emails.

The morning of the meeting, Mark hasn't read the briefings I prepared for him. Andrea's insistent that I brief him in the car, on the drive to the presidential palace, and she'll message me when Mark is ready to depart. I wait, watching the clock, assuming we're supposed to arrive before noon, to get through security and past the press scrum.

At 11:23 A.M. my phone pings. It's Andrea:

"Here? We are leaving. Soon. About to be in cars. Where are you? We are in the garage loading."

I'd been waiting in the lobby for an hour. I head down and text, "In lift. Here. At S1. Where are you?"

"You are not at S1. I'm at elevators. We are ready to go. Where are you?"

Something was badly wrong. That's when we all realize that they're at the Bogotá Marriott and I'm at the JW Marriott Bogotá. Two separate hotels, far from each other.

I'm told to meet Mark at the presidential palace. I google and learn that the hotel I'm currently standing in is forty minutes away. The hotel Mark is currently in on the other side of Bogotá is at least fifty minutes in traffic and that's being optimistic. The meeting with the president is now due to start in less than thirty minutes.

My mind and my body process the horror of what is unfolding

separately. There are no taxis at the hotel. Before I know it, I'm starting to run. Vaguely in the direction of the palace. It's hot and muggy. I'm desperately scanning the street for taxis.

My phone rings; it's a very nervous Derick, from the comms team, at the palace. He's wanting to know when Mark and I are going to arrive. When I explain I'm not with Mark and I'm not anywhere near the presidential palace, Derick calmly asks what I need. Transport.

"Didn't someone hire a van?" Derick directs me to run down a main *calle* toward the palace in the hope that the driver can spot me. I take off my heels and run barefoot as fast as I can, conscious that every second could be the difference between making it or failing. Little stones jab into my feet. Eventually, I see a white van and we speed to the palace.

I watch with dread as the van's clock ticks past noon. When we get to the palace, military police block us. Of course. I should have realized I couldn't use an unmarked white van to charge into the Colombian president's palace.

After clearing this up, I'm whisked from the van to pandemonium in the palace, and marched directly to a stern man in a green uniform replete with medals. He's red-faced with anger. He doesn't bother with the usual pretense of diplomatic niceties. He just demands to know where Mark is.

I can't answer because I genuinely have no idea where Mark is. But President Santos is waiting to receive him. I can't even bear to look at the time or look at Derick. He sidles up beside me and explains that it's worse than I think and that the president is clearly pissed, after waiting for ages.

The minister of information technology approaches, the man whose ministerial van I'd ridden in for our road trip through the Colombian jungle. He'd stuck his neck out to make this meeting happen during the middle of peace talks. He looks crushed. This is not good for him.

I try to assure the minister that Mark is nearly here at the same time Derick takes a call from Andrea, wherever she and Mark are. Derick recaps the call to me in a whisper—Andrea has told the president's office that Mark's flight was late landing and tells Derick that we should do the same. I'm stunned she thinks this lie will work. Doesn't she realize they can check? Who does she think controls the airspace? They flew in last night.

When Mark does finally arrive, we're marched upstairs to the president's office. No one acknowledges our lateness, but it is clearly understood and extremely uncomfortable.

We sit down. Mark seems awkward and off his game just making small talk. The president opens by telling us he has to go talk to the FARC. He explains they're at an especially difficult stage; there'd been a deadly bomb attack a few weeks before, and the whole thing is at risk of collapsing. He says he wants to build support in Colombia for the peace process and wants Facebook to help him get this over the line. Mark seems flustered, with the wide eyes of a man who has not read his brief. He isn't prepared to talk about the FARC. But he offers to do all Facebook can to facilitate the process. (Facebook doesn't do anything significant. In fact, months later, after the peace process is concluded, Joel refuses to allow FARC-related content on the platform, despite direct requests from the president's office.)

We all can feel this meeting will be over any minute even though it has hardly begun. Mark brings up Internet.org, tries to explain how it will help people in remote parts of Colombia. We'd put two Colombian government sites in the app—one for agriculture and one for education—and Mark pitches adding more. Santos is noncommittal and ends the meeting after less than ten minutes, saying, "We can't keep the press waiting any longer."

We decamp to a different room, where Santos interviews Mark onstage for a little over a half hour. The original plan had been for an hour and a half; they were supposed to take questions from entrepreneurs and press in the audience, and then exit together. Instead, Santos gets up and walks out, along with his retinue. Mark is left standing onstage alone.

Before this meeting, the minister and the president said Colombia would lead Internet.org globally. They'd put all government services into the app, not just the couple we launched with. We talked about sending the minister around the Americas promoting Internet.org. After this, we can't get them to do anything.

22

Hunger Games for the 0.001 Percent

Here's something you don't see in Davos: children. In fact, everyone seems like they're middle aged or old or very, very old. But in 2015 I decide to bring my eleven-month-old daughter, Sasha.

Davos is what people call the World Economic Forum—the annual meeting of the high-flying people who think they run the planet—billionaires and world leaders and celebrities (the Clooneys, Kevin Spacey back in the day, Bono of course). It's a festival for the important and the self-important, held in the ski town of Davos, Switzerland.

One of the conceits of Davos is that the logistics are incredibly difficult, and that's if you're a billionaire with a large staff. It's a ridiculous place to hold anything. The location is high up in the remote Swiss mountains in the dead of winter. Getting there requires a flight to Zurich followed by a long drive through treacherous icy, windy roads, or train, or—if you're one of the top attendees (and not staff like me)—helicopter. The town is tiny, one main street surrounded by ski chalets. The scarcity of hotel rooms, restaurants, and convenience stores seems to be the point.

I've managed Facebook's presence at Davos for years, but this time, Tom's also going to be there, on assignment for the *Financial Times*. So we have to bring the baby. When I confide in other staffers about this plan, they say, alarmed, "Don't let Sheryl know. She needs to know all your attention is on her." Which told me all I really need to know about Sheryl's real attitude to combining work and motherhood. In fact, when a woman I work with closely expresses surprise upon learning I have a child, she tells me, "Good job!"—openly admiring the fact that she'd had no idea—and I feel a flush of pride. Both of us acknowledging the success (and the necessity) of the subterfuge.

I decide we'll be smuggling our daughter to Davos. Tom disapproves but suggests no alternative. We decide reluctantly that the only thing to do is to bring our nanny to watch Sasha while we're working. We've never traveled with her before and it feels like a big ask, but she's excited to go.

We're traveling in the dead of winter and the baby gets sick. After 4:00 A.M. in the seventies-inspired faux log cabin of the Sheraton Hotel Davos, when Sasha vomits into my hair again, as the three of us lie in bed exhausted and unsleeping in the stiflingly hot room, Tom turns to me and says, "This is, beyond doubt, the worst idea we have ever had. I am never coming to Davos again." And he keeps his word.

Around this dull Swiss town, the World Economic Forum has constructed a byzantine social structure where they control the minimal resources available. These are then dished out by their grace and favor according to status. Everything at Davos—every speaking slot, every car pass, every drinks invitation, every meeting room, the distance you sit at dinner from the front table—is distributed according to social status. The ultimate type A personalities at Davos understand these minute power calibrations and spend their time comparing each and every one, constantly striving for more. So you overhear people saying sniffily that they're surprised that a certain prime minister is staying in the Hilton Garden Inn rather than the

Seehof Hotel, or that a celebrity mistakenly tried to cut a line for a panel, too uneducated to realize they were pushing past a Nobel laureate. The narcissism of small differences.

In other words, the WEF has weaponized the concept of status envy to create a Hunger Games for the 0.001 percent. Maybe that's why they all seem to love this place. It's like the status Olympics—a chance for them to measure themselves not just against their own industry but across business, politics, entertainment, and media. A bunch of the richest people in the world.

Know who this setup is not so great for? Anyone trying to do their job with a baby in tow. Know who it's made for? Sheryl Sandberg. At Davos, every cell in her body is tingling, primed and hard at work weighing, assessing, and measuring whom we should stop to speak to, who gets a selfie, whom we share information with or give swag to, and who has committed some past slight that renders them ineligible for even a polite head nod. And they're all doing this! Being around all this constant calculation is exhausting.

Since I arrived at Facebook, we've made Davos into the moment each year when we pause and assess how things are going around the world for Facebook. We go into it with a "bible" I take months to pull together, summarizing every issue of importance to Facebook, and preparing talking points. It's like taking Facebook finals each year. We come out of it with an email Sheryl writes, after meeting with politicians, regulators, and journalists at the conference, setting the policy direction for the year ahead.

This year at Davos, Sheryl and Joel are taken aback to hear—from their own kind—that things are not looking so rosy for Facebook. Joel emerges from a meeting with a senior editor of the *Wall Street Journal* looking like someone has handed him a grenade ready to explode. The guy told him, "Everyone's currently going after Google but you're next." He warned Joel that media, regulators, and high-level politicians around the world are all lining up to start to "rein in Facebook." One of Sheryl's former Treasury colleagues tells her,

"You all are two years away from being as hated as the investment banks."

The Italian prime minister tells us that he and his counterparts in Europe are struggling with unemployment and slowing economic growth, and the tech companies are seen as leeches, sucking money out of their countries and not creating jobs, making investments, or paying tax. At dinner, the UK chancellor of the exchequer George Osborne hits the same note, saying that Facebook isn't "paying its fair share." I agree with this. Facebook deploys something called a "double Irish" to avoid paying taxes. It's something Google and Apple do as well. The way the double Irish works is that when one of these companies makes a dollar selling ads (or iPhones in Apple's case) in Italy or Germany or elsewhere in the European Union, that revenue can be shifted to Ireland for tax purposes, and then on to a tax-haven country like Bermuda that charges no taxes at all. To do this, the companies have to set up subsidiaries in Ireland and transfer their foreign IP rights to those subsidiaries. What Ireland gets out of the deal is big Google and Apple and Facebook operations located on their soil, with thousands of local employees earning good wages. Those employees pay taxes to Ireland, even if the tech companies don't. After years of controversy and opposition, the EU had just forced Ireland to shut down the boondoggle a few months before Davos.

This makes our next meeting with Irish prime minister Enda Kenny particularly important. Before Facebook, I'd never been in the rooms where the sausage gets made with world leaders. I'd assumed WEF would be like my experience at the United Nations, where for all its flaws, things still had a feeling of idealism to them. A sense that is absent in these Davos meetings. There's no pretense that Facebook is out for anything but ourselves. It's brazen. By this point I know I shouldn't be surprised but it still makes me recoil.

We get together in the WEF Strategic Partners Lounge, a bland room in the Davos Congress Centre packed with temporary furniture. Unlike the setting, Kenny is charming, a charismatic man who occasionally recites poetry from memory or sings in the raucous dinners he hosts each year at Davos. "Ahh, the beautiful ladies of Facebook," he says as he greets Sheryl and me. Coming from another man, this would be creepy. Somehow, from him, it's almost charming. He hugs Sheryl, embraces me. Kenny has a sense of mischief. One year at Davos, tipsy after dinner, he breaks me and Sheryl's assistant Sadie into a beyond-exclusive wine party thrown by an obscenely wealthy private equity guy, telling us, "Come, you'll never have better wine in your life." He barrels past security into a dark room where a bunch of somber-looking men are sipping from glasses and literally taking notes, declaring brightly, "Someone get these gorgeous ladies some wine." And we're begrudgingly handed the most expensive wine I've ever tasted in my life.

Kenny has been one of Facebook's firmest allies since the beginning, and the Irish have gone above and beyond to court our business. Sheryl often tells the story about how she decided to locate the Facebook European headquarters in Ireland in 2008, after the Irish government gave her a special phone when she landed in the country on her first business trip. The phone connected her to someone in the Irish government who could solve any problem or address any accommodation she needed. Every time she meets an Irish politician she brings it up, and sure enough she starts this meeting by praising the phone and telling the prime minister, "I told folks at the White House that they should be like the Irish government, because you are so good to business. That phone!"

Kenny starts with some feel-good chat on how much the government is relying on Facebook to reach citizens, and how Facebook is positively impacting Ireland. Then we get down to brass tacks. With the EU quashing the double Irish, is Facebook going to stay in Ireland?

Google and Twitter have publicly committed to keeping their operations going, but Facebook hasn't.

Sheryl says, "I appreciate that there was substantial pressure and scrutiny this year on global tax rules and arrangements," and thanks Kenny for his "careful" and "considered" handling of it. What she's thanking him for is an additional five years of double Irish for Facebook and the other tech companies that Kenny had somehow wangled. We're protected from tax until 2020. But what comes after that?

I feel sorry for him. I know that's not the right response to tax avoidance, but Ireland has severe austerity measures in place. This man needs the economic boost Facebook's international headquarters provides. It's hard to know what he can give that will satisfy Sheryl. He'd already promised her at Davos three years ago that even if European countries make him tax Facebook, he won't raise the corporate tax above what it is now in Ireland: 12.5 percent. (In comparison, it's 35 percent in the US.) Of course, 12.5 percent is a lot more than nothing, which is what Facebook is currently paying.

Kenny starts explaining the pressure he's facing. "Now, you know Ireland had no choice but to comply with what these other countries. . . ."

Sheryl interrupts. "Did you know Facebook has over five hundred employees from fifty-four nations based in Dublin, and we've just leased a building with capacity for over two thousand employees?"

"Have I told you about the Knowledge Development Box?" Kenny asks with a twinkle in his eye.

"Sarah, stop taking notes," Sheryl instructs, knowing Kenny's about to tell us how he's going to keep the gravy train going for us. She doesn't want it written down. My notes can be subpoenaed. So this part of the meeting will be "off the books." "Is this the thing that you told Marne you were focused on, to make us happy? The IP initiative?"

"Oh yes," replies Kenny, before he describes a new tax scheme that will allow companies like Facebook to separate out "income from intellectual property" and pay half of Ireland's already low tax rate. "Details are still being negotiated."

"We'll have our team help shape them," Sheryl insists.

So is this what it looks like when a company conspires with a government to avoid paying taxes? I know Kenny's just trying to do right by his people and keep a bunch of jobs in Ireland. But still. It doesn't feel right, this backroom deal.

Before the meeting closes, Prime Minister Kenny has a favor to ask. Europe is steaming about privacy and Facebook, and they're about to adopt a law—the General Data Protection Regulation—to crack down on how Big Tech uses personal data. Exactly who will enforce this law is still being negotiated. Kenny wants it to be Ireland. We do too. But we've got a problem because no one believes Ireland will be tough enough on the tech companies. With good reason. Kenny needs to make it seem like his regulator—the Irish Data Protection Commission—is on the case right now, doing proper oversight, a watchdog Europe can trust with this responsibility. "Ireland's been criticized," he says, which is true, and asks if we can assist in "building up the credibility" of his regulator by talking publicly about its audits of Facebook privacy, and the changes we've made because of it. In other words, we should tell the world the lapdog has been a pit bull. Of course Sheryl agrees to this.

As soon as the prime minister leaves, Sheryl turns to me and says, "Taxes."

"Were you not happy with what he offered?"

"Maybe. But whatever happens in Ireland, taxes are coming our way throughout the world. Especially in Europe. I don't think we can escape it. The current tax structure is too hated to last."

It's Joel's first time at Davos, a place he assumed he was going to hate because (in his words) "my people"—that is, Republicans—hate this sort of globalist gathering. But instead, he's having the time of his life.

I find him scooping up tiramisu out of a large catering-size glass dish that he has lifted out of the buffet and is eating all by himself, with a fork, in the middle of the congress center.

"Hey, look at this! Everyone said there wouldn't be any food at Davos and I'd be hungry for days and look at me. I've got a whole tub of tiramisu. I love tiramisu."

"See, isn't Davos great," I respond, almost successfully masking my sarcasm. "I thought 'your people' didn't come to this particular shindig."

"So did I, but it turns out there's a bunch of people I know here."

"Your country club friends? Harvard? DC? Bush administration? Federalist Society friends? Supreme Court? General global elite?"

"All of it."

He smiles triumphantly and scoops up another forkful of tiramisu.

As darkness falls in Davos, I half skid, half run back to the hotel to order some room service ice cream and quietly sing "Happy Birthday" to Sasha before she goes to sleep. It's exactly a year since I received the request for talking points for Davos while I was in the stirrups about to deliver her. I bundle this sweet baby into bed and myself back into snow clothes to race back to brief Sheryl and Joel on their next meetings. I am questioning all my life choices. I want to be at home, with my baby and my husband and my new "mom friends." Surely having a kid and a career is not meant to be like this? I know I'm expected to work as if I don't have children, but I didn't expect it would feel like this. There's a grief to it. I'm still committed to the mission, but it feels like the cost is too high. Though this is what Marne and Sheryl both do. This is the *Lean In* workplace.

And I haven't learned the difference between knowing when to quit and knowing when to persevere.

Joel is very impressed with what he calls his "sweet boots," cowboy-inspired snow boots that set him apart as a Republican in this liberal elite milieu. He sends me a photo of himself wearing the boots, saying, "Look how smaht [*sic*] my boots are. I think I might be able to get away with wearing them to meetings? What do you think?" He regularly asks me to admire the boots and in subsequent emails to me refers to them exclusively as his "stylin' boots." As we move from meeting to meeting across Davos, he makes a point of racing off in his boots and telling me to "hurry and catch up, you're not pregnant now."

Just before midnight he realizes he's lost them and throws a late-night tantrum. He copies me on an email to other staff titled FYI that simply states, "SWW lost my sweet boots," so I understand the extent of his displeasure. Despite the fact I had nothing to do with him losing his boots. And this is how I find myself—when I want to be cuddled up in bed with my sick birthday baby—crawling on my hands and knees through the various coatracks at the congress center in Davos to find the boots—which he accidentally left at a coat check. At 12:58 A.M., I email him, "I have your boots."

It's not always the things you think that will bring you to your knees.

In Sheryl's Davos apartment, she starts to prepare her "Lessons of Davos" email that she'll send to Mark and leadership when we fly out. This will set our policy direction for the rest of the year.

I suggest that she tell leadership we need to take the storms on the horizon seriously. European leaders are telling us that things aren't right—they've noticed Facebook is making gobs of money from their citizens and that isn't translating into jobs or money for them. They're not happy. At the moment they're being reasonable and asking Facebook to find a way to invest, but it's clear that's going to change. I actually believe it's only fair that Facebook should pay more taxes, and that's what I suggest. It's not a crazy idea. Starbucks had just volunteered to scrap its tax-dodging tactics and pay more tax in the UK, agreeing to contribute as much corporate tax in 2015 as it did in its first fourteen years in the country. Compromising now on taxes is not just the right thing to do, I say. Giving a little now is smart strategy; it might prevent worse regulations and taxes later.

Sheryl ignores me, as if I hadn't said anything. Seriously, it's so off the map she doesn't even bother to respond. Instead she taps out her conclusion to Mark and the rest of the Facebook executives: "The best thing we can do is invest in getting policy-makers to use Facebook to communicate and politicians to win elections."

This is how Sheryl wants us to address the growing hatred toward Facebook and the regulations and taxes that are likely to come. Facebook has an ace that the other tech companies don't; we can make Facebook essential to electoral success. The more that politicians are indebted to Facebook, the better it is for us: "Where policy makers have a positive experience using Facebook for campaigns or governance, they're more open to partnering with us to address policy issues." It's a shift that will have far-reaching consequences.

After this, Facebook invests heavily in campaigns and elections around the world. Sheryl directs Joel to hire teams in Asia and Latin America and Europe. They'll coach politicians on how to target specific messages to specific sorts of voters, and they'll sell them ads. Make them reliant on Facebook for their power. This is what Joel's been wanting to do for a while now, and what he has been doing on a small scale. Now he gets a mandate to supercharge it. As he launches into this hiring spree, I fight it best as I can. I think this approach will only end badly. I think we'll get too close to people who lose . . . which could alienate whoever wins. And in other places, I think we'll get too close to objectionable people who do vile things and win office with our help. That won't be good for Facebook in a different way. Either way, we're complicit. Enabling. I think it's best to stay as neutral as possible. Or at the very least let a different part of Facebook handle it. Not the part of Facebook that is responsible for all policy and content decisions. But I lose every fight. Nobody's listening to me.

23

Making Sure This Thing Flies

By April 2015, Internet.org is stalled. Mark's said he'll do whatever it takes to make it a success, and invests inordinate amounts of his own time. But only nine countries have rolled out the app since it launched nine months ago.

I pitch him attending the Summit of the Americas in Panama, where he can meet lots of heads of state and prime ministers in one place. And to supercharge Mark's time at the summit (and elevate him above the other CEOs who'll be there), I've negotiated to have him participate in a panel, alongside President Obama and the presidents of Mexico, Panama, and Brazil (our target countries!). It's been a torturous process to get agreement to have Mark onstage with presidents, but the Panamanians have been helpful accomplices. That is until the White House heard what I'd done. They're furious for reasons I never uncovered, but I think they don't like the power dynamics of Mark onstage with Obama and other presidents. As a result, Mark's ousted from the panel, but they put him in the front row of the audience with the president of Coca-Cola and some other CEOs, and at one point, Obama points to Mark sitting there and says, "I'm glad that my friend, Mark Zuckerberg, is here. Obviously, what he's done with Facebook has been transformative."

Mark is handed a mic to ask a question. He takes the opportunity to promote Internet.org and ends by asking each of the presidents on the panel, "What more can we be doing together to connect everyone in the world?" See what we did there? Mark's momentarily leading them in discussion.

The Mexican president responds, "Digital inclusion is the new alphabet." President Obama adds that "governments need to work with the private sector." He then goes on to give an unexpected example suggesting that in Central America young people, instead of joining gangs, can start internet companies using social media.

Mark's thrilled. He's got presidents lining up to reinforce the importance of connectivity. As the session concludes, Mark and I try to leave our front-row seats but we're sucked into a vortex of people. They're thrusting business cards, calling his name, requesting selfies, and trying to move me out of the way to get to him. I need to hustle Mark out of there to his next meeting. But we can't make any headway through the crowd. Any direction we go, another person appears and I feel us being pushed back into our seats. It's a relief when Mark's security team materializes and pushes people back so we can walk toward the backstage exit. Except we're still not making progress and the circle of people around us starts pushing against Mark's security. His bodyguard senses the danger and starts to forcefully move people out of the way. There's discontent among the crowd as it becomes clear that Mark is leaving the venue, not doing selfies. As his bodyguard forcefully shoves a group of men to the side, a plaintive voice cuts through:

"But, but, but . . . I'm the president of Guatemala."

The people around us fall silent at the cri de coeur and stop jostling—waiting to see how this will unfold. Mark looks at me like, What's the diplomatic protocol after you've shoved the president of Guatemala? And before I can say anything, I see the smile playing on his lips. That's definitely *not* the diplomatic response, and everyone else sees it too. We stand there for what seems like an unreasonably long time before security hustles us out. For years afterward, any-time there are too many people getting into a van or a room is too crowded, there's always someone on the team who'll pipe up with plaintive indignation, "But, but, but . . . I'm the president of Guate-mala."

The hubbub around Mark at the summit continues. The president of Panama stands in front of the press with Mark to announce Internet .org's entry into Panama, and other heads of state are reaching out to ask for Internet.org in their countries. Everyone's talking about the importance of connectivity. Telecom operators who'd refused to engage with us in the past now want to host Internet.org. It's like Internet.org has become the new cool thing no one wants to be left out of, among these national leaders. It's a very different conversation from what we were having before the summit and way better than we'd dreamed. Thirty new partnerships for Internet.org are put in play during the summit. Mark and Javi generously give me the credit for this and report back to Sheryl that I'm a "policy badass." They're so impressed with my ability to pull strings around the world that when a massive container ship emblazoned with the words NEW ZEA-LAND appears in front of us during our tour of the Panama Canal, they're sure I had something to do with it.

We have other adventures in Panama. Drinks at a spectacular rooftop bar. An unexpectedly fun, drunken dinner in a historic build-ing where Javi mistakes the word "delicacy" for "delicatessen" and Mark has to patiently explain that delicious food is not described as a "delicatessen." This is the trip where we go to the state dinner with the scantily clad people at the archeological site. Mark messages me to thank me—which is completely uncharacteristic; he doesn't usu-ally thank his own staff—for making the road trip productive "and also fun," with a smiley emoji. It occurs to me, when does Mark ever get to have much fun?

In the midst of all this positivity and goofing around, a few strange things happen that I register as odd and potentially troubling. The first is Mexico. We thought we had convinced the Mexican president to launch Internet.org after our meeting last year but, like so many of the Internet.org launches, it has stalled out. Even more worrying is the president of Brazil. We learn that she has serious concerns about Internet.org that we need to address. In fact, the meeting with her becomes the most important of the summit, because Brazil is our biggest target in this hemisphere. It's the largest nation in Latin America and half its population is still offline, which makes it critical for Facebook and for Internet.org.

Brazil is also at the forefront of internet regulation globally. It's one of the few countries that was quick to grasp the risks of social media and swiftly move to regulation. Instead of accepting Facebook's line that the government doesn't have authority over us, they've passed internet regulation that's comprehensive and has teeth, far ahead of any other country. It gives them explicit jurisdiction over Big Tech on everything from tax to privacy. They back it up with enforcement. When their courts declare they will block our service, we believe them, because they do.

To top it all off, Brazil's president Dilma Rousseff is someone other leaders in the region listen to and respect. If she turns against Internet.org publicly, it could kill the whole thing. The Brazilian press is reporting that she's going to make her decision soon—either to partner with Facebook on Internet.org or to "protect" internet users in Brazil by keeping it out. We've heard that activists are set to protest if she picks us. And despite all our efforts, we still don't know which way she's leaning.

It was difficult to get any time on Rousseff's schedule for an appointment, but I wrangle an hour at 4:00 P.M. on Friday, the last day of the summit.

And then . . . an impromptu meeting with President Obama is added to the schedule, to start at 3:45. Which is exactly when we're supposed to be driving to President Rousseff. I find out about this minutes before it happens. Someone from the White House must've offered it, and I'm sure if anyone on our team asked Mark, he'd have said yes.

Mark had originally wanted Obama to come with us on our side trip to the Panama Canal. Andrea messaged me and Joel, "Any chance that he would visit the canal with us? POTUS I mean? That could be epic . . . leaders, standing in the middle of physical connectivity and innovation." As if I somehow have the ability to swing a cameo from President Obama whenever Mark might want it. Joel politely pointed out that since Mark is suggesting this less than a week before the summit, he'd be very surprised if Obama's schedule would allow for a road trip to the Panama Canal.

Instead, this impromptu presidential meeting happens in a secure area of the convention center where they're holding the summit. I deliver Mark into the room before Obama gets there, hoping he'll say "stick around" like he does so often. Not this time. I wait in the corridor. When Obama arrives, he leaves his people outside also.

I wait. We should be in our van right now, I think.

Soon it's 4:00. Our meeting with President Rousseff is supposed to be starting. I get a message from the Brazilians that their president is waiting and wants to know where Mark is. It's excruciating.

I message Derick—Mark's communications guy—who's closer to the room, chatting with some Secret Service guys: "Please get him out asap."

He responds, "They are behind closed doors."

I obviously know that they are behind closed doors. I'm standing less than ten feet away from Derick. I just don't want to be the person who interrupts this meeting.

"Knock on the door," I message.

He ignores my message. I march over to where Derick is standing beside a scrum of security guys and pull him away, saying, "You have to go in there and get him out."

"I can't do that. He's with the president of the United States. There's a Secret Service agent right here blocking the door. I'm not going to interrupt them. You do it."

"Derick, I'm not fighting with you. He simply can't keep the president of Brazil waiting any longer. It's a disaster."

"Good. I'll watch you do it."

I move toward the door where Mark's bodyguard Brooks Scott is standing watch, next to a Secret Service agent.

"You need to go into that room and get Mark out," I urge Brooks. "I don't have time to get into it but for protocol reasons it is critical you retrieve Mark now."

I'm obviously trying to make this sound as official as possible, but he doesn't buy it. He knows he doesn't take orders from me. We're all in a standoff, looking from one to the other—me, Derick, Brooks— when I hear the unmistakable noise of a door handle being pulled down. I don't even know if it was my hand that did it. The door swings open and Brooks enters the room so quickly I barely see him move. That's instinct and training; if someone can get to Mark, he has to get there first. I follow him. I look back and see Derick standing in the door frame.

I imagine both President Obama and Mark are surprised and unused to this sort of interruption, but honestly, my mind goes blank today when I try to conjure the exact moment. I remember them sitting toward the back of the room at a table covered by a white tablecloth with blue detail. Obama perched at one corner of the table and Mark close beside. Plain chairs. Both completely relaxed and somehow unsurprised to see me. I don't hear what they're saying, just the pounding of blood in my ears. I walk over and say something—I don't remember what—along the lines of "We gotta go." Mark has no sense of urgency about the president he has waiting. He continues to shoot the shit and loiter with this one for a little bit longer. I do remember it's agonizing, watching him slowly summon himself to go. Finally I get him out of there and rally the rest of the team to get out of the conference hall as quickly as possible.

Of course we're late to meet President Rousseff, but she's gracious about it. Treats it like no big deal. This is a woman who'd been tortured by a military dictatorship, she'd been a guerrilla leader, so I frankly didn't expect her to be the kind of person who'd engage in a lot of chitchat. But she talks to us with warmth, asking with genuine interest about our trip to the Panama Canal (without Obama). When Mark presents her with a Facebook hoodie with a Brazilian flag sewn on, she seems genuinely tickled and puts it on right away.

"I came here to Panama just to meet you," Mark says, which is awkward, given how long we've kept her waiting while he hung with Obama. She doesn't bat an eye. He presses on. "Brazil is so important as a leader for the internet and is so influential. Facebook can help you achieve your goals to bring the benefits of the internet to all the Brazilian people. Our program is called Internet.org."

Unsurprisingly, she already knows the name, and as they get into the substance, Rousseff transitions from charm to a steely grasp of the technical aspects of internet regulation. A trained economist, she asks pointed questions that Mark has a hard time answering about zero rating—where services like Internet.org get subsidized by telecoms, which underpins the whole project. She deflects Mark's efforts to get her to endorse or partner with us to launch the Internet.org app and instead asks for *real* ways to provide free internet in Brazil. She wants infrastructure. She wants investment. She wants drones deploying the internet to remote parts of the Amazon.

And she's right. Facebook could have offered these things. Facebook is investing in internet drones and is currently building a prototype. But when we message the team to see if we can agree to testing the drones in Brazil, they tell us no: "Right now we need to stay focused on making sure this thing flies." I think they already suspect the drones are not going to happen.

Mark starts to get desperate. "I think we could get there quickly by launching the Internet.org app instead this quarter. My schedule is tight but I will come to Brazil in June to launch with you." He offers e-government services and local content. "I have a team ready to make that happen."

President Rousseff is inscrutable. She warmly welcomes Mark's offer to travel to Brazil and says some positive things about the Internet.org app but doesn't commit to anything. And before we know it her team are insisting she has to leave.

Days later she tells the press that she and Mark limited their conversation to Facebook building internet infrastructure in Brazil and didn't discuss Internet.org or zero rating. Not true at all, but at least she's giving a clear signal where Internet.org stands with her. She says that Mark will come to Brazil in June to negotiate a partnership but that "we have to think in our interests."

I share this with the Facebook team. Joel responds, "Oh man. Cold feet already. The battle is joined and we need to start fighting back."

24

California Time

One of the unexpectedly stressful things about traveling with Mark is the repeated questions about why I'm not based in California, closer to him and the teams. These are friendly, teasing, but I know he's serious about this.

Three weeks after Panama, I'm back with Mark and our friend, Japanese prime minister Abe, at Facebook's Menlo Park headquarters. Abe's made good on his promise to visit us, dropping by after his state visit with Obama. He's now one of many heads of state who want to stop by Facebook's HQ.

"This is success," I explain to Mark as we discuss the Abe meeting. "Facebook and meeting with you is becoming a standard thing for heads of state to do, when they visit the president. Like a West Coast White House."

"You're going to be out here all the time, then," he says. Mark's not someone who jokes, but this is his version of an amused poke at me.

"I already am," I respond.

"Then save yourself the trouble and just make it permanent. I don't see what's so great about New York. . . ."

"Then you don't know New York. . . ."

"I grew up there."

"New York City, not the suburbs, Mark."

"What would you know? You're from New Zealand."

I don't take the bait and we move on. No one from the policy team is based in California. They all see the world's center of power as Washington, DC. And Mark hasn't asked anyone from the team to move to California, so I figure it will all blow over. But part of me worries that Mark has understood what I see, that power is shifting and Silicon Valley is starting to assert itself on its own terms. A place political power players have to visit. A few weeks later, completely out of nowhere, I receive this message:

From: Mark Zuckerberg
Sent: Friday, May 29, 2015, 5:54 P.M.
To: Sarah Wynn-Williams
Subject: Thank you

Sarah,

Thanks for all that you are doing around the world to build important relationships for Internet.org.

You've set up many critical meetings with Heads of State, which is pretty much impossible to do. You created a rally in Indonesia, got the meet and greet with Kirchner [the president of Argentina] and you've worked hard to keep things moving forward despite our challenges.

I'm really optimistic that we'll achieve our goals, and you work [sic] is a really important part of connecting the world.

Mark

Every fiber of my being wants to stay in New York with the life we've built there, but when I read this I know we have to move to

California. It may not look like much. An encouraging email from a boss. But like I said, Mark doesn't send these. He thinks that if you work directly with him regularly you should know you're good at your job. You don't need affirmation. And combined with the drumbeat of comments about moving, I assume this email is his way of saying it's time to relocate. And he's choosing to flatter me into it, rather than force me. But he's capable of either.

Weeks later when I've sorted the logistics and let him know I'm relocating, he sends the sort of gracious email that would be normal from another sort of boss but surprises me from him.

From: Mark Zuckerberg
Sent: Thursday, July 02, 2015, 1:39 A.M.
To: Sarah Wynn-Williams
Subject: MPK [Menlo Park]

I'm glad you're moving to MPK and I'm looking forward to working together more closely.

Thanks again for everything you're doing. We're going to have a big impact all over the world.

Mark

Note the timestamp. Typical.

25

Muppets and Monsignors

September 2015 ends with a big week for Mark on the two projects most important to him: China and Internet.org. He also gives the keynote speech at Oculus Connect, the conference we've organized to promote Facebook's investments in virtual reality. Each of these disparate threads represents a different vision for Facebook's future. If any one of them comes through, we'll be a very different company.

First up during that week is Chinese president Xi Jinping.

I was confused months earlier when Vaughan and the China cheerleaders inside Facebook announced that President Xi would begin his state visit to the US at Facebook's headquarters, to announce our entry into China. A Facebook page that Vaughan and the China team helped establish just for the visit, #XiVISITUSA, had somehow amassed over five million followers. I found that odd. More people are into this visit than the entire population of my country? Who are they? Facebook isn't even available in China. What exactly had been done to the algorithm to boost the audience? Will we be offering this incredibly valuable service to other heads of state? Don't we need to be honest about it?

The team apparently put a lot of effort into protecting the page. Something other heads of state, like the Mexican president hit by the poop emoji storm, would have loved. And the team worked toward offering VIP service for other Chinese Communist Party pages.

Then, in mid-August, we hear from Condoleezza Rice's consulting firm—which we've hired to help with China—that the Chinese president will *not* be visiting Silicon Valley on his visit. This is news to Vaughan and the rest of Facebook. Joel responds in an email, "If accurate, seems like a strong signal they aren't on a late September timetable" to announce our entry into China. Debbie forwards me his email with this comment: "Exactly what you said." She's another China skeptic.

Xi chooses Seattle, the home of Amazon and Microsoft, to start his visit. Ouch.

Vaughan keeps hopes alive of a meeting between Mark and Xi in Seattle, suggesting it will be the time and place where Facebook's entry into China is announced. Then this is scaled back to a "pull-aside" at a group meeting and no announcement, and finally a "longer than normal handshake," which Mark is prepared to fly to Seattle for. They're desperate.

The handshake does happen, but in a particularly galling setting: the Microsoft campus, during Xi's tour of the facilities. I'm not with them, but watching the video, it's hard to tell if it's "longer than normal." They're together for less than a minute. In contrast, Xi holds a closed-door meeting with thirty American and Chinese CEOs, including Jeff Bezos and Tim Cook. Mark is not invited.

Having invested so much to get this handshake, Mark posts a photo of it on his Facebook page, making it sound like he actually was allowed to attend the meeting with the other CEOs:

Today I met President Xi Jinping of China at the 8th annual US-China Internet Industry Forum in Seattle. The Forum is an opportunity for CEOs of technology companies to meet with government officials from the US and China to discuss common issues for the future of our industry.

He adds at the end:

On a personal note, this was the first time I've ever spoken with a world leader entirely in a foreign language. I consider that a meaningful personal milestone.

But there's a problem with the photo he posts. It's from an angle where you see Mark's face, and the back of President Xi's head. This is a breach of protocol. I'm not there because I try to avoid all things China. But the moment I see it, I know there's going to be trouble, and sure enough, panic ensues at forty thousand feet on Mark's private jet when the Chinese government contacts them over the spotty internet connection to let him know they're furious about it. Instead of creating a positive first impression with the president of China, they've created a diplomatic crisis. We're banned from China, barred from the meetings with the other tech CEOs, confined to a one-minute handshake, and even that, they've screwed up.

Next come agonizing discussions about whether to leave the photo up. But every person on that jet has been on the receiving end of requests to remove embarrassing things from Facebook, and they're all acutely aware that taking something down can attract way more attention and controversy than simply leaving it up. They continue debating the entire flight, and as they land the realization hits that the photo is already everywhere across the internet. The damage is done. They leave it up.

Two days later, at a state dinner in the White House, Mark gets another chance to speak with Xi. In Mandarin, he asks Xi if he'll do him the honor of naming his unborn child. Xi refuses.

The next day, Saturday, September 26, Mark addresses the United Nations, hoping to rouse excitement for Internet.org. As always, I try to get him the most high-profile speaking slot possible. At the UN that means the morning. The earlier you are, the more important you are. I manage to book him between the president of

Argentina and the prime minister of the UK, and then Mark's assistant Andrea nixes it. The United Nations isn't important enough for Mark to do an event before noon. He still doesn't like getting out of bed early. We compromise with a later slot. The day before the event at the UN, when Elliot sees which presidents are scheduled to speak before and after Mark, he suggests pulling out. This is before tech companies were engaging with the UN, and I find no one on my side in wanting Mark to speak there. The whole thing is being treated as if Mark was indulging me by agreeing to do it in the first place, like he was visiting my hometown as a favor or something. "These heads of state are not particularly impressive, no?" Elliot writes. I feel myself bristle, as a citizen of one of those "not particularly impressive" nations. In the end, he decides that a photo of Mark addressing the UN will be worth the indignity, and we don't cancel.

We're going to the UN because we're trying to influence their Sustainable Development Goals. They update these every fifteen years. They're targets to do things like reduce global poverty and illiteracy and inequality, and promote gender equality. Back when I first started at Facebook, Marne and I tried to get the United Nations to add internet access (or any reference to the internet) to the UN's seventeen development goals. At first, we were literally laughed at — "You mean you're here from some internet site to tell me that giving people the internet is more important than ending child mortality? Or eradicating hunger?" But now the draft goals for 2015 include a few references to connectivity. Internet access is definitely not a UN priority. But at least they're acknowledging it.

To push them further in this direction, I pitch a "Connectivity Declaration." It's a petition anyone can sign online, stating that "internet access is essential for achieving humanity's #globalgoals" and pointing out that "half the people on this planet don't have access, especially women and girls." It calls on "leaders and innovators from all countries, industries and communities to work together as one to make universal internet access a reality by 2020."

In my mind, we're not just doing this because it'll create more Facebook users and promote Internet.org. It really seems like a tangible way we can use our power to make the world a better place. In retrospect, staggeringly naive.

Facebook spends over $1 million on full-page advertisements championing the Connectivity Declaration in the *New York Times*, the *Wall Street Journal*, and other publications around the world, and I'm astonished how many people take it seriously and sign up. We get a bizarre bedfellows party of celebrity endorsements from Shakira, Stephen Hawking, George Takei, Bill Gates, and Charlize Theron. Real NGOs like the United Nations Foundation sign on. We partner with Bono's ONE Foundation, because Bono is a friend of Sheryl's, and write an op-ed for Bono and Mark to place in the *New York Times* setting out our connectivity agenda in more detail. Everyone's surprised when Bono wants to edit it.

We spend millions more building a giant "innovation pop-up" in the plaza right in front of the UN, a big glass structure with screens depicting the connected world and videos of people who've recently gotten the internet, along with an array of VR headsets, an Instagram wall, and the extremely large wing of a drone prototype that we're hoping will someday deliver internet from the air.

Mark delivers his speech to the United Nations General Assembly and gets generally glowing press for it. CNN's website: "Mark Zuckerberg: Internet Access Can Eradicate Extreme Poverty." Reuters: "Facebook Founder Calls for Universal Internet to Help Cure Global Ills." *Wired*: "Zuckerberg to the U.N.: The Internet Belongs to Everyone." I'm thrilled these things no one else wanted to do have all worked.

But then we have a lunch at the United Nations Private Sector Forum, with Secretary General Ban Ki-moon and German chancellor Angela Merkel. Mark's nervous sitting next to Merkel, because Germany has several open investigations into Facebook privacy issues dating back to Marne's Holocaust meeting with the German ministerial delegation, and has been one of the most suspicious and effective regulators of the internet. Before the speeches, Merkel is caught on a hot mic pressing Mark to remove antirefugee posts from Facebook in Germany. She's just opened her borders to hundreds of thousands of Syrian refugees, she's under significant political pressure, and the torrent of racist anti-immigrant posts is damaging her popularity and making her job that much harder. Mark is heard on mic agreeing, "We need to do some work" on this hate speech.

Then, when he gets onstage to deliver his keynote, it's a surprise to everyone including me when Mark announces that Facebook will be "working with UNHCR [the United Nations High Commissioner for Refugees] to bring the Internet to refugee camps." I've never heard anyone breathe a word about this at Facebook. Neither, apparently, has Elliot, Facebook's policy head, who sends out an email to the team asking, "Does anyone know where the offer of wifi to refugee camps came from?"

No one does. Even the head of Internet.org, Chris Daniels, was blindsided by this and writes, "We would appreciate a discussion on these announcements before they are announced."

Apparently Mark made this up.

Maybe he'd been planning to announce this for days, and for some reason didn't want to discuss it with all of us. But it also seems possible that it was an ad lib, made up on the fly to quiet some inner discomfort after Angela Merkel scolded Mark for worsening the refugee crisis. Maybe he thinks everyone just freestyles at the United Nations.

At the luncheon, there's no time to think through what Mark's refugee camp announcement means. We need to show Bono around our innovation pop-up and then rush across Manhattan to Central Park.

Central Park is mobbed. It's the annual Global Citizen Festival, and sixty thousand people have shown up on the Great Lawn for a kind of thinking man's Davos music-and-ideas concert. The lineup includes Beyoncé, Coldplay, and Stephen Colbert.

I think Mark will love this: crowds, celebrities, young idealistic attendees. He's talked about wanting to play a stadium. But I'm the only one who wants him to do it. Elliot, Joel, Andrea—everyone else is adamantly opposed. There's too much happening this week with Xi's visit, the state dinner, and the United Nations. They want me to let it go. But I know they haven't asked Mark, and I'm convinced this satisfies something he's been wanting ever since his request for a riot, so I don't let it go.

To make the timing work and get Mark a slot onstage after the UN luncheon and the pop-up, I'd asked the festival organizers to move Big Bird. They initially said no, insisting that my Big Bird problem created issues for Malala and Beyoncé. Then they relented and moved Big Bird so he's right before Mark. Big Bird's fine with this, but the Facebook team does not think that this sets the right tone—Elliot doesn't want Mark to follow a giant yellow Muppet—so I need Big Bird moved again. I'm still scrambling to solve that when Mark emails saying that the pope's going to be in New York that same day and, on top of everything else, he'd like an audience with His Holiness.

I email a monsignor I've worked with in the past to ask about meeting the pope, and ask Big Bird if he can swap with Bill Nye the Science Guy. That would work for Mark, Malala, Beyoncé, and maybe the pope. But my hopes are dashed when I'm informed that Big Bird can't take the stage after dark, and that Big Bird and his team are not prepared to do any more accommodating for Mark Zuckerberg.

Andrea latches onto the idea that all our scheduling problems will be solved if Mark simply provides a video for the Global Citizen Festival rather than appearing in person. She proceeds to get the video filmed. I continue to push for Mark to do it in person and beg her not to submit the video, but the most I can secure is a promise that we'll make a decision on the day of the event. Which seems unnecessarily fraught to me. My position is that Mark will definitely want to get in front of a huge crowd. Her position is that it's going to be chaos getting from one place to another in New York during UN week. Meanwhile, the pope's representative responds, "Send Mark to Rome if he wants an audience with the Pope."

I guess we're all staking out our positions.

When we arrive at Central Park, we're ushered into the penned-off area for the performers. Common is laughing with Olivia Wilde in the corner and Usher is casually taking photos of some of the beautiful women lounging around. Leonardo DiCaprio is sharing our green room, talking to Mark about some charity thing he wants Mark to support. But I can enjoy none of this because I'm utterly exhausted. I'm three months pregnant with my second child and have felt sick for every day of those three months. I'm also worried I'm going to bump into Big Bird, who I hear is mightily pissed at me about the whole schedule thing.

I excuse myself to get a front-row position for Mark's speech and leave Andrea and Mark in the green room.

As Bill Nye the Science Guy wraps up, having successfully switched the slots, I watch the steps where Mark will take the stage. There seems to be some sort of weird commotion between Andrea and the stagehand; she's arguing with him and he seems to be giving as good as he's getting. I race over, but before I get there I see Mark bouncing up the steps onto the stage and surveying the crowd of tens of thousands. They all seem weirdly excited by the Science Guy or Mark. I can't really tell. Perhaps both. Out of the corner of my eye, I catch sight of Big Bird backstage and immediately feel every muscle in my body tense.

Mark takes the microphone and seems to be looking for the teleprompter, and maybe that makes him miss a beat or maybe the setting sun is in his eyes, but just as he starts his speech there's some weird feedback. His words are repeating but they're a little bit different. What is happening? He stops talking and just stands there, frozen, but his voice keeps going. I realize to my horror that somehow a giant projection of his face is speaking. It's the video Andrea submitted. It's booming out and Mark is now looking around desperately, like an animal in a trap. The audience is confused. I want to throw up. I can't look at him in case he makes eye contact with me. I start to call every person I have ever connected with at the festival to tell them to stop the tape. No one picks up.

What is a very short video feels like it grinds on for eternity. Mark awkwardly looks at the crowd. They stare back at him. I wonder, just for a moment, if Big Bird is behind this. The video ends and I wait for Mark to crack a joke or say something to the audience. But no, he just quietly backs down the stairs on the side of the stage while still facing the crowd. It reminds me of the GIF of Homer Simpson backing away through a hedge.

"What happened????" I rush over to him and Andrea.

"We needed to do his face and change his shirt. . . ." I mentally kick myself. I know about his sweating issue. Along with a change of T-shirt, Andrea now carries these blotting papers with her everywhere and blots Mark's face when he sweats. "I told them to wait while he changed."

"But they can't wait," I interrupt her. "They squeezed us in. They need to set up the stage for Beyoncé and Malala."

I'm not sure why but this guts me. Maybe because I'd pushed so hard to make it happen. Maybe because I'm utterly exhausted and not quite in control of my emotions, thanks to the pregnancy. I'm worried I might cry, and I know that would not be professional or proportionate.

"Look, this is my fault, I should have stayed with you," I say. Knowing that I had, somewhat shamefully, left them alone by the stage to avoid Big Bird.

"Sarah, Dre, look, this is my fault," Mark says earnestly. He's looking deep into my eyes. "No, seriously, it's my fault."

"It isn't," I insist. "I should have been able to stop the video. . . ."

"Look, Sarah, if I was good at speaking or even improvising this wouldn't be a big deal. I would have said something. I would have engaged the crowd. I need to work on this stuff. It's me, not you. Really."

If I was worried about crying before, I'm even more worried now that I'll cry at his kindness. He's never tried to comfort me before. He's surprisingly . . . tender?

"You've done an amazing job, really. I would never have thought we could do any of what we've achieved today. Focus on all the impact you've had, Sarah."

As we transfer from van, to helicopter, to private jet, Mark continues to reassure me—it's the most human he's ever seemed—and by the time someone cracks a Big Bird joke at my expense, I'm fine.

Monday morning Mark emails the team, wanting a Facebook post about his United Nations announcement, his plan to bring Wi-Fi to refugee camps. He suggests we use a photo he's found of a grinning white engineer surrounded by refugees in Tanzania.

I don't want to be the only person pushing back against this terrible idea, so I ask Dex Torricke-Barton to point out the white-savior problem to Mark. He emails Mark, "Would not use this photo—optics problematic for diversity (prosperous white guy saving the poor black kids)."

I respond as politely as I can manage on the bigger problem—Mark announced an initiative at the United Nations that doesn't seem to exist. The way I put this is that it's not the time to post, as we're "right at the beginning of this program with limited substance." Everyone agrees not to post for now.

Elliot meets with some of the Internet.org people to discuss how to implement what Mark promised and get Wi-Fi into refugee camps. They decide we shouldn't be giving away Wi-Fi for free but should instead create a "sustainable business model" where refugees will pay. Joel hears about this, and he writes the group, "Apologies for the ignorant question, but do the refugees in these camps have a source of income?"

This is when it really hits me. There's not going to be any meaningful Wi-Fi delivered to refugee camps by Facebook, like Mark has announced at the UN. When we left New York I'd never felt more connected to Mark, and now I feel stupid. The United Nations still means something to me. Despite its flaws. I'm the one who suggested he go there to lay out his vision for making the world a better place, and it feels weirdly personal that he'd be so cavalier or cynical to make this announcement there without it being ready to roll out. In fact, he has not even discussed it with his team before he speaks. Like, what kind of person does this—promises to help people most in need without a plan in place or having discussed if it will be possible?

At this point I'm still a true believer in Facebook's mission to change the world. And I had thought my role in it—my contribution—would be to get Mark to engage internationally, meet with real heads of state. I thought that would teach him to exercise political power responsibly. Make reasonable compromises when needed, on privacy, protecting children, and whatever mattered. Build a company that would make money, sure, but also be a good citizen of the world.

But now it occurs to me that maybe Mark isn't on the same page at all. Somehow, introducing him to global leaders and putting him on the world stage at the United Nations is having the opposite effect of what I'd hoped. He seems to be giving less of a damn. Saying things because they sound good. Posting things because they look good. Looking back now, I regret having enabled this.

It gives me a bad feeling in the pit of my stomach.

What unfolds next with Internet.org only makes the feeling worse.

26

The Wicked Witch of the West

Sixty-seven digital rights groups around the world have joined forces to oppose Internet.org. They summarize their objections in an open letter to Mark Zuckerberg. For starters, they point out—correctly—that Internet.org doesn't actually deliver the full internet. Instead, users get access to a handful of apps and websites that have been approved by Facebook and local service providers. This violates basic principles of net neutrality, the idea that everyone should have equal access to all the information and services on the internet, and the ability to create content and innovate without asking anyone for permission. Reducing the internet to a few stripped-down apps also makes it that much easier for any government to control and censor the information reaching its citizens.

There's a hastily organized videoconference between Chris Daniels, who runs Internet.org, and digital rights representatives. It doesn't go well, full of accusations, anger, and vitriol on both sides.

The problems identified by the digital rights groups are so cartoonishly awful that I initially assume they have it wrong. But I discover they are right. They point out that none of the websites on Internet.org—including the stripped-down version of Facebook—have the basic kinds of security and moderation we use everywhere else. So terrorism, hate speech, fraud, spam, and sexual content all go unchecked. You could be organizing a terrorist attack or inciting people to violence on Facebook. Internet.org prohibits encryption that could protect users from government surveillance or fraud or cyberattacks. There's no two-factor security protecting people's data and identities. It pushes all these problems onto the people least able to solve them.

In short, Internet.org entrenches the digital divide between the haves and the have-nots, by delivering a crap version of the internet to two-thirds of the world. The two-thirds least digitally literate and able to cope with it. What Mark's running, in the digital rights groups' view, is a bait and switch. He's pretending in his lofty speeches that this is all about connectivity and handing people the tools they need to better their lives, when in fact he's delivering nothing even close. The whole thing, in their view, is a power play to sign up more people to Facebook.

When they lay this out, Chris feels personally attacked, outraged that they're questioning Facebook's good intentions. The way he sees it, Facebook choosing which websites can be accessed from Internet .org is just like Apple's App Store or the Google Play Store dictating what apps are available there. We're making an app and negotiating a deal so people can get it for free—what's so evil about that? By the end of the meeting he's red-faced and angry and telling the digital rights groups that "they're trying to dictate the content of Internet .org," which is exactly what they're accusing Facebook of.

The meeting rooms in Facebook's offices all have cutesy names (Guns 'n' Rosegarden in DC, I'll Be Bak Choy in Singapore), and our goal of convincing human rights groups of Facebook's good intentions is perhaps not helped by the fact that the name of the meeting room, Wicked Witch of the West, is displayed, without explanation, under Chris's talking head for the entire meeting. (I point this out to him afterward, and within days the name of the meeting room has been changed.)

I leave the meeting convinced that we're on the wrong side of this one. I feel like Mark is wrapping himself in a cloak of moral superiority when he pitches Internet.org, pretending it's advancing human rights and solving the digital divide, and what he's delivering is so far from that. It's ugly. This isn't Facebook as a force for good or Mark acting responsibly. I, perhaps foolishly, write an email to the leaders of Internet.org arguing that we shouldn't pretend that we're trying to save the world with Internet.org. Let's just admit we're doing it to get more users. Elliot quickly shoots back:

> I think any move away from "public good" will be frustrating for Mark, since he views internet.org as both a growth [get more users] AND a brand [philanthropic/good for the world branding].

At the very least, I argue, we should change the name. The digital rights groups are right when they say the name is deceptive. That's so much of their problem with this project. Internet.org isn't the internet, and ".org" suggests that it's a nonprofit enterprise, which it isn't. Let's be honest about what this is and is not. Also: we'll never get into one of our key countries—Brazil—if we don't change the name. Their Ministry of Justice has declared the name is misleading and barred us from using it in Brazil.

I bring this up with Mark many times. He deflects, blames me for not doing a better job managing the Brazilians, or tells me the name Internet.org is his choice and he has good reasons for choosing it.

The tussle grinds on for weeks. I keep pushing and after weeks of meetings, marketing research, PowerPoints, product road maps, and fights with every layer of Internet.org leadership, we end up in a tense showdown with all the Internet.org guys in Mark's personal meeting room at headquarters. Mark doesn't disguise his anger at the situation and lack of progress on Internet.org. He's combative, and at times surly, rehearsing all the arguments I've heard ad nauseum over the months we've been debating this, but it feels personal because I'm the only one opposing him. I'm the only one urging compromise with our opponents on this issue. And, unsurprisingly, I'm the only woman in the room. I try to convince Mark that by giving in on this point, we'll score wins that are more important to us. He can't accept the need to concede on anything. He wants to win it all. After railing against the name change for over twenty long minutes while we sit in silence, he ultimately concedes to changing the name in Brazil only. He suggests the name Free Apps (and freeapps.com).

The problem is that in Brazil the app isn't free; users have a minimum balance requirement and tax payment. It takes another month of arguing before we arrive at our new name: Free Basics. That'll be what Internet.org is called, not just in Brazil but everywhere.

27

Street Fighter Tactics

The problems in Brazil are bad, but the problems in India are worse. Facebook launched Internet.org in India in February 2015. At that time, of the four billion people in the world who weren't connected to the internet, one billion lived in India (although that changed rapidly in years to come). India was always a top priority for Internet.org. But after a promising start, things quickly unraveled. The government's Telecom Regulatory Authority (TRAI) started to flex its significant power and announced it was going to look into programs like Internet.org and get the public to weigh in on whether they should be banned. Some of our Indian partners on Internet.org—like Flipkart (India's Amazon) and NDTV (India's CNN)—knew this meant we were probably doomed, and hurriedly pulled out of the app. Sheryl tried to reassure the Facebook leadership:

> Our policy team is directly engaged with the government, include [sic] Prime Minister Modi's office. We're lucky this is happening in a place where we have very deep senior relationships in the government, but it's still going to be hard. If we lose this in India it will send all the wrong signals in Latin America.

Angry at losing on the name change to free basics, Mark keeps instructing the team to "go on the offensive" against governments. No one really understands what he means, but I have a sinking feeling that it's not going to be good.

On August 21, 2015, Mark assembles all the senior men working on what's now called Free Basics and me in his conference room named the Aquarium. The guys are pretty tense and Mark addresses the group like a general addressing his troops—one who is displeased with their performance.

Mark opens the meeting by talking admiringly about what he calls "street fighter tactics" that Uber is employing against politicians around the world and how successful they've been. I'd thought there was a general agreement that Facebook didn't use these underhand tactics and we certainly didn't admire them.

Uber weaponizes their drivers and riders, creating strikes, protests, and transportation chaos, forcing authorities to the table. They're sponsoring the soccer teams of the children of key Brazilian senators responsible for decisions that impact their business, insisting on having UBER plastered across their kids' uniforms. They propose compiling opposition research on journalists. It's dirty. But what becomes clear the more Mark speaks is that not only does he not judge what Uber is doing, he's judging us for not doing it. Mark believes Facebook could have a lot more leverage with politicians than Uber ever could, and we're failing him by not using these tactics.

He launches into a spiel about Emperor Augustus, his favorite emperor, who led the transformation of Rome from a republic to an empire. He talks about "offense." He wants to mobilize Facebook users. He wants pro-Facebook activists. He wants protests.

Then he talks "defense." He wants lists of adversaries, whether they're companies, individuals, organizations, or governments. He wants to know how we can use the platform and tools we have to win against these adversaries. He doesn't want us to constrain ourselves to our usual Internet.org tools. He wants us to leverage *all* of

Facebook to find the right things to offer our enemies in order to pull them over to our side. He wants us to invent ways to use the platform and the algorithm to pressure them. He wants to establish a team within Facebook to figure out how to build the tools that will use the algorithm and platform to pressure adversaries, including politicians who oppose us, to bolster the policy team.

I try to catch Joel's eye to see if he's also shocked by what he's hearing. He won't look at me. He looks chastened, not surprised. As if he's heard all this before.

"When you say 'adversary,' who do you mean?" I raise my hand and ask tentatively, a little concerned about what will happen to anyone on one of these lists.

"Anyone who opposes us is an adversary," Mark responds firmly. Not acknowledging that when it comes to Free Basics, that's basically everyone. All I can think is how horrified politicians would be if they knew Facebook was harnessing the platform and its power to put the screws to their thumbs.

He's angered nearly every human rights group we work with, they're now on the list of adversaries, and he's about to torch all the trust we've spent years building with politicians and leaders around the world. And he doesn't care. In fact, he's doubling down and compiling an enemies list, going after anyone who raises reasonable concerns about Internet.org. After years at the company, I'd never seen him go on the offense like this, with such ferocity and hostility. There's no idealism there at all, not about Facebook or Free Basics or anything. This isn't the revolution I signed up for. This isn't who I thought Mark would become, when I first tried to coax him into international politics. I don't want to be part of any of that. But I'm pregnant and showing and it's no time to start looking for a job. So I make a decision. Up till now, I've done everything I could to help Facebook grow. But now is a turning point. For the first time since I pitched this job to Facebook, I won't exhaust everything I have to deliver what my bosses want. I won't do all I can to develop creative strategies to advocate and convince governments and civil society that they're wrong because I don't think they are. Instead, I'll focus my efforts on Facebook's leadership, keep raising objections in meetings and emails at Facebook. I'll execute Mark's orders halfheartedly—focusing on the ones I agree with and not putting particular effort into the others. I'll no longer try to do the impossible to make things happen for Facebook. When civil society groups and the Brazilian government point out problems with Free Basics, I won't try to buy them off with "thoughtful partnerships." I will keep bringing their issues—that there's no encryption, no privacy policy, and no moderation of content on Free Basics—to the teams responsible for them at Facebook, knowing they probably won't fix them. And they don't.

This feels so weird to me. I know how much Mark wants Internet .org and believes in it. But I tell myself I joined Facebook because I believed the platform was a force for good that would change the world. I didn't join for Mark.

It doesn't take long for an actual "war room" to be established. But just for India, because I refuse to do it for Brazil.

Soon they're cranking out advertising campaigns across TV, newspapers, cinemas, radio, and billboards in India. Spending tens of millions of dollars, not including the dark-post (targeted nonpublic posts for specific users that only they would see) advertising on Facebook itself, which is aiming to reach over 50 percent of adult users in India. There are separate SMS campaigns. Their strategy—laid out in an "India Action Plan"—calls for them to "galvanize actual (*or at least the appearance of*) public support," the italics give the game away somewhat here. So there are op-eds. User stories. They organize protests—or riots, as some in the marketing team joke—in support of Free Basics. When I ask that team how they managed to get people there, why on earth Indians would feel so strongly about a poorly designed Facebook product with many flaws that they would march in the streets for Internet.org, one of them tells me it was by promising free T-shirts. I don't know if he's joking. They activate the megaphone that Mark wouldn't let Sheryl use for organ donation. It warns, "Free Basic Services are at risk in India," and tells users to show their support by liking the page. Mark writes to Prime Minister Modi trying to arrange a meeting. Sheryl calls the minister in charge of the internet; Joel and the India team organize outreach to other politicians. There's lots of travel back and forth to India.

The Indian regulator, TRAI, has a new chairman and in mid-November he announces that he wants to make a quick decision after the agency has dithered for nearly a year. For the second time, the regulator asks the public to comment on four questions concerning net neutrality and zero rating, which together will determine whether Free Basics lives or dies.

We have six weeks. Mark had told the team to leverage every tool Facebook has, so all Indian Facebook users now see a pop-up when they log in:

> Unless you take action now, India could lose free access to basic internet. Tell the TRAI you support Free Basics and digital equality in India. A small, vocal group of critics are lobbying to have Free Basics shut down on the basis of net neutrality. Instead of giving people access to some basic internet services for free, they demand that people pay equally to receive access to all internet services—even if that means 1 billion people receive no services because access costs too much.

The megaphone has a large purple button prompting all Indian Facebook users to email the regulator. Clicking on this sends a form letter supporting Free Basics into the official "public consultation."

To create virality, the team designed it so that clicking on this would also notify a user's friend list that they had submitted a letter to the regulator. As if this were not intrusive enough, many users complain that even if they declined to send the message, merely lingering on the page caused Facebook to send all their friends a notification saying they had written to the regulator. This feat of engineering resulted in nearly 17 million submissions to TRAI by January 7, 2016. Well, 16,987,204 emails to be precise.

So there's shock and panic on Sunday, January 10, when TRAI announces that it's received only 1.4 million submissions.

"So the reported numbers are off by a factor of 10?" Joel queries.

The guy responsible for the campaign tells him yes. "We were monitoring logs on this and as far as I know 16.9M emails were all actually delivered."

This prompts further digging. Then a discovery. It looks like something stopped the emails from actually being sent out. Some sort of technical glitch. They're trying to figure out what happened but it's a complex system.

The period to comment has ended and the team agrees there's no way TRAI will accept more comments after the deadline. The atmosphere at Facebook's headquarters is funereal. Everyone's like, "Someone's gonna get fired. Don't know who it'll be. But someone's gonna get fired." Leaders leave crisis meetings to "comfort their teams." There are bouts of collective disbelief. How, after spending tens of millions of dollars, the war room, the advertising campaigns, the daily crisis meetings, Mark's many visits to India, Modi's visit to Facebook, how had Facebook stumbled right at the finish line by messing up the technology to deliver these comments? We're a technology company.

A few days later, a breakthrough. The team figures out what happened. Someone at TRAI—whoever controlled the email address for the public comments—simply opted out of all emails from Facebook. This happened back on Wednesday, December 16, between 9:00 and 10:00 P.M. PST. There's a record of it on Facebook's logs. In the hour before they opted out, over 200,000 emails were sent to them. In the hour after, it dropped to 251.

Mark and some of the brightest tech minds in the world devoted months to this, and some low-ranking official in India outfoxed them simply by clicking an opt-out box.

Elliot immediately flies to India to try to convince TRAI to take the 17 million submissions. He reports back to Mark and Sheryl, "This was a contentious discussion with lots of anger and frustration by TRAI's team—they felt that we exploited our position as gatekeeper." The regulator was furious that Facebook's viral submissions didn't actually answer the four questions the regulator had asked. Why should they accept them as actual public comment? The TRAI felt like Facebook had reduced a democratic public consultation to a popularity contest and abused its platform and power. Nonetheless, Elliot convinces them to accept all 17 million comments—which of course are all the same exact comments, 17 million times over—on a flash drive. He returns to California confident that he's won this, and writes to Mark and Sheryl, "It's difficult to believe that TRAI will come out with a blanket prohibition of zero rating." Free Basics will survive in India.

A few weeks later, on February 8, 2016, the regulator published its decision. Free Basics was banned. Completely struck down. A blanket prohibition of zero rating. Effective immediately. Which feels like a special "fuck you" because it means Facebook has to figure out how to shut it down in a day. They could've given the team a small grace period to turn the thing off.

In our meeting when we learn the news, Elliot looks defeated and humbled in a way I've never seen him. It takes him weeks to shake it. We've never lost a fight this big.

Internet.org has two other priority projects, and they both crash and burn—literally—within months. In June, the Aquila prototype, a drone the size of a jet airplane that is supposed to deliver Wi-Fi and stay in flight for a year, smashes to earth during a test flight. A National Transportation Safety Board review of the accident said it crashed because it was flying in stronger winds than it was built to handle. The website the Verge showed this report to an aviation expert who criticized the fact that Mark was there for the maiden voyage, saying it put pressure on the engineers to fly despite the high winds. "I never would have approved flying in those conditions—and certainly not having the CEO coming in to witness it."

Three months later, on September 1, Elon Musk's SpaceX rocket explodes on the launchpad, completely destroying the Internet.org satellite it's supposed to be putting in orbit. Mark posted,

As I'm here in Africa, I'm deeply disappointed to hear that SpaceX's launch failure destroyed our satellite that would have provided connectivity to so many entrepreneurs and everyone else across the continent. Fortunately, we have developed other technologies like Aquila that will connect people as well.

Aquila, of course, was the drone that crashed on its maiden flight.

After this, Free Basics doesn't die immediately. It launches in a few more countries: Nigeria, Madagascar, Algeria, Belarus, and unfortunately Myanmar. (That becomes a particular disaster that I'll get to in a bit.) But there are no more daily crisis meetings, no more war room. Mark and the other senior leaders simply disappear from the effort and turn their attention elsewhere.

28

Lean In and Lie Back

Sheryl's absence from the Internet.org fiasco is not unusual. By this time she's absent from a lot. What's more surprising is that it's a twenty-six-year-old who steps into her role.

Rather than appointing an experienced chief of staff, Sheryl hires a number of young graduates who fulfill a hybrid administrative/advisory/personal assistant role. These positions attract ambitious graduates who want to be close to power. Part business, part lady-in-waiting. Over time they begin to wield significant power themselves, becoming more of a consigliere than an assistant.

Of these hires, Sadie is the gold standard. An Ivy League graduate, good-looking, with a ruthless efficiency in building the perfect résumé. She took a creative and apt shortcut to the job by working at Sheryl's Lean In Foundation. If anyone embodies leaning in, it's Sadie.

I like working with her and we become friends. She's smart, charming, and way funnier than most of the self-serious super-achievers we work with. She thrives in the role, confiding with delight, "You would not believe the things Sheryl's delegated to me to decide." We live in the same neighborhood in San Francisco and commute to and from the office together. Weirdly, Mark has his San Francisco house not too far from ours. When I ask him why we never see him in the neighborhood, he explains it's because he can't get planning permission for a place to park his helicopter so he rarely uses the house. We might live in similar places, but we are living completely different lives.

I'm delighted when Sadie announces she's coming to Davos with Sheryl in 2016. I'm surprised when someone from Mark's personal communications team shows up midway through a Davos planning meeting to discuss Sheryl's social media strategy for the trip. I ask Sadie what he does and she whispers that I do not want to know. I promise to leave it alone if she lets me know the general area. She pauses and carefully chooses her words.

"He manages engagement for Mark and Sheryl's social media using all of Facebook's tools," she says evenly. "You don't want to know any more than that."

"Does this explain why they have millions of followers and ridiculous amounts of engagement on their posts? Are they gaming the algorithm?"

"You don't want to know," she says.

The expectation to Lean In sits heavy, particularly now that I'm in the final stages of pregnancy. The doctor wants to induce me at some point in the next few weeks. I raise the possibility of skipping Davos, given the risk of flying to Europe when I'm on the cusp of giving birth, and the response from Sheryl's office is being told I should make sure I have a doctor's note clearing me to fly, which is not the outcome I'm hoping for. Travel is taking a toll more generally. When I explain this to Tom, he insists on coming to my doctor's appointment and once there explains I've been traveling and working too much. He tries to convince my doctor not to write the note. He fails. So, one more time, I try raising my concerns about traveling so late in my pregnancy with my bosses. In response, I get an email from one of Sheryl's assistants:

The flight attendant assigned to the trip worked previously in the medical field and has credits towards her nursing degree. The private jet operator also has MedAire and there are medical kits on board.

I write back:

Thank you! I'm really hoping that none of this is necessary. . . .

Her response:

You and me, sister.

Not very reassuring.

This year everyone at Davos is focused on terrorism. This is just two months after suicide bombers and gunmen killed 130 people in Paris, including 90 at a concert in the Bataclan theater. Sheryl emails the leadership team from Davos breathlessly highlighting how terrorism is working to Facebook's advantage: "Terrorism means the conversation on privacy is 'basically dead' as policymakers are more concerned about intelligence/security." In other words, this is a moment when governments are more interested in surveillance than people's privacy. Which is good for Facebook's business.

A "good visit with the boys" is how Joel summarizes our meeting with British prime minister David Cameron and George Osborne. Joel emphasizes that he and Sheryl "made the case that we were doing a lot on terrorism" and got a chance to rant about how Facebook's competitors were not, which Joel acknowledges is "admittedly a cheap shot but felt good." Joel's pleased that both politicians try Oculus and that Osborne particularly is impressed with Facebook's drones, though Joel notes, "not as much as Blair . . . Brits do seem to love a good unmanned aircraft." But the point when I realize that Facebook's meetings with politicians are changing is when I see that Cameron and Osborne don't want to confront Joel and Sheryl about any regulatory issues. What they want to talk about—and ultimately request—is Facebook's support against the Brexit vote.

They're not alone. More and more politicians are explicitly requesting that Facebook put its thumb on the scale. The causes range from reelection to indigenous broadcasting content, but the expectation is clear. Some are less delicate than others and accompany the request with a threat to regulate if the request is refused. All the requests speak to the changing power dynamic.

Once we're airborne on the flight back from Davos, Sadie and I start to churn through meeting notes, thank-yous, follow-ups, and a first draft of the "lessons from Davos" email Sheryl will circulate to leadership. There's a separate room with a large bed in it, next to the main cabin, which is very much Sheryl's domain. Sheryl emerges from this room and announces that she's going to sleep and that we should all sleep now so we adjust to the California time zone. Sadie and I exchange a look because we both know that even if we work hard for the twelve hours it'll take to get back to California, it'll be tough to complete all the work we have to do before we land, and Tom and Sasha are not going to be happy if I arrive back from this trip and then try to work throughout the weekend. We politely decline. Sheryl seems miffed that we're not taking her advice but returns to her room, and we return to our work.

We're an hour out of Zurich when Sheryl emerges back into the cabin in her pajamas.

"What are you doing? I'm going to bed." As if it isn't obvious that we're preparing all the emails that'll go out under her name.

"Lots to do," I say cheerily.

"But it's better if you rest now so you can get back on California time," she insists.

"I'm okay," I respond. There is only one bed in the jet and Sheryl is obviously using it.

"Sarah, come to bed." Her tone hardens.

I look around at the others to check if they heard what I did.

I shake my head and she repeats her instruction. "Sarah, come to bed."

We're at a stalemate. I look around desperately for support from the others but everyone's looking away.

On the long drive from Davos to Zurich for the flight, Sheryl and Sadie had taken turns sleeping in each other's laps, occasionally stroking each other's hair, while I tried to make myself as small and invisible as possible, feeling uncomfortable with what I was seeing. I hoped my enormous bump made it clear that my lap was not available for my coworker or boss. Regardless of motivation, it was not a position I felt I (or anyone else working with Sheryl) should be put in. I make pleading eyes at Sadie hoping she might be up for another close moment with Sheryl. Sadie shakes her head.

Sheryl sees this silent exchange and snaps, "Sadie's slept over lots of times and I'm not asking Sadie. I'm asking you."

I don't want to do this for all the obvious reasons—it wouldn't be right for a male COO to ask for this and it's not right for a female one to—but one thing that popped into my head, I'll confess, is that I'm scared of something that happened on a flight a few weeks before this, from Tokyo to San Francisco. So exhausted by work and pregnancy, I fell asleep before the flight even took off, and woke up with a start. Everything around me was white. I couldn't get my eyes to focus and I couldn't see a thing. Just white. It reminded me of what I saw during my father's leisurely drive to the doctor after the shark attack when I really thought I wasn't going to make it. I go into a complete panic. Maybe I'd pushed myself to my limit and had a medical emergency, maybe it was a pregnancy side effect, or maybe I was having a breakdown. Maybe I shouldn't be flying so heavily pregnant. I tear at whatever my white confines are and as they fall and the interior of the aircraft reappears, a flight attendant rushes over. In the most exquisitely polite terms, she explains that I had been snoring so loudly that I was disturbing other passengers, and the enterprising Japanese crew had erected a small white tent around me to try to muffle the sound. I was mortified. I tried to explain to her that I never normally snore, it's only because I'm so uncomfortably pregnant.

As Sheryl is insisting that I get into the bed with her, I'm worried about many things, including that I'm so exhausted after working around the clock for Davos that there's a reasonable chance I would horrify Sheryl by falling asleep and snoring at antisocial levels.

I look at Sadie for guidance. Her face is completely blank, as if she has vacated her body. I'm on my own here. No; it is simply impossible for me to get into bed with Sheryl. I'm resolute.

I tell her no, I can't. But people say no to Sheryl so rarely, she doesn't know what to do with this. She retreats to her bed, making no effort to hide her frustration and resentment.

I know something has broken between us. I know consequences will follow, but I don't know what they'll be.

Sadie tries to console me, she tells me things will be fine, but there are unspoken rules with Sheryl about obedience and closeness. Those closest to Sheryl are rewarded. Marne and Sadie often appear in her unwanted designer clothes; both assumed plum seats on boards that Sheryl had been asked to serve on. There are courtside basketball tickets and introductions to celebrities. Sheryl lends them the keys to her vacation homes.

Sadie is very conscious of the benefits of being Sheryl's "little doll," as she calls it and having Sheryl tell her she loves her. She's the one who explained to me the benefits of "being on the pedestal." She's acutely aware of others she shares that with. But she's also very aware of the expectations that come with it. How carefully calibrated the rewards and demands are.

Sheryl recently instructed Sadie to buy lingerie for both of them with no budget, and Sadie obeyed, spending over $10,000 on lingerie for Sheryl and $3,000 on herself.

When Sadie tries another of the bras Sheryl purchased her for the first time, she emails her.

"This bra is INCREDIBLY beautiful and fits perfectly. So grateful. This is my breasts equivalent of flying privately for the first time."

"Happy to treat your breasts as they should be treated," Sheryl responds.

Sadie confides she's never spent this much on single items of un-derwear in her life, messaging Sheryl that the experience is "a total *Pretty Woman* moment (the good one not the one where they kick her out). I feel like the fanciest twenty-six-year-old in the world."

Sheryl responds by asking her twenty-six-year-old assistant to come to her house to try on the underwear and have dinner Later the invite becomes one to stay over. Lean in and lie back.

At times Sadie shares with me how stressed out she is about her relationship with Sheryl. I urge her to find a new job somewhere else, where her life would be less enmeshed with Sheryl's. She says she's shared her concerns with Elliot and another senior manager, and they've also counseled her to escape from Sheryl.

When the plane lands in California, it's pouring rain. We stand scat-tered around the jet with Sheryl's black car idling nearby and the rest of us scanning the Uber app and juggling umbrellas while waiting for our luggage to be returned by the overworked staff. Sheryl walks purposefully toward me. I think she'll make a conciliatory gesture or extend a thank-you for what was a challenging but successful week at Davos. I raise my umbrella politely and she leans in close.

"You should have got into bed." Then she turns her back and stalks off toward the waiting car. I just stand there, rain soaking into

my hair and running down my cheeks, my protruding belly collecting raindrops.

Oh, I think to myself. I'm probably going to have to leave this job.
Almost all policy at Facebook runs through Sheryl. If she writes me
off, I won't be able to get anything done. Problem is, I really can't
quit right now. I'm weeks away from giving birth. At this moment, it
doesn't seem like much of a choice.

Alert to the new danger Sheryl poses, when she sends me an email
thanking me for my work at Davos on Monday and Joel echoes it, I
decide it's best to tell him what happened in the plane. After I do,
he simply instructs me not to tell that story to anyone. So I tell his
boss, Elliot, who laughs nervously and then gives me essentially the
same advice. I decide to confide in Debbie, who is underwhelmed by
my fears, telling me that "half the department" has been in Sheryl's
bed by now. She is joking, like, hey, this is less of a big deal than you
think (and you're less of a big deal than you think—classic Debbie)
and trying to reassure me. But it doesn't help. I start to notice Sheryl
icing me out.

29

Citizen Sanchez

On some level my life was going "Americanly." I was living "the American dream," bootstrapping from nothing to private jets with tech titans. Although the reality of that dream was darker than I expected.

A few days after we arrive back from Davos, I report to the US Citizenship and Immigration Services offices in a filthy part of San Francisco. The place is run-down, with chipped paint and cheap carpet, the staff carefully protected behind thick glass windowpanes. It feels like a cross between the visitor's room in a prison and an airport departure lounge, with a list of case numbers on an electronic screen, enforced silence, bureaucratic posters, and overtly heavy security presence.

For a variety of complicated reasons, I urgently need to secure American citizenship. Facebook's legal team have helped me with the process, but now I need to ace the exams. While I genuinely enjoyed learning about the aspirational foundational documents of the United States of America, I'm worried about the civics portion of the test. Ten questions that could be on anything from American history of the 1800s to American holidays, constitutional rights, or national symbols. The practice questions include things like, "What is one promise you make when you become an American citizen?" the correct answer being to "give up loyalty to any other country."

I've told Joel I'm taking off the day for the test and that I'm worried about getting the questions wrong. While I sit there, I get an email from him. I'd responded to an administrative request from Joel's assistant, reminding her and Joel that I had taken time off for my Americanness test but would respond as soon as that was done. Joel removes his assistant from the email chain, replying:

Did you get the dirty sanchez question? I hear that is on the test like 10 percent of the time.

I don't know what "dirty sanchez" means and I make the mistake of googling it. I immediately regret doing that.

It's not the first time he's said something to make me uncomfortable. In Panama when we rounded a corner too quickly and I accidentally bumped into his hip, he said, "Don't worry, you didn't touch anything precious." After he approves a new position on my team, he emails me, "Who is your sugar daddy?" (Which I guess is Republican policy wonk for "Who's your sugar daddy?") Another time he writes me saying, "I will personally buy you 'something nice' (niceness TBD by the beholder/buyer) if you responsibly spend" all your budget. As these things go, these are all pretty mild, but his dirty Sanchez question is a new low, totally inappropriate, and I think, this is getting worse.

This all hits as I'm stewing in anxiety about the citizenship test, desperately trying to memorize the foundational texts and the more perfect union that US citizens strive for but sometimes fall short of. All the aspirations they contain.

I get the first question wrong. It's the date of our wedding. Trying to start things off positively, the officer examining me allows me another guess. Wrong again. Cautiously, he offers me a third opportunity to tell him when my husband and I were married, and when I fail to guess correctly he moves on.

The mood in the room has definitely darkened.

I manage to answer all the other questions correctly, and at the end the officer seems genuinely happy for me. Nice guy. He leaves to print out something to get me to the next step of this process, and then returns to the room looking like someone has died.

"There's a big problem," he says. "When did you arrive in California?"

Turns out the State of California requires me to be a resident for ninety days before I can become a citizen, and I'm seventeen days short. This is something Facebook's lawyers should've noticed. I should've just waited to apply. Now I'll have to start the entire process over again. We only have five months before Tom's visa runs out and he has to leave the country. That's way less time than the citizenship process usually takes, so Facebook's lawyers will have to apply for some sort of special rush petition with Citizenship and Immigration Services. Whether we get to stay in America depends on them.

Just one more reason I can't quit my job right now.

30

Poker Face

It's February 2016, and just weeks ago in Davos, leaders from around the world were very explicit with Joel and Sheryl and me. They worried terrorists were being radicalized on Facebook, hate speech was proliferating, and Facebook was not partnering with them to figure out what to do about it. They wanted to find new ways to tax Facebook. Internet.org is basically dead at this point because it couldn't get past governmental scrutiny.

We're in shit with governments all around the world.

Joel, Sheryl, and Elliot agree that things are bad enough that the board needs to know. We need to get their attention and make them understand that the threat of regulation is real; there will be pain and it's coming soon. Internet.org proved governments are one of the few things that can change Facebook's growth, products, and business overnight.

I'm still clinging to the ever-diminishing hope that we'll drop the street fighter tactics and start to engage in a much more open conversation with governments about how social media should operate in their countries. In other words, grow up. I know Joel and Sheryl and Elliot see this differently. They'd play hardball way more than I care to (and maybe they're right about that in some cases). But even they see that something has to change. Maybe Facebook's board of directors can be the turning point and put us back on the right path.

I'm authorized to write up a presentation for the board. We'll make the threat of regulation and its impact on the business real for them, and then ask them for $55 million and sixty new staff members for the policy team around the world.

The board meeting is held in a conference room at headquarters that we use all the time. It looks out over the parking lot and scrubby marsh. A decidedly unglamorous setting for some of the most powerful people in Silicon Valley. It's way more casual than I expected, almost disturbingly so. I'd pictured it more like a Wall Street boardroom, or maybe the jury room in *Twelve Angry Men*, people in suits earnestly and thoroughly sifting through reports, spreadsheets, and data. Instead it's more like a coffee break at a college campus. Sheryl is perched cross-legged on her chair in yoga pants, and Mark wanders the room in his standard jeans and T-shirt, occasionally pausing to scroll through his phone. There's no fear in the room. No uncomfortable power dynamics. No tension. Probably because the structure of the company gives Mark complete and utter control, dual class shares, and a voting majority, making him basically untouchable. Mark and Sheryl speak to the board the same way they speak to me. They're the ones in charge here.

Before they get to my item on the agenda, I watch them, fascinated by the roles that each of the board members carves out. PayPal cofounder Peter Thiel, who is more all-American clean-cut than I expected, plays the role of provocateur. Former White House chief of staff Erskine Bowles takes a scholarly approach, weighing his sparse words and interventions. Netflix cofounder Reed Hastings is the sober businessman. Gates Foundation CEO Sue Desmond-Hellmann—who looks like she just finished a hike—is like a commonsense schoolteacher speaking up to get the discussion back on track. Venture capitalist Marc Andreessen acts as if he found his way into the room by accident and spends most of the meeting playing with his phone. Physically bigger than anyone else, he has a boyish air that seems out of context in a board meeting.

Joel, Elliot, and I don't even stand to give our presentation. We lay out our case that things are bad and about to get much worse, especially outside America. Politicians and governments see a borderless internet as a threat. Facebook is seen as competing against homegrown industries like publishers, telecom operators, and local tech companies. And they'll use everything from antitrust regulation to privacy regulation to crush Facebook.

Our goal is to frighten the board into dramatic action, but they don't seem very frightened. Their response is "deals." What do these different players want? Especially the decision makers, the regulators, and politicians. And what can Facebook "offer them"? What will head off regulation and change the global narrative on Facebook? This is very different from the vision I had of our teams around the world constructively working with governments and not trying to buy them off. We tell them, basically, give us the money and the people and we'll figure it out. They say yes.

Then the board gets into a conversation about what other companies or industries have navigated similar challenges, where they have to change a narrative that says that they're a danger to society, extracting large profits, pushing all the negative externalities onto society and not giving back. People suggest various analogues that don't seem to fit very well and then Elliot finally says out loud the one I think everyone's already thinking about (but not saying): tobacco.

That shuts down the conversation and they move on to the next agenda item.

A few days later I have my performance review. It's all going well until Joel starts talking about how I'm confusing to him. "In many ways you fly under the radar," he says. "Like in all the Internet.org stuff, you know. You show up, you understand all the complexity, and you've got this amazing poker face and you'll just sit there taking it all in, and when the moment's right you drop in the perfect advice or the reality check or whatever it is that we need at that time. It's amazing. And then sometimes it's just the complete opposite and you have absolutely no poker face."

He pauses and I try to control every muscle to make the perfect poker face, and say in an expressionless, even tone, "Could you perhaps give me an example?"

He pauses, thinks, and then says, "Oh yeah, I've got a great one."

I can tell he's thrilled with whatever he's about to say next. I use all my self-control to not react and to keep my poker face anchored in place. I pick up my pen and indicate I'm ready for him to go on.

"The board meeting. That was a classic."

"Could you say more?"

"Yes," he enthuses. "You're in a meeting with Mark, Sheryl, and the entire Facebook board and there were a couple of times where I saw you, in fact the whole room saw you, rolling your eyes."

"Do you happen to know when that was?" I ask as neutrally as possible, keeping my eyes straight on.

He pauses and thinks but can't seem to place it. We sit in silence until I decide, perhaps injudiciously, to speak.

"Was it maybe when one of our board members was suggesting to our largely Jewish leadership team that Facebook needs to get much closer to the far-right political parties in Europe because that is where the power is shifting to?"

This was the proposal that we should use the election support and campaign tools we were offering to US presidential candidates (and that Donald Trump was using aggressively in his 2016 campaign)—and offer them to the Alternative für Deutschland, the far right in Germany, and to Marine Le Pen and the Front National, the far right in France. Getting closer to these political parties and helping them into government would be the most effective way to stop govern-ments from regulating Facebook.

I say this realizing that my poker face is slipping.

"Well sure," Joel says. "But whatever it was, you can't be rolling your eyes and making faces at the board."

That's true and I apologize for it. By way of explanation, I tell Joel that I understand that some board members think fascists could solve our regulatory issues and we need to cozy up to them right away. And that I'd expected more pushback from the rest of the board.

Other than that, Joel tells me, great review!

I do not roll my eyes in response.

31

A Heartwarming Story

In March 2016, a Facebook vice president in Brazil, Diego Dzo-dan, is arrested on the way to work. This is because WhatsApp—which Facebook owns—refused to hand over messages in a Brazilian drug trafficking case. I'd worked closely with Diego, a charismatic Argentinian, and liked him. Smart, savvy, and a genuinely nice guy with an impeccable sense of style.

A few months before his arrest, WhatsApp had been blocked for two days by the Brazilian courts for similar reasons, and during those two days, Telegram (a rival messaging app) picked up 1.5 million users in Brazil, reaffirming Mark's conviction that Facebook must avoid being blocked at any cost. After that block, Mark wrote a Face-book post to rally Brazilians, saying, "Please make your voice heard and help your government reflect the will of its people." People did what he asked for and started contacting President Rousseff's of-fice, which was unfortunate because she had nothing to do with this block. It was ordered by a Brazilian court. The president's chief of staff reached out to express the president's displeasure.

I relayed this message to Mark and recommended he delete the post or, at the very least, edit out the line urging people to contact the government. After he struck the line, the president's office leaked to the press that Mark had changed his post at their request. Which was embarrassing. Mark was furious they talked to the press and made him look weak. So there was bad blood between the two sides, even before one of our executives was sitting in a jail cell in São Paulo.

That post has come back to haunt us now, in Diego's case. Before Diego was arrested, our legal team went in front of a judge and argued that he should not have a Facebook employee arrested for something WhatsApp did. They're separate companies. Diego has nothing to do with WhatsApp. The judge doesn't buy it. He says of course Facebook and WhatsApp are the same company, and as proof, in his ruling he quotes Mark's December post calling on Brazilians to "make your voice heard" after WhatsApp was blocked. So it's fine to arrest the most senior Facebook employee in Latin America for something WhatsApp did.

He really wants those WhatsApp messages.

At the request of the head of sales, Mark somehow manages to get a Facebook Messenger message through to Diego, who responds quickly, "Thank you Mark! It's an honor to receive this note. Everything is fine here and the legal team is doing a great job. This is our part in making the world more open and connected. . . . Count on me!"

Mark loves this and emails a few of us:

Diego's reaction ("you can count on me!") to being arrested for upholding our stance on protecting our community is deeply heart-warming.

Do you have an issue with me writing this up as a short story to post on my page? I think this story says a lot about our protection of our community, our culture and our technology.

I mean, I guess it does, but not in the way he thinks. Instead of helping figure out how to do everything possible to get Diego out of jail, Mark wants to turn this into a teachable moment for users and governments around the world.

He puts together a draft post:

I have a heartwarming story to share.

To protect our community and keep you safe, all messages
you send on WhatsApp are encrypted. This means your messages are so secure that we couldn't access them even if we
wanted to, and neither can governments or hackers.

Of course some governments that want access to your messages don't like this, and yesterday Brazilian police arrested Diego Dzodan, the leader of our Sao Paolo office, for protecting
someone in our community and not turning over messages
we couldn't access ourselves.

Hard for me not to interrupt here to point out that "someone in our
community" is an accused drug trafficker who's threatened to assas-
sinate the judge in this case. In an email, Elliot points out to Mark
that "we will face criticism couching this as 'safety for our community.'" Mark went on to draft the rest of his post.

As soon as I heard about Diego's arrest, I immediately sent
him a message to let him and his family know we were doing
everything we could to get him freed. He sent me the most
amazing reply from jail:

"Thank you Mark! It's an honor to receive this note. This
is our part in making the world more open and connected.
Count on me!"

Wow. So powerful. That's from someone on our team in jail
for protecting our community.

I know I can count on Diego, and hopefully you can also feel a little safer communicating with your friends because you know people like Diego are fighting for our community and you know you can count on them too.

We all try to explain to Mark why posting this is a terrible idea. For starters, it's hard to frame our actions as "protecting our community" when the government wants these WhatsApp messages to prosecute a criminal organization that murders and kidnaps people. To say nothing of the active assassination threat they've made against the judge.

And from a legal point of view, the post would be disastrous. In an email, our general counsel says this is not the moment for Mark to pick a fight with Brazilian law enforcement:

> This risks inflaming LE [law enforcement] in Brazil and heightens the risk that Diego personally faces (the case is still active) and all other employees in Brazil face. The situation there is fluid, the judge is unpredictable, and this could get worrisome quickly.

Elliot points out that if Mark posts this message, he'd be destroying our main defense to get Diego out of jail. They've concluded that our best shot is to go into court and again argue that WhatsApp is a different company from Facebook, so it's wrong to jail a Facebook employee over WhatsApp messages. In his post, Mark's admitting the two companies are the same company, with him at the head. The general counsel says that if the judge saw Mark's post, it would sink that line of defense and "make it harder to release the next person who gets arrested."

I read those words and get a chill. The next person who gets arrested? Now these guys are building that into their business plan?

Mark is not bothered. He still wants to post. Elliot sends him a breathless email stating, "The consensus (rare) among your advisors is to NOT post this—too complicated in Brazil and may meaningfully jeopardize Diego and our teams in the country." Mark pushes back and asks Elliot to draft an alternative post that might not be as damaging, which Elliot sends him, advising again that even the alternative "risks triggering a negative reaction from the court" and "the danger created by sharing this post in Brazil outweighs its benefits outside the country."

Throughout all of this, Mark could not be more disappointing. Despite saying in his note that "we are doing everything to get him free," he doesn't seem to be worried about Diego in the slightest. He seems to see this, first and foremost, as an opportunity to write a great Facebook post. A heartwarming story. If he cared even slightly about Diego's welfare, or felt responsible for him as his boss, he wouldn't be insisting on posting his little message to the world, something that could do great harm, before he goes out to dinner. He'd be doing everything possible, calling Brazil's president, calling the many Brazilian legislators I introduced him to when he was lobbying for Internet.org, and begging them to make public statements supporting Diego's release. Doing all the things I'm doing. That kind of pressure coming from him would be more effective than coming from me. I make this case with Elliot, who's talking to Mark, telling him a general should stay on the field with his troops.

While everyone's arguing about the post, Diego has his day in court.

It comes down to an appeals court that thankfully issues an order at 3:30 A.M. releasing Diego, less than one full day after he was arrested.

I come away from this feeling disgusted with Mark, and truly seeing him differently. That could've been me in jail—in Myanmar, South Korea, Thailand, or any of the other places I've traveled for Facebook.

Or it could have been any member of my team. And I guess I had this last vestige of hope that at the moment one of us was locked up, the cavalry would come to save us. Or at least one of the world's richest men would do everything in his power. But when it happens, when one of his employees is sitting in jail, instead of doing everything he can, as the most powerful person at the company, Mark obsesses over some stupid post and then goes out to dinner. This seems such an obvious failing of a basic test of normal human decency.

Five years earlier when I arrived at Facebook, Mark didn't have a theory of how he and the company should be in the world; he didn't really have developed opinions about policy or politics, beyond "sign up more users." The rest of Facebook's leadership wasn't very different. Mark really couldn't be bothered to care. Now he's developed priorities, and they're mostly pretty horrible and ignorant of the human costs.

My original hope that when he started to exercise power on the world stage, meeting with presidents and prime ministers, it would be an education in responsibility and accountability—that's really turned out to be a bust. He disappoints again and again.

This thing with Diego confirms something I didn't want to admit to myself: I have to leave Facebook. I start calling around looking for a new job. For so long now, I've been able to convince myself that I can do more good inside Facebook than outside, but now I understand I probably can't. My problematically pregnant state makes this complicated. Realistically, how am I going to land and then start a new job when I'm days away from giving birth? I feel trapped.

32

What to Not Expect
When You're Expecting

One of the random places I'd traveled in service of Facebook was João Pessoa, a remote city in northeastern Brazil. I hadn't thought about it much since. Not until I read a *New York Times* article tracking the development and discovery of something called the Zika virus. This was before there was a lot of interest in Zika, but because I'm pregnant I read the article in detail. There's something about it that unsettles me but I can't place it.

It's later in the day when I'm unloading the dishwasher that I connect the discomfort with the trigger. The article was focused on mothers and babies in Paraíba State, which had seemed vaguely familiar. Tentatively I type "João Pessoa State of Brazil" into my phone and Google quickly returns, "João Pessoa, port city, capital of Paraíba state." I immediately feel a stabbing, sick feeling in my stomach—not from the baby kicking.

This place is remote. It took more than twenty hours of flying to get there from San Francisco. I force myself to reread the newspaper story. It describes the mothers of Zika babies as "ghosts—mute, expressionless figures in corridors holding babies whose foreheads seem to have vanished." I'm typing different queries into Google hoping I'll find something to convince me there's nothing to worry about, but it does the opposite. João Pessoa is at the heart of the Zika outbreak, there are hundreds of cases, and the number of children with suspected microcephaly is increasing tenfold weekly.

I can't even think about how I'm going to tell Tom. He didn't want me traveling to all these weird places when I was pregnant, and I'd blithely assured him he was wasting his worry on nothing. I'd had no idea I was at any risk. Of course I wouldn't have gone if I was.

It feels like this job is taking too much from me, permeating every-thing, poisoning everything.

It takes a while to get an appointment with my doctor and the wait is agony. When I don't feel the baby's kicks for a few hours, I convince myself it's because of microcephaly. Being pregnant is al-ready an experience full of fear and guilt for me—am I eating right, doing enough exercise, getting enough rest? And now there's this searing, sleep-depriving knowledge that I'd unintentionally put my baby in harm's way, and the crushing fear and guilt that go with that.

It's hard to think about anything else.

When I finally see my doctor, I can tell she's underwhelmed by my concern. She explains that ever since the *New York Times* piece, she's been inundated with middle-class mommies who've been to Florida or Mexico on vacation who are worried they now have a Zika baby.

"But I was in João Pessoa earlier in my pregnancy."

She's unmoved.

"It's the epicenter of the outbreak."

"Did you even have a mosquito bite?" she says, still skeptical. I pull up a photo of my body covered in them that I'd sent to Tom during the trip, worried that I'd been bitten by bedbugs.

Still unimpressed, she grudgingly books me in for an ultrasound. She cautions that they still don't really know much about the disease and that means both diagnosis and treatment are difficult.

The day of the ultrasound, as I lie prone on the chair, feet in stirrups, the technician peppers me with questions about why I traveled somewhere so dangerous. I bristle and tell her I didn't know about the risk, and we fall into an awkward silence.

"How do you diagnose it?" I ask.

"We haven't diagnosed any here. I don't think there's been a Zika baby born in the US yet. . . ."

That "yet" hangs in the air.

"What are you looking for?"

"Calcification around the eyes, head size, anything abnormal. You heading back into work?"

Why was she trying to change the subject? What was she seeing on that screen?

In the end, they don't spot anything, but they also tell me that they probably wouldn't be able to diagnose it while the baby's still inside me. As one of the doctors put it, "We don't really know exactly what we're looking for anyway."

After months of quiet Zika-related terror, just a week after Diego's arrest, I'm more than relieved to deliver a healthy, Zika-free baby girl in March 2016.

But as she's placed in my arms I can't stop shaking, and as I keep trying to grip her more firmly the shaking intensifies. Worried I'm going to drop her, I quickly hand her back to Tom. I try to stop the shaking, but after many hours of labor I'm exhausted and can't seem to control my body.

The nurse who was there for the hardest parts of the delivery, Lauren, is still around. With long brown hair and a kind face, she's been a source of comfort throughout.

"It's okay," I reassure her. "I'm actually okay. I'm just tired."

She doesn't accept my assurances and instead gets more blankets and remains in the room, ostensibly tidying things, but something feels off. Why is she still here?

"Lauren—is the baby okay?" She strolls over to perform a cursory check on the sleeping newborn.

"She's beautiful and she's okay." She returns to tidying. I feel so broken that I can't even remove my feet from the stirrups they were in during the delivery. I sink into an exhausted silence. Eventually, under questioning from Tom, Lauren admits that she's worried about the amount of blood I'm continuing to lose. She starts to weigh the towels that have been placed around me to collect the blood that continues to flow and calls for the doctor on duty. After that doctor, others arrive. My shaking evolves into convulsions.

By now I know it's serious; Lauren keeps cleaning up the blood but it's flowing thick and fast. I feel drained and hollow, beyond exhaustion. The basics of existing—breathing, listening, and feeling—are thick, heavy, almost insurmountable tasks.

The room fills with various doctors and nurses who barely acknowledge me as they plunge needles and attach me to machines. A new nurse pushes Lauren to the side when she arrives, but I manage to grab Lauren's hand and beg her with my eyes not to leave the room. I periodically remove my oxygen mask to ask Tom and Lauren to check on the baby, who remains peacefully in the corner.

Time slows down as pain expands. It radiates from my swollen belly but I can see that all of me is swelling up. The new nurse attached a blood pressure cuff to my arm when she arrived; it feels like it's burning through my swollen skin. Every time I summon the energy to remove the mask and try to speak, to tell her to fix the cuff, she scolds me, dismissing me and replacing the mask without even glancing at the cuff.

The medical team keep pushing Tom back into the corner but he fights his way forward. I manage to nod toward my arm, and Tom immediately grasps what's going on when he sees the cuff like a rubber band depressed between red swollen skin that looks and feels as if it is about to burst. The nurse also dismisses him when he tries to call her attention to it. He hauls the lead doctor into the corridor and insists that this nurse is removed and Lauren is returned to my side. I keep thinking how awful it must be for him to sit watching all of this unfold.

Eventually one of the medical staff remembers the baby and asks to have her removed. I try to protest, removing the oxygen mask to object, my body still craving to hold her, feed her, see her.

But I'm silenced, the mask replaced, and the baby removed. I feel like I'm starting to succumb. It's hard to breathe, even with the oxygen mask.

I motion for Tom to come and remove my mask. "Get Debbie, get Sadie, get them to come here, for you, for the baby." As I start to consider how bad this might get, I want someone here to look after Tom. I don't want Tom to be alone for what I suspect is about to happen. I'm dying.

I hear my doctor ordering lots of blood product and threatening to go and get it herself if it doesn't arrive faster.

I fight to stay conscious. What no one tells you about those final moments as you battle to hold on is how seductive unconsciousness is. How, when you've reached the end of exhaustion, there's something so wonderfully inviting in succumbing to the sleepy comfort of numb unconsciousness. The respite. How each time you fight to pull yourself out of the calm nothingness, you're plunged back not just into consciousness but physical torment. Bright lights, frantic voices, the struggle for each breath, and complete searing pain. I fight with everything I have to try to stay awake. The idea of never holding my new baby is too awful. Of never seeing Sasha again. To say nothing of leaving Tom alone.

I reopen my eyes in an operating room.

"I think she's back with us," I hear someone say, and I start to look around for Tom and Lauren but my head is heavy and I can't bring anything into focus. My doctor comes into view and welcomes me back, saying something about how an anesthesiologist was about to knock me out so it's lucky timing that I joined them now. As if I'd just arrived at a neighborhood barbeque.

I ask repeatedly for Tom, I need him, and wheeze, "No anesthetic."

My doctor looks confused, then explains that I'm in an operating room undergoing emergency surgery and it's very serious. I summon all my energy to say, "If you have general anesthetic . . . you can't breastfeed . . . for three days." This urgent need to breastfeed; funny how raw and powerful these basic maternal instincts are. Even when I am incapable of anything else.

"Sarah, I don't think you understand the situation." My doctor pauses—maybe not wanting to tell me I'm dying? She then explains that Tom has already consented on my behalf.

"I have to feed my baby. You need consent. My consent. Not his." I'm desperate to stay conscious and see and hold and feed my baby. "Not his," I insist.

"Sarah, you're very, very sick. . . ." I can tell my very capable doctor is both bemused and frustrated, arriving at an impasse that will rob her of precious time. She tries a different approach.

"Someone give her a pen," she says.

And before I know it a pen comes into my line of vision. I reach for it but realize I can't control my body. My hands won't connect with the pen. When I get close to it my fingers can't grasp it.

"Sarah, are you able to get that pen and sign those forms?"

I'm frozen, my voice is stuck, and I feel thick, suffocating terror. Defeated, I shake my head no. An anesthesiologist moves into position and before I can register what is happening, a numb dark blackness moves through my body, stifling the thoughts and feelings I'm desperately clinging to as signs of life.

The next thing I see are white walls. As my eyes focus I see a clock on the wall and a whiteboard with the message "Call Sadie" scrawled on it. There are incessant beeps and dings but everything else is enveloped in a thick silence.

The pain cuts through the grogginess but it's a different type of pain. I feel almost as if I'm choking. My stomach is an empty bump. Where's Tom? Where's my baby? I'm alone.

Sadie emerges through a curtain. She seems completely at ease, as if she's been here for days.

"You're awake!" she exclaims excitedly.

"Where's Tom? Where's the baby?" I gasp frantically. She strains to hear me. "The baby, where's the baby?"

Sadie shakes her head. Then, very slowly, as if talking to an elderly relative, she says, "I can't hear you. You have a machine in your throat helping you breathe. You're in intensive care. You're on life support. You're very sick."

I try to say "baby" loud enough to break through the pipe in my throat, but she continues to shake her head. "Tom," I try. "Where's Tom? Tom."

Sadie shakes her head again.

It doesn't make sense. Tom should be here. The only reason he wouldn't be here is if there was something seriously wrong with him . . . or the baby.

Panic spurs a burst of adrenaline and I hoarsely yell "baby, baby, baby" into the void of the ventilator. Sadie tries to placate me by putting together words in sentences that make no sense. She says nothing about the key point of where Tom and the baby are. Maybe our baby's dead? The very thought of it makes me claw at the machines, trying to remove the ventilator from my throat so I can leave and find my baby. Before I can, medical professionals hurriedly appear and I realize too late that, in their rushing and pushing of buttons and turning of switches, I've been sedated.

When I wake again Debbie's sitting beside my bed.

She pulls a notebook and pen from her stylish designer handbag. I reach for it and my hands fail me, again. Debbie pushes the pen into my hand and the notebook under it. I know I have to play it cool or I'll be knocked unconscious again. I can barely move my hands but I scratch out, "Am I tied to bed?"

Debbie nods. Two clear plastic restraints tie me to the bed. All I want to do is leave this ICU and see my baby.

"I worried about her. Can I hold her?" I write strenuously but trying to play it casual.

Debbie gently but firmly shakes her head no. I don't know if that's because of me or because of the baby. I feel as if the floor is falling out from under me.

Soon Tom walks in. I'm so relieved to see him I can feel tears in my eyes, but the ventilator makes it difficult to actually do the other parts of crying; sobbing makes me choke against the tube in my throat. When Tom looks at me he starts to cry. I've rarely seen Tom cry.

"I'm sorry; I don't know why I'm crying. I haven't throughout everything," he reassures me, as if I would somehow think less of him. "It's just they told me to be prepared because you might not . . ." He breaks off as his tears well up. "But you made it. And Xanthe's okay."

I'm confused.

"Xanthe?" I write.

Tom looks down, a hint of shame in his face.

"You named the baby?" I write, incredulous. I can feel Debbie shift silently on her chair, suddenly uncomfortable.

"Um, Xanthe Juliet, middle name for my mother, but . . . we can change the name," he says hurriedly.

At that moment, his phone buzzes and I can see a notification saying, "Xanthe is due for her next feed." And I know, in that instant, that her name will never be changed.

Tom fills me in on some of what I missed while I was in the coma. Apparently, I'm in an intensive care unit at a completely different hospital from where I was when I was last conscious in the operating room after giving birth. From what I piece together, at some point before, during, or after labor I suffered an amniotic fluid embolism. He explains that means something entered my bloodstream—either amniotic fluid or some part of the baby like fetal cells or hair—and stopped the blood from clotting.

He tells me I had more than thirty-five blood transfusions, the entirety of all the blood currently in my body more than three or four times over. Tom says they just kept pumping more blood and blood products into me but the blood just flowed out. After hours of doing this, nothing was working. It was just after midnight, and they tried one last intervention. Something went right and my body started responding. He tells me I'm lucky, the doctors saved my life.

After a few days, I'm finally reunited with Xanthe. The moment I ached for, holding her properly for the first time, but instead of relief, I'm overpowered by a sense of guilt. That from the outset I've failed this sweet defenseless baby who has been in the other hospital's nursery all the time I was in the ICU; both of us in the care of strangers.

Dying in childbirth while working in Silicon Valley is like being killed by a horse and carriage or consumption or a duel. Something that belongs in a different century or a different country. Weeks before this I was playing ping-pong in virtual reality with Mark Zuckerberg and the prime minister of Singapore. How did I go from that to nearly dying the sort of silent death you see in a nineteenth-century novel?

And yet it's not. In fact, it's a very modern American way to die. The US has the highest maternal mortality rate in the developed world. Shockingly, it's on the rise.

When it's time to go home, I'm rolled out of the hospital in a wheelchair because I still can't walk. Lauren, who helped get me and Xanthe through so much, sends me a note:

"I hope that someone tells her one day how hard you fought for her life and your own."

I have no idea how we'll cope. I can't walk, because my back was somehow damaged when I was moved between hospitals. I'm still losing blood and incredibly weak from that. Tom's exhausted and due back at work soon, our families are both in other countries, we barely know anyone in San Francisco. I have no idea how we'll look after a newborn and a toddler.

It's still only a few weeks after Diego's arrest and I know I should be looking for another job. Coming so close to death only reinforces my feeling that I have to leave Facebook. I think about it constantly. But it's hard to move that forward when I need to give all I have to this sweet baby. When I'm physically wrecked. How do I do it?

After less than a week at home, I hemorrhage while putting Sasha to bed. Tom finds me in the bathroom in a small pool of blood and calls an ambulance. After two days, I check myself out of the hospital, but I continue to lose blood every day. I hide the extent of it from Tom because I can tell he's already at the breaking point, but each time I use the bathroom there's so much blood I feel like I need to roll out crime scene tape. Lacking that, I just carefully wipe everything in the bathroom clean, to hide the evidence that something is very wrong.

33

Do We Have to Go into This?

I'm not well. I continue to lose significant amounts of blood for months and struggle to do basic activities. I get to the supermarket with the baby and toddler and realize I don't have the strength to walk through the aisles, so I head home, stopping on benches to rest along the way. There's a quiet desperation to everyday life.

None of this seems to matter to Joel. He knows full well that I'm still on maternity leave, sick and on strong pain medication, and yet messages and emails from him and his assistant pile up daily. Less than two weeks after I am discharged from the hospital, they set up a weekly meeting with me. Because I'm in California and he's in Washington, DC, they're videoconferences, but he starts to take them sprawled across his bed rather than in his office. He's in a T-shirt and who knows what else. I tell myself the family photos surrounding his bed are proof he's a family man and I shouldn't feel weird about it.

"Does me being in bed when we chat make you feel uncomfortable?" he asks repeatedly, and it's hard not to feel that's the point.

One day he pushes further. On one of our regular video calls during my maternity leave, he asks me how my health is. I keep my answer brisk and professional: I'm still very sick, I'm going to need more surgery.

"But where are you bleeding from?" he asks.

My mind races. There is no way he doesn't know.

"Seriously? Um, well, it's the same place I've been losing blood from all along."

"What place?" he presses, insistent.

"Do we have to go into this?"

He stares me down from his bed, propped up by voluminous pillows, and asks again about where the blood is coming from.

"I'm not really comfortable."

"Come on, Sarah," he pushes.

"Well, it's not my eyes. . . ."

He starts to get angry.

"I have to go." I exit the videoconference and call Tom. Then I call Debbie and tell her too. I trust her and she's been at Facebook for years.

She has no advice for me.

Elliot, Joel, and others in senior leadership chip in together for a night nanny for a few weeks, which on one level is so thoughtful— it's thousands of dollars that we absolutely couldn't afford—and on the other feels like a message of "get back to work." Tom suggests we refuse the gesture but that feels rude.

During maternity leave, Joel presses me to join a "leadership offsite" in Hyderabad, India, that's scheduled a few weeks after I'll return to work. It looks like a waste of time. The focus is team building—it's lots of tourism and meals—not making any real decisions.

And honestly, I'm scared. The blood loss continued for a long time, months after the baby was born. I'm very weak. The doctors didn't know why; they suspected an artery had been incorrectly fused to a vein during the crisis, but they couldn't tell without operating. By the time my return-to-work date nears I'm postsurgical but recovering slowly, and I don't want to do it. My body isn't strong. There are still unresolved issues. I'm still losing blood; medical professionals struggle to draw blood at every regular blood draw and no one knows why. It's a twenty-hour flight. I'm afraid of hemorrhaging again, and the medical advice is that I should not wean the baby, whom I don't want to leave, until I'm fully healthy.

Raising this with Joel is excruciating.

"On India," I start nervously. "I know you want me to, so I'm planning to go, if I can figure out a way not to wean my daughter. Although if you don't need me, I'd prefer to stay."

"You mean breastfeeding?" he asks.

"Yes," I say.

"Explain breastfeeding to me." He looks expectantly at me.

"What?"

"Explain breastfeeding to me."

Ugh. This, again.

"I need to keep up my supply in order to continue breastfeeding," I say as neutrally as possible, trying to keep things professional. But this doesn't satisfy him. He continues to push.

Eventually, I shut the conversation down by telling him I'll explain my concerns directly to his assistant. I tell her how badly it went with the breast pump in Turkey and my worries for India. This persuades no one. I'm sent a breast pump and booked for India.

I return to work in August 2016. My first day back, Joel decides to do a performance review, as he says "it's performance review season." A quick Google search confirms my suspicion that you are not supposed to be given a performance review of your maternity leave. In fact, I understand that pushing someone to work during their maternity leave is against the law. Nevertheless.

"You weren't responsive enough," he says.

"In my defense, I was in a coma for some of it."

"It's not just me, Sarah. Some of your other colleagues found it challenging to engage with you."

"I mean, you know, I was in hospital, in a coma and near death, but I accept that this did make it hard to engage with me at times."

Irrespective, this leads him to conclude that there were "issues limiting my effectiveness" and both he and my peers say I was "difficult to work with during this period." Sadly, he notes that he is unable to put a formal performance rating in the system to accompany this feedback because I was "out of the system" for most of the performance cycle, but he wants me to know that if he could, it would be bad.

I don't really understand what is happening and it's only the first day back, so I reach out to the policy team's HR person, Stacey Tomey. Over Zoom I see that her home office is decorated with framed menus from Michelin-star restaurants she's dined in.

"I've had to work a lot during maternity leave."

"I'm aware," she responds. It takes a minute for that to sink in. They knew. I'd thought Joel was doing this and no one knew.

"I'm worried about India, especially pumping." I explain my fear that I'll start hemorrhaging again during forty hours in the air. I let her know that the idea of me traveling to India while I'm still having medical issues is causing a lot of stress in my house. I don't reveal the extent of Tom's distress.

"You can fly with me," she offers. "That way if anything goes wrong you'll have someone onboard."

That might be helpful only if Stacey could obtain a medical degree before the flights. Otherwise, what exactly is she going to do if there's a postsurgical medical emergency?

"You can lean on me and Joel's assistant Erin." This is her solution to both the medical issue and Joel's behavior. When the two of us meet up with Erin in India, she christens the three of us "the tripod" and sets up a "tripod" group chat.

At the opening "strategy meeting" in Delhi, Joel gathers his leadership team and asks us each to identify the biggest risks for the company over the coming year. Predictably Erin Egan, head of privacy, says "privacy." Kevin Martin, who's in charge of Internet.org and connectivity efforts, says "internet connectivity." And so on.

When it's my turn, I try to talk about a disturbing new trend in how politicians are using Facebook. The day before the offsite started, the Filipina journalist Maria Ressa published a groundbreaking series. It outlined how the new president of the Philippines, Rodrigo Duterte, had weaponized Facebook to propel himself into power. He was an outsider candidate running against insiders, but using paid ads and a network of social media volunteers, his campaign chipped away at facts, with political pages masquerading as credible sources of information to pump out half-truths. Combined with the power of bots, fake accounts, and trolls on social media, they fabricated an alternative reality that manipulated people by sowing fear, uncertainty, and doubt. The campaign harnessed Facebook's algorithm, which optimizes for eyeballs and doesn't distinguish between fact and fiction.

Maria Ressa brought all this information to my team before publication while I was on maternity leave, but my bosses didn't really get it. They did nothing.

Duterte is a brutal political figure who said he would enforce law and order by allowing—or possibly collaborating with, given he claimed to have thrown someone out of a helicopter—death squads who've killed over a thousand people. He's praised the murders publicly. And he's far from the only leader using Facebook in troubling ways. Juntas in Thailand and Myanmar are using enterprising methods to suppress speech, incite fear, and spy on their citizens. They falsely claim that Facebook shares user information and data with them to suppress dissent on the platform.

The Facebook presidents are no longer "good guys" and "friends of the United States" like Joko Widodo, Enrique Peña Nieto, and Justin Trudeau. Regimes that want to control and censor their populations now understand the power of Facebook to monitor what's being said about them and who's saying it. Duterte's playbook of misinformation and trolling has been so successful, of course others will imitate it. We've been cozying up to these candidates and happily making money off of them, and we really need to rethink. By this time Brexit has already happened and the leadership at Facebook are steadfastly avoiding acknowledging any role Facebook may have played in that. There are some important elections coming up, including the US election next month.

That's the moment I lose the room. It's blank looks everywhere. Joel listens, eyes darkening.

"Thanks, Sarah, I think we've got a few more immediate things to worry about. We'll let the US team handle the US election."

I know that the way he sees it, US politics is outside my expertise and very different from whatever I'm seeing in what he calls "tin pot" countries like the Philippines, Myanmar, and Thailand. Also, and maybe more importantly: everyone in this room understands we're making record amounts of money off the Trump campaign, with all its misinformation and trolling. As far as Joel's concerned, Facebook doesn't need to worry about outsider candidates like Trump. In fact, they're great for Facebook because of how much money they bring in, and Joel cares about that. If they're peddling outrage and stretching the truth, well, Joel understands that outrage and stretching the truth are just part of the game, part of politics. Joel was at the Brooks Brothers riot, after all.

Outrage is a lucrative business for Facebook right now, a month before the election, and Joel's determined that his team contributes to Facebook's bottom line. I remember seeing his name as the first one to like an internal post from our political ads team—the one he created—celebrating the record spending by Republicans in the Iowa caucuses. And when the team posted that Ted Cruz's Facebook strategy has "put money in all of our pockets and that's what we call sweet, sweet coin," underneath it read, "Joel Kaplan and 22 others like this post."

If anything, Facebook rewards outsider candidates who post inflammatory content that drives engagement. We charge less money for ads that are more incendiary and reach more people. Trump is using our system the way it's designed to be used. From my point of view, that's incentivizing and rewarding the worst kinds of political ugliness.

Joel doesn't seem to care at all, it's all money. And what harm does it do? He tells us it's clear Clinton's going to win anyway.

34

The Facebook Election

Joel's wrong. Everyone's wrong. So I'm curious to walk into Facebook headquarters a month later, the morning after Trump's victory.

There's a hastily called meeting for the policy and communications teams to discuss how everyone feels about the outcome. I'm surprised that Joel and Elliot have thought to do that. It shows a sensitivity to people's emotions that is normally notable by its absence. Joel later confides that they set it up because there was an ugly situation in the London office after the Brexit vote a few months before. Most of the policy team was openly devastated and it wasn't handled well. The few who wanted Britain to leave the EU felt personally attacked by the rest of the team, and it spiraled, leaving bad blood between the two groups. Joel wants to avoid a repeat now with Trump, between the Republicans who dominate his office and the rest of Facebook, which is mostly Democrats and a lot of libertarians.

All the policy and communications teams in Silicon Valley are crammed into a meeting room that's too small, with the DC office projected on the large white wall at the end of the room. Elliot struggles to find the right tone for the political operatives assembled, some of whom have been embedded with Trump's election campaign, and settles on some vague opening monologue about the importance of democracy and tolerance. Joel is upbeat—visibly happy about Trump—and struggles to contain his disdain for the collective out-pouring of grief in the Silicon Valley headquarters. We'd all walked by crying young staffers on our way in.

A Republican on the DC team had told me that Joel had "cut checks for everyone except Trump." And Joel admitted that he hadn't voted for Trump. So I ask him later in our one-on-one why he was so joyful on the call when he was a very public Jeb Bush supporter.

"You're looking at the election all wrong." Joel's tone is mildly patronizing. "If you look at Trump's agenda it's the Republican agenda. It's the things we want. The things I want. It's tax cuts. It's less government. He'll get it done. Trump's got the Senate. He's got the House. It's a decisive victory. He can do things. Great things. Not only that, it's going to be great for tech and for business. Hands off, all systems go."

He pauses, as if to check that I understand that this is good.

"Sure, there are some things on the margin thrown in that I'm not wild about," he concedes. "But the bulk of it is what the party wants, what I want."

I nod. Which he takes as acceptance of his point.

"My actual issue with the election is that Trump won't go far enough on the things that really will make a difference."

"What are those?" I ask, already knowing but wanting to hear him say it.

"Cutting entitlements," he responds firmly. "The biggest weak-ness with Trump is that without touching Social Security, Medicaid, Medicare, he's not going to meaningfully change that much. That's the biggest disappointment with this president. But on the whole, it's a great outcome."

In contrast to Joel, some of the senior distraught Democrats who address the assembled group talk about their grief, pain, and fear of the future following Trump's win. It's hard to ignore the eyerolls exchanged by some of the Republicans on the DC team who forget that their faces are being magnified and projected on the wall.

One of the younger employees in California raises her hand and says timidly, "I worry for my friends who are Black and Hispanic."

She doesn't mention how "All Lives Matter," a slogan created as a negative rejoinder to "Black Lives Matter," keeps popping up on the Facebook graffiti walls all across campus (or that Mark and Sheryl's response was that "we have to assume positive intent"), or the TRUMP SUPPORTERS WELCOME posters that materialized everywhere. Most of the employees at headquarters are in their twenties, they're on Facebook all the time posting their political opinions, so there's been a roiling political tension at the company for months. There's a prolonged silence, with Elliot and Joel both avoiding any eye contact, before a white, bearded guy in his early twenties stands up and says, "I want to be an ally."

As he continues, sharing his feelings about the election and his thoughts about being Black, or gay, or Muslim, or a woman in America in 2016, the faces of the DC office projected across the wall are exquisite contortions. I find myself inadvertently making eye contact with others in headquarters who—like me—are scanning the room, forensically searching for a Black or Hispanic face among the sea of fresh white faces, hoodies, and Patagonia vests. There are only a few.

Instead, Joel shuts down these concerns, stating firmly, "There are a lot of good guys in the Trump administration who want to do what's best for America."

Another question comes from a young woman who probably has a different idea from Joel about what's best for America: "I'm worried about what's going to happen to immigration. What do we do about people who don't have immigration status?"

Elliot praises the question and makes a few bland statements. I'm lost in thought about how many men there seem to be in the DC office projected on the wall and whether they would also describe themselves as "good guys" and how they're still struggling to contain their shocked delight at the outcome of the election when I tune in to hear, "Sarah will have some thoughts on this, as she's had difficult immigration challenges."

There's a moment of silence and everyone turns to me. I don't respond because I assume he must mean some other Sarah who would be qualified to address the question in some way. Then I realize he means me. He's throwing the ball to me so he doesn't have to talk any more about Trump's immigration plans.

"I don't think the issue is New Zealand immigration," I say. "But I do know—"

Joel jumps in, alert to the fact I'm going off script, and assures everyone that Facebook will look into this.

From the crush of people in the back corner of the room in headquarters, someone asks, "Is it our fault? 2016's 'the Facebook election.'"

It's a relief to hear someone give voice to what I had been thinking. In the lead-up to the election, this was the constant message inside the company. We called it "the Facebook election" internally, and the company had committed to dominating this election like no other. We all know hordes of people across policy, communications, sales, product management, and engineering who've been working full time on elections. In presentations everyone's been talking for months about how powerful Facebook is and how effective it is as a tool to influence people and change minds. How we're in the "business of democracy." Not to mention Joel's constant quest for our teams to be adding to the bottom line of the company by selling political ads.

And yet Elliot looks baffled. He pushes off the question as if the mere suggestion is preposterous.

"Facebook's role and our role as employees is to make the world more open and connected. That's never been more important than it is now," Elliot concludes, and then shuts down the meeting before any follow-up questions are asked.

They're sentiments that are echoed by Mark onstage at the Techonomy conference days later. Where he states categorically that the suggestion fake news on Facebook influenced the election is a "pretty crazy idea" and then follows up by saying that the "idea that that had any impact in the election is pretty out there."

35

Angry at the Truth

Mark Zuckerberg is mad. When he arrives at the airport, he's fuming about the suggestion he had any responsibility for the election results. We're due to leave for Peru, for the Asia-Pacific Economic Cooperation (APEC) summit.

I'm nervous. It was my idea that Mark should travel to Lima for APEC. While I was on maternity leave, he'd emailed me, finally taking the initiative on foreign policy. Specifically, he'd been thinking about how the world is governed:

> I'd like to learn more about this area—how the UN and the different international governance institutions came into existence, what power and levers do they have to get things done, what are their limitations and whether these are intentional or these organizations are being marginalized, why they're set up as a federation of nations as opposed to a democratically elected international body, etc?

> One specific topic I'm interested in is why no one is arguing for a significantly stronger international government or system. That is, today's system seems relatively weak—it has a small budget, it is beholden to nations as opposed to being elected or controlled

directly by people globally, etc. Today it seems there are two primary proposals for how large countries want to interact with the international system: continue as is, or increasing isolationism. I'm curious why there isn't a serious third option of strengthening this system further, and what would be potentially required to make that happen. I'm looking for any recommendations on how to learn about this: book recommendations, people to talk to or invite over for dinner, or other resources to check out.

What I take from this is that he's feeling Facebook's rising power globally. He has politicians from around the world wanting to come see him and kiss the ring—the way they do with, say, Rupert Murdoch. He has this global network, more political capital and more wealth than he can possibly spend, and he's wondering what he can use it for. What are the other institutions that cross national borders? What powers do they have, compared with Facebook? His speeches increasingly talk about "global community." He knows Facebook has a budget that's larger than many nations' GDPs and is not "beholden to nations." He could buy all the politicians of a country or many countries if he chose to wield this power freely.

And so, I thought, if he's thinking about using Facebook to do something else, something more, in countries around the world, and he's wanting to understand how the international system works—or doesn't—he needs to see it up close. With that in mind, I pitch going to APEC. It's bigger than the international conference I took him to in Panama. Vladimir Putin and Xi will be there, and this time Mark wouldn't be showing up as a salesman, trying to push Internet.org or Facebook. I wanted to put him in situations that he'd be in if he were a head of state. I'm quietly hoping these leaders will knock him around a little, get real with him about their problems with Facebook, so he's forced to grapple with the harmful effects it has in many countries.

Mulling over what Mark seems to be imagining for himself on the global stage, a vision popped into my head of Mark presiding over all the heads of state in a meeting at APEC. A session where Mark and the most powerful leaders around the world have some sort of reckoning and forge agreement about some basic rules of the road for the internet. It was preposterous to even think of it. No one would agree to elevating just one CEO, raising him to the level of the most powerful heads of state in the world, and having him preside over them. The White House had nixed him even being onstage for a panel at the last big summit he attended. But I told myself it was a good starting position for the negotiations with APEC on how Mark would participate. If I ask for that, once they stop laughing, they're at least going to consider giving me some of the other things that I actually stand a chance of getting.

So I was shocked—after months of negotiations—to get what I'd asked for. As we prepare to take off for Peru, I still can't believe it's actually going to happen, Mark running a meeting of presidents and prime ministers exactly as I saw in my original vision.

Although we're actually not about to take off because Mark didn't bring his passport.

A small group of Facebook executives mill around the bland, beige terminal, which looks like a place that dispatches rental cars to middle managers rather than private jets to tech titans. Mark's pissed off. By now, I can't work out whether it's just about the blame Facebook's getting for the election result, Trump's election, the forgotten passport, or having to go to Peru in the middle of it all. I worry it's the last one. He was up for it when I pitched it. He even suggested that we should see if the Obamas wanted to do a trip to Machu Picchu with him.

Irrespective, he blames other people for all of those things, including forgetting the passport. I guess that's what it's like to live in a bubble, like Mark does. But a bubble implies flimsy transparency, a diaphanous space where you can see a normal life just beyond your grasp. And what Mark inhabits is more like a thick opaque dome, a murky fortress that separates him from the rest of the world. When you have so many other people doing things for you professionally and personally, you stop taking responsibility for any of it. Max Weber said that dealing with unintended consequences of your actions is what political responsibility is. This guy can't even take responsibility for leaving his passport at home, let alone influencing the US election.

Andrea throws herself on the grenade, declaring that it's all her fault the passport isn't here and that she should be supervising "Mark's home staff" more closely. Notable by its absence is any suggestion that it could have occurred to Mark that a passport might be helpful to visit South America.

Elliot suggests, "Sarah, could you contact the president of Peru to see whether we can get Mark in the country without his passport?"

"Yes," Mark agrees quickly, "that would be good."

"Even Mark Zuckerberg still needs a passport," I gently tease Mark. It doesn't go over well. Fortunately, before I'm peer-pressured into making the call to the president of Peru, Mark realizes he doesn't have some medication he needs. The decision is made to push back the flight departure time while someone, not him, goes to get it.

This isn't the first medical crisis to hit the trip. And not just because of my ongoing medical issues. One Sunday a few months earlier during "maternity leave," I received an urgent call from Elliot.

"It's Peru, it's in trouble," he informs me gravely. "Mark and Priscilla are trying to conceive," he shares in a whisper, never mind the fact we're on a phone call and no one can overhear us.

This immediately feels too intimate. Like we're courtiers of conception admitted into the royal bedroom.

"Riiiight," I say warily.

"Well, you can guess the problem," he says conspiratorially. I'm guessing the dates of the summit don't work out with the dates of ovulation, but that is way too much information for me. CEO conception plans are definitely not part of my job description. I let his statement hang there unanswered.

"Zika," he says. There's no way that Mark can expose himself to Zika or push back his plans for a second child. Mark had once told me that he wanted a "tribe" of kids, so I understand his reluctance to delay.

Elliot had been talking to Mark and the current guidance was to wait three months after travel to a Zika-infected area before trying to conceive, so either the trip should be canceled or we should look at serious measures to protect him from exposure.

At this time, Lima barely had any Zika. Neither Elliot nor I mention that Facebook sent me to ground zero of the Zika outbreak while I was pregnant, but it hangs in the air. Elliot asks me to see what the Peruvian president's office can do to stop Mark from getting Zika. Confidentially, of course.

I assure him I'll do everything I can.

In reality, I don't even know how one broaches the idea of asking a presidential office to safeguard your CEO's sperm. Particularly when you've already asked them for quite a lot lately. I raise it in the vaguest of terms and make it sound like it's me that's worried about Zika and conception. The lovely people I've been working with from the government of Peru seem confused, knowing I have very recently given birth, have been gravely ill, and at the time am supposedly on my maternity leave—like, what sort of person am I? It's very awkward, but I decide to let them believe I am fecund and wanting a third child. It seems easier despite the shame. Naturally, there's little they can do to help, despite best intentions.

And so Facebook is considering extreme measures, or "operation perfect sperm." After a meeting about Zika risk that I'm not included in, Andrea sends me a photo of a head-to-toe netting "bug suit" from an army supply shop that the team thinks Mark should wear. I picture Mark meeting with President Obama, Mark's face obscured behind the gauzy net of the costume, the president pausing briefly to remark on the texture of the net and novelty of the net handshake, making some dad joke about "nothing but net." I respond like Andrea's suggestion is a joke and hope it is.

After Mark talks through every possible Zika mitigation method with the head of the Centers for Disease Control and other experts, things get more extreme. We change our plans to reduce time on the ground to an absolute minimum and decide to build a "controlled structure" on the site of the APEC conference center where ventilation, exposure to others, and bug mitigation can be overseen by Facebook. Limited exposure to the outdoors, sealed rooms, and controlled air supply. I think they're joking about this too, but before I know it I'm negotiating with the Peruvians for some land near the conference to be dedicated to Facebook.

We're a company that's been accused of "digital colonialism," and recently board member Marc Andreessen fired off a series of tweets suggesting that India was better off under British colonial rule. Constructing a Silicon Valley replica in Peru on the grounds of the APEC conference to meet with the heads of state of the world's most powerful nations is not a good look. But any concerns I raise are dismissed.

A large Facebook pop-up is dutifully erected onsite next to the conference center. It's grander than any of the places that heads of state are meeting in. It replicates Mark's meeting room in Menlo Park down to the exact snacks stocked in the "micro kitchen." If the bubble Mark lives in was previously metaphorical, the Facebook pop-up makes it a real physical structure.

At the airport, after a few hours, we finally board the private jet. Mark sits in his leather chair, incensed. He cannot stop talking about the election. It's him, Elliot, a woman from the comms team, and me in a little quad of chairs that face each other. Mark and Elliot have it out. Everyone else in the cabin is pretty quiet.

Elliot's communications team had briefed Mark going into the

Techonomy conference, and Mark's still seething at how his remarks there—that it's a "crazy idea" that Facebook influenced the
election—have been universally rejected, even mocked. A headline
in the *New York Times* that week sums it up: "Mark Zuckerberg Is in
Denial." I agree. Mark still stands by what he said. He believes it! It's
remarkable that a person who founded one of the most powerful
companies in the world, a business premised on the notion that it
can influence the brand of toothpaste you buy, has such difficulty
accepting that the platform where the president-elect spent vast
sums of money had any influence on the election. But this is where
he is. Having tried and failed with the "let Mark be Mark" communications approach, Elliot's mission for the flight is to pull him out of
this denial and figure out what in the world he should say about all
this, going forward. He can see the crisis in a way Mark can't.

Over the course of the ten-hour flight to Lima, Elliot patiently
explains to Mark all the ways that Facebook basically handed the
election to Donald Trump. It's pretty fucking convincing and pretty
fucking concerning. Facebook embedded staff in Trump's campaign
team in San Antonio for months, alongside Trump campaign pro-
grammers, ad copywriters, media buyers, network engineers, and
data scientists. A Trump operative named Brad Parscale ran the operation together with the embedded Facebook staff, and he basically
invented a new way for a political campaign to shitpost its way to
the White House, targeting voters with misinformation, inflammatory posts, and fundraising messages. Boz, who led the ads team, described it as the "single best digital ad campaign I've ever seen from
any advertiser. Period."

Elliot walks Mark through all the ways that Facebook and Parscale's
combined team microtargeted users and tweaked ads for maximum
engagement, using data tools we designed for commercial advertisers. The way I understand it, Trump's campaign had amassed a database, named Project Alamo, with profiles of over 220 million people
in America. It charted all sorts of online and offline behavior, in-

cluding gun registration, voter registration, credit card and shopping histories, what websites they visit, what car they drive, where they live, and the last time they voted. The campaign used Facebook's "Custom Audiences from Custom Lists" to match people in that database with their Facebook profiles. Then Facebook's "Lookalike Audiences" algorithm found people on Facebook with "common qualities" that "look like" those of known Trump supporters. So if Trump supporters liked, for example, a certain kind of pickup truck, the tool would find other people who liked pickup trucks but were not yet committed voters to show the ads to.

Then they'd pair their targeting strategy with data from their message testing. People likely to respond to "build a wall" got that sort of message. Moms worried about childcare got ads explaining that Trump wanted "100% Tax Deductible Childcare." Then there was a whole operation to constantly tweak the copy and the images and the color of the buttons that say "donate," since slightly different messages resonate with different audiences. At any given moment, the campaign had tens of thousands of ads in play, millions of different ad variations by the time they were done. These ads were tested using Facebook's Brand Lift surveys, which measure whether users have absorbed the messages in the ads, and tweaked accordingly. Many of these ads contained inflammatory misinformation that drove up engagement and drove down the price of advertising. The more people engage with an ad, the less it costs. Facebook's tools and in-house white-glove service created incredibly accurate targeting of both message and audience, which is the holy grail of advertising.

Trump heavily outspent Clinton on Facebook ads. In the weeks before the election, the Trump campaign was regularly one of the top advertisers on Facebook globally. His campaign could afford to do this because the data targeting enabled it to raise millions each month in campaign contributions through Facebook. In fact, Facebook was the Trump campaign's largest source of cash.

Parscale's team also ran voter suppression campaigns. They were targeted at three different groups of Democrats: young women, white liberals who might like Bernie Sanders, and Black voters. These voters got so-called dark posts—nonpublic posts that only they would see. They'd be invisible to researchers or anyone else looking at their feed. The idea was: feed them stuff that'll discourage them from voting for Hillary. One made for Black audiences was a cartoon built around her 1996 sound bite that "African Americans are super predators." In the end, Black voters didn't turn out in the numbers that Democrats expected. In an election that came down to a small number of votes in key swing states, these things mattered.

Mark quietly takes it all in. At first, he's skeptical and pushing back, but that gradually turns into curiosity. He starts to ask questions, trying to understand the mechanics of it all. He doesn't seem upset that the platform would be used this way, not in the slightest. If anything, there's admiration for the ingenuity of it. Like, these tools were there all the time for anyone to use this way. How smart that they figured it out.

I'm horrified to hear it laid out like this. I'd heard it before, a few days after the election, at Sheryl's business operations meeting, and had the same reaction, a sense of sticky personal revulsion, knowing I work at the company that did this. I can't imagine how I would feel if I had created the company. I honestly think I'd have a nervous breakdown right there on the private jet, trigger an emergency landing somewhere over Mexico. It's so ugly. What a thing to be responsible for.

When all this was explained to Sheryl at that business operations meeting, once she grasped what Trump's campaign did, her immediate response was not horror but that it was brilliant and innovative and do you think we might have a shot at hiring Trump's guy Brad Parscale to come work at Facebook? No one said anything. After an awkward moment, chastened, she shifted gears: "Of course that's silly. He can have his pick of jobs right now." A pause. "But maybe there are others from the Trump campaign we could bring inside Facebook?"

Mark appears to reach an altogether darker conclusion, but not immediately. Through this whole flight, he's still mulling over everything Elliot laid out for him. Still occasionally pushing back but definitely intrigued.

But before we land in Peru, Elliot doesn't just need Mark to accept how central and instrumental Facebook was in putting Trump into office. He also needs to convince Mark to tell the world that he understands the role Facebook played in the election—and that things are going to change. Elliot wants Mark to post this on his Facebook page when we land, and he wants him to include a concrete action plan listing changes that Facebook will make to address misinformation. That's what the world knows about and people are upset about, all the fake news on the platform.

Mark is adamantly opposed to doing a post, but starting about halfway into the ten-hour flight, he starts to engage Elliot about what he *could* say. They begin drafting. By the time we land in Peru, Mark and Elliot are still locked in battle. Mark's fighting back against every one of the measures that Elliot is pushing. They argue as we get off the plane. They argue in the car to the hotel. They argue in the elevator up to Mark's suite. They continue arguing in his suite. Mark sees the very idea of this post as bullshit capitulation. A shakedown by the press, which blames Facebook for "stealing their livelihood." As far as he's concerned, the press keeps inventing one fake Facebook scandal after another, trying everything they can think of to damage the company, because of how it's decimated their businesses, and they've finally found something that might stick.

Elliot tells Mark that if he thinks that's the real issue, then we should beef up the profit sharing Facebook's doing with news organizations. Buy them off. Or at least be a little fairer. A year before this,

Facebook created something called Instant Articles, which shared ad revenue with newspapers that posted content on the platform. We could go a lot further, Elliot tells him. Mark's not into that.

A few staffers watch them argue and offer suggestions. But I'm silent. What's the point? Mark sees how Facebook threw the election to Trump, and now he's arguing over a bunch of possible changes at Facebook that won't get to the heart of the matter anyway.

Hours after we get to the hotel, Mark's post goes up and it's almost laughably on the nose:

> The bottom line is: we take misinformation seriously. . . . We've been working on this problem for a long time and we take this responsibility seriously. We've made significant progress, but there is more work to be done.

It's a very equivocal post. With this next sentence, for instance, the first half is all Mark and the second half Elliot: "While the percentage of misinformation is relatively small, we have much more work ahead on our roadmap." But Mark does state plainly in the post that Facebook has to do a better job catching misinformation and can't rely on users to complain about it first. Elliot pushed Mark to announce that we'd work with journalists and fact-checking organizations. Mark doesn't commit to that. Instead there's a vague promise to "learn from" fact-checking organizations and to "work with journalists and others in the news industry to get their input," particularly about fact-checking. He also doesn't commit to labeling stories that we know are false but says that we're "exploring" it. When some commenters notice the timestamp on his post, he decides to address them: "For those asking why I posted this at 9:30pm, that's when I landed and got into in [sic] Lima last night."

Part of my pitch for attending APEC was the opportunity for Mark to meet with President Xi of China. By this point, Mark had been trying to meet him formally for years, with no success, and his eagerness to make it happen was only increased by the screw-up in Seattle where Mark posted the photo of the back of Xi's head. While I didn't believe in Facebook's strategy for entering China, I did see value in a meeting between the two, if only as a reality check for Mark.

A formal bilateral meeting wasn't going to happen. But maybe I could wangle some kind of "spontaneous encounter" or "pull-aside."

To achieve a spontaneous encounter, I had to get Mark in close proximity to President Xi. State dinners were obviously out after our experience in Panama. And President Xi, like the pope, wasn't going to come to Mark. But I was able to negotiate Mark a slot for a keynote speech right before President Xi's keynote speech and convince APEC to make the "connectivity revolution" the theme. Even more important, I was able to secure dressing rooms next to each other. This gives us the best opportunity in years for Mark and Xi to meet. We game out different ways of making it happen, rehearse multiple times what to say, and get to the venue unreasonably early to give us as much time as possible to make the connection. I'm primed and ready to be wingman again, only this time without the mojitos.

When our security team lets us know that Xi is on his way, we move outside our dressing room, into the cavernous event space, poised for our "spontaneous" encounter. Mark braces himself— ready for one of the more consequential moments of his career—as Xi's security detail arrives. It's a phalanx of men, in identical gray uniforms, marching in formation past us. Mark stares in disbelief, mouth open. They just keep coming, dozens and dozens of them. It's almost comical. Just when you think there could not be any more, more step in.

As Xi approaches, the thick line of men moves into a formation. They create an impenetrable dividing line between his dressing room and ours, one that stretches all the way down the hall to the entrance. A human Chinese wall.

President Xi is so obscured that he doesn't even have to risk making eye contact with Mark. The troops are now still and silent enough that we can hear Xi's footsteps as he goes by. Soon he's safely ensconced in his dressing room and the door is shut, and the human wall silently files out, leaving Mark, me, and the rest of the small Facebook group loitering outside the dressing room wondering what we just witnessed.

I find it hard not to admire Xi for so completely outmaneuvering us. The Chinese clearly went to the organizers just like I did and asked, "Where will the president be backstage? Who else will be around?" And when they learned it would be Mark Zuckerberg, they took serious precautions. I'm about to compliment their foresight and their sheer commitment—the boots on the ground—that made that happen. I've never seen anything like it. But then I realize Mark's feelings are hurt. His pride is wounded. He's not used to people avoiding him so overtly.

"Uh, I guess that pull-aside isn't going to happen," he laments awkwardly. No one knows what to say in response.

Mark gives his keynote. Hours later we head to a different stage, the one where Mark will preside over a group of heads of state. We've scheduled some time to head back and prepare in our bubble beforehand, but Mark has no interest in doing that. Gone are the days where he would pepper me for information about voting systems, term limits, agenda, and the motives of presidents and prime ministers. We're back to the early days when Mark would tolerate no more than a sentence or two whispered to him before he entered a room or a written briefing no longer than a text capable of being read with one glance at his phone. Inside the Facebook bubble there's a constant churn of presidents, business executives, and continued election fallout chat. No one is paying any attention to Diego Dzodan, Facebook's vice president of Latin America, who stays in close proximity waiting to be noticed. I'd asked Diego to travel here from Brazil, partly because he's our most senior employee in the region, but mostly because he went to jail on behalf of the company and he deserves some face time with the CEO. Like meeting the Chinese, I see value in Mark grappling with the issues he represents in person.

When Mark's meeting room clears, I bring Diego in. I guess I'd been expecting Mark to go over and greet him. It's immediately clear that Mark has no idea who Diego is. I introduce them and Diego gets the standard wan smile. This poor guy had literally put his body on the line and gone to jail in Brazil for Facebook, and Mark effectively blanks him until I remind him of this fact. There's then a supremely awkward exchange where Mark thanks him in a stiff and perfunctory manner with none of the passion that was in his "heartwarming" Facebook post. He doesn't really want to take the time to talk to Diego, and everyone can feel it.

Diego's soon shuffled to the side in favor of some new crisis that requires Elliot. Someone remembered that Ivanka Trump is scheduled to present an award at the Breakthrough Prize, Mark's award ceremony designed to turn scientists into rockstars. Suddenly, after Trump's election, Mark doesn't want her there, but no one knows how to disinvite her. They're gaming out different ways to get a message to her using some combination of Yuri Milner, Jared Kushner's brother, and Karlie Kloss, his brother's girlfriend. Diego returns to his corner.

When we arrive at the Grand Hall for the roundtable with presidents and prime ministers, the first leader to approach us, fittingly, is New Zealand prime minister John Key. So much has changed in the five years since Mark stood outside his conference room and told me and John Key that he didn't want to meet John Key. So much has changed since the time when world leaders made Mark scared and sweaty, since he doubted their relevance to him or Facebook.

Key now tries to cut in as Mark and Elliot continue to discuss the Facebook post about the election, and it seems to take Mark minutes to register that John Key is speaking to him, not just mumbling beside him.

"What is he saying?" Mark asks me, while John Key continues to talk at him, perhaps wanting me to translate his New Zealand accent into American English.

"Tax, Mark. He wants you to pay tax in New Zealand."

"Oh." Mark nods blandly, and turns back to Elliot. The president of Mexico joins our group.

"Have you met the president of Mexico?" I ask John Key.

"Enrique, Sarah, please," President Peña Nieto chides, as he interrupts John Key to get Mark's attention. He's double-booked for the session and came by to personally apologize to Mark for missing it and to get a photo with him. Canadian president Justin Trudeau approaches and also asks for a photo, as does Australia's prime minister, Malcolm Turnbull. It's like Mark's a kingmaker, and they're there to bend the knee.

I drag Mark into the Grand Hall for the session he will chair. It's a vast space, with large red screens reminiscent of the Chinese flag projecting the APEC logo. In the middle of the room a circle of wooden tables has been assembled, with microphones, chairs, and nameplates for each of the presidents and prime ministers. At the center is Mark Zuckerberg. I sit directly behind Mark, with Elliot perched beside me.

Once we're settled in with all these heads of state, it's surprising how many are familiar faces. People I've met either with Mark or in my own role. We know that many of the global leaders we've built relationships with are coming to the end of their terms; some are already gone, and in some cases we've already successfully transitioned to their successors. I'm struck by the impermanence of importance. And yet Mark could conceivably continue to hold his place chairing world leaders for another fifty years. He'll see these leaders off and the generations of leaders that follow them. Like the queen.

After Mark's opening remarks, I'm expecting a rough ride from the assembled presidents and prime ministers. A few had told reporters they saw the session as a chance for "confrontation with Mark

Zuckerberg" about taxes, misinformation, the decimation of local journalism, privacy, and online harm to children. And that was all before Donald Trump was elected with Facebook's help. I am braced for a reckoning.

It is not a rough ride. It's a bubble bath.

"How do we build the next Facebook in our country?" softballs a prime minister.

"How does connectivity help in actual day-to-day governance? Why should it be a priority for my government?" queries Michelle Bachelet, president of Chile, one of the first to formally oppose Internet.org.

Before Mark has the opportunity to address this, the solicitous Canadian prime minister Trudeau jumps in to explain how the internet can be used to deliver social programs electronically, how there are productivity gains if benefits can be paid directly into bank accounts without the need for going to a bank, how social infrastructure is moving online. He's repeating some of the talking points we'd said to him in our chat before the session.

As other prime ministers and presidents intervene to show their tacit support for Mark, I notice that the newly elected president of the Philippines, Rodrigo Duterte—who credited Facebook with his election—is conspicuously napping.

What's odd is that no one raises Trump's election and the role Facebook played. But I belatedly realize it makes sense. These leaders are all in the business of getting elected. They, like Elliot, Sheryl, and basically everyone except Mark (although he seems to be changing his position), probably believe Facebook was instrumental and they don't want to piss off the guy who made that happen. I'm sure that Trump's election elevated Mark in their eyes. He's the powerbroker and they want to stay in power. They understand that one of their most important assets—their voice—is political capital that is ultimately controlled by Mark. So they spend the session complimenting Mark and suggesting ways they can work together with Facebook.

But Mark doesn't seem to absorb it. As he sits in the chair leading this conversation with heads of state, it's like his mind is elsewhere. He seems preoccupied and barely listening. When he does listen, he'll turn to me and ask me for the answer to the question and sometimes the question itself. He's phoning it in. Suddenly, I'm leading a Q&A with the leaders of the free world. I can't believe this is happening.

It's strange. Instead of enjoying what should be the pinnacle of my career, I'm also preoccupied. I spent so long trying to help Mark get comfortable with presidents and prime ministers and get him operating as a global player. Presiding over a room full of the most powerful people in the world should have been a career highlight for both of us. But what I'm seeing is that the more comfortable he gets, the less he cares. As his importance compounds, his regard diminishes. He sails through the whole session, presiding over some of the most powerful people in the world as if none of it matters. Uninterested.

Obama hadn't made it to the roundtable. When we told Mark he was double-booked, Mark responded, "I guess it doesn't matter, he's a lame duck anyway." Which sounded like he didn't care but we all knew better. When we first started planning this trip to Peru, Mark was fixated on traveling to Machu Picchu with President Obama as a "farewell road trip." As if I could just add in a presidential jaunt to one of the Seven Wonders of the World on the side of a roundtable with the leaders of the free world. Before I know it, Mark offers to leave his Zika control bubble and drive across Lima to meet Obama.

We arrive at the Pontifical Catholic University of Peru, where Obama was doing a town hall, one of his last international public events. After the slick Facebook APEC pop-up, the place seems gargantuan and dilapidated, buildings with peeling paint and rotting wood. With Obama soon to be out of office and Mark fresh off chairing APEC's heads of state, Mark definitely has a little swagger on the way in. The power balance is shifting.

We're not allowed to accompany Mark into the meeting. So a few of us are loitering outside when Mark bursts out of the building and strides off even angrier than he was at the start of the trip.

It's a walk across the university campus to get back to where our vans are parked. Mark is moving quickly, silently fuming. By the time we crowd back into the van, he's raging. There's a scramble to fit us all back in, but no one makes the usual "But, but, but . . . I'm the president of Guatemala" joke. We had prepped him for a meeting that would focus on Obama's legacy, but we ended up with a meeting focused on Mark's.

"Fake news, he kept going on about fake news and misinformation," Mark steams. "He doesn't get it. He's got it totally wrong, totally out of proportion. He said that Facebook's playing a destructive role *globally*. And I think he actually believes that."

Elliot shakes his head sympathetically.

"'Not taking it seriously.' That's what he said. I'm not taking these threats seriously enough." Mark quivers, furious. "I told him fake news wasn't a big thing on Facebook. It's less than one percent of what's on the platform. That it wasn't fake news that swung the election for Trump. And that realistically there's not an easy solution. I mean, what does he want me to do?"

Elliot agrees. "I think we'd very quickly run into free speech issues with any action we take."

"And you know what Obama's focused on?" Mark says incredulously. "The next election . . . already."

"They've only just lost this one," Elliot says.

"Yeah, he said he was 'warning me' that we need to make serious changes or things are going to get worse in the next presidential race," Mark says.

"Warning me," he repeats, incensed. Angry that Obama had taken him to task on the role Facebook had played in the election and beyond.

Mark replays fragments of the conversation as if trying to beat them into submission. He's blindsided by Obama's criticism and inflamed, reiterating again and again how Obama's a lame duck, as if that's the salve to the wound. But it seems to me that's what allowed Obama to speak his mind so freely.

Under his anger, I can tell Mark's genuinely hurt. I think he likes and respects Obama. He's also completely unused to frank criticism from anyone more powerful than him. There are so few who fit that description anyway.

36

Rosebud

Mark broods for much of the flight. When he suggests a board game, I agree to play explicitly on the condition that I don't have to let him win. He thinks I'm joking. When I trounce him at Ticket to Ride, he accuses me of cheating. This irks me. I mean, I understand that he's used to everyone going easy on him, so it's logical to him that anyone who beats him must be cheating, but does he really think I wouldn't be able to beat him fair and square?

He challenges me to Settlers of Catan. A couple of other staffers join. I win. He does it again.

"You definitely cheated that time," he says loudly. I see members of the team who are pretending to sleep covertly tune into what is happening. I know he's competitive and not used to losing, and he's working out his anger over Obama and being blamed for throwing the election results for an entire country. But still.

"I didn't cheat," I hear myself say before I can stop myself. "And actually, right up until that last move, you were going to win. You had multiple ways to win." I pause to demonstrate on the board the moves I thought he was going to take or, more accurately, the moves I would have taken in his position. I see him sit back, for the second time that day getting some unexpected pushback (or the third, if you include Xi avoiding him), as he takes in the different strategies I lay out.

"But this is like everything," I say ill-advisedly. "You're so focused on winning every single battle you forget the war. You were so focused on winning the longest road just then, you weren't paying attention to the rest of what was happening on the board." I fail to stop. "Sometimes you have to lose something to win the more important thing. If you try and win everything, you end up losing. You could be strategic about giving some things up. I mean, some people call it compromise, but if you don't like that word you can think about it as a 'strategic loss' or 'strategic retreat' or whatever. But this is why we keep having massive issues. You're so used to being the winner who takes all."

"An example," he challenges me. "Give me an example."

"Sure, there are too many to choose from." I mean this with all my heart. We seem to be in a constant can't-see-the-forest-for-the-trees situation. I think about Facebook's refusal to cooperate in sharing even the smallest amount of data with researchers or compromising just a little on taxes or actually educating regulators about our products rather than taking advantage of their lack of understanding of our technology. All of which would build some trust and goodwill.

"Just pick one," he presses.

"No problem. How about changing the name of Internet.org? How many times did we have to come to you and say it was a problem and it was going to attract regulatory scrutiny and make everything harder and it didn't need to? And how many times did you push back? You wanted to win that battle so badly, and it's just a name, and by the time you realized that and actually agreed to call it Free Basics, it didn't really matter. We'd burnt up all the goodwill we had with regulators and they were against the whole thing. If you'd just lost that battle upfront, accepted that regulators have some actual real power, and accepted we needed to change the name, we would have stood more of a chance of actually making Internet.org happen."

He leans back in his seat and considers this. There's a tense si-

lence. By now, those who were pretending to doze to avoid the board
games have given up the pretense entirely. I'm filled with regret for
having been goaded into this confrontation and not showing the def-
erence generally expected from women who work for Mark, but the
accusation of cheating pushed me over the edge. Finally, he speaks
slowly.

"That's fair," he says.

Nothing more. That's the end of the conversation.

Instead, talk returns to legacy. It's a familiar topic. Mark has become increasingly obsessed by his own legacy in recent years. Things
he can be remembered for besides Facebook. This is what's occupy-
ing him so much of the time I'm around him, and fills his conversations, not new products he wants to launch or new places he wants
to drive Facebook. His foundation, the Chan Zuckerberg Initiative,
launched less than a year ago.

"I want to talk about purpose," he declares. "For the commencement speech." He's giving the commencement speech at Harvard in
a few months, and he's focused on that more than any Facebook issue or product. In fact, for months he's been raising this commencement speech. It seems to be the only thing that brings him joy. The
comms team staffers start taking notes as he riffs on high-minded
themes, global connection, and freedom. This seems to cheer Mark
up. By the time he brings up his personal challenge, he's having a
great time.

Each year Mark does a public "personal challenge" that is heavily
promoted on Facebook. Previous years included learning Mandarin
or eating only meat he's killed himself. This year, for his 2016 challenge, he's made an AI assistant for his home. To show it off at the
end of the year, he wants to put out a "humorous video" with the AI
voiced by a celebrity. The more he talks, the bigger the idea grows.

"We should do the video from my perspective," he declares.
"We'd need to film it pretty fast. We're nearly at the end of the year.
It would be good to do another video from . . ."

"Priscilla's perspective?" Derick suggests.

"I was going to say the AI's perspective, but that could be funny. Maybe Priscilla would learn that the AI only listens to my voice. Like she's trying to command it in different places around the house and it just ignores her."

I have thoughts on "Priscilla not having her voice heard" in her own home but I know enough about expectations of women at Facebook to keep silent. Mark thinks it's hilarious.

"Maybe we can have users vote on who should be AI's voice?" he says, eyes lighting up. The team keeps trying to lower his expectations, given the tight deadline.

The conversation switches to what he's going to announce for his 2017 challenge, which he wants to do soon. I'm only mildly curious about this. Maybe he could focus on all the pressing problems confronting Facebook? Do something about the way misinformation spreads, or the way populists are using the platform, or how the two issues combine with authoritarian and populist leaders using misinformation to trigger violence in the real world, like in the Philippines? But it turns out he's already decided.

"I know what my 2017 challenge is going to be," he says firmly. "I'm going to visit as many states as possible. Get on the ground. Meet people. Understand what they're looking for."

My antenna goes up. Mark is not someone who particularly enjoys travel or, in fact, people. And I know he's hoping to have another baby in 2017, so this doesn't make any sense as a personal challenge.

"Are there any states in particular you want to go to?" I ask tentatively.

"Iowa, New Hampshire, South Carolina, Ohio, Pennsylvania."

Ugh. The traditional stops for presidential candidates. Someone asks if there's a particular time he's looking to go to those states and he responds that he'd like to start as soon as possible. I can't bring myself to ask directly, "So you're going to run for president?" Like saying the words will bring it into existence. So I go instead with the only slightly more veiled, "You're not looking to go eat fried butter or whatever at the Iowa State Fair?"

"Yes," he pronounces. "I'm going to Iowa." There's a moment as this sinks in. It feels as if all the air has been sucked out of the plane. "Can we do that first?"

The comms team staffers start to quickly enable. Logistical questions: How fast can they launch this tour, how many early-voting states can they reasonably cover, what order, what do they do in each state, what stakeholders do they need to reach out to, what images do they want to convey? I keep trying to catch Elliot's eye but he avoids me. I move to the empty seat beside him.

"He can't run for president," I whisper when I think Mark is sufficiently distracted. Elliot's the one person on the plane with an air of fatherly authority; he seems like the best person to quash this quickly. "Elliot, he listens to you, he just told us he's planning to run for president of the United States. You have to stop this."

Elliot shifts back in his seat and shakes his head.

"This is a horrible idea," I press.

Elliot shrugs and says, "Mark gets to decide his own personal challenges. It's not for us to intervene, Sarah."

I think he's telling me to be quiet, to drop it, to know my place. And I realize that everyone around Mark is like this. No one's going to try to talk him out of it.

Mark's still bothered by the Facebook post Elliot made him write about the election. He doesn't want to move the company closer to the media industry or allow it to assume more media-like functions, such as editing or fact-checking.

Mark starts talking about how the lesson from the 2016 election is that the mainstream media failed and blaming Facebook is just opportunism by a media ecosystem that wants to scapegoat Facebook for its own failure, and its own problems.

Talk turns to how he would solve it. He wants to remake the American news media. What's unsaid is that he already has remade the American news media, by inserting Facebook at the center of it, driving down ad rates for newspapers, and distributing their stories using their content to boost time spent on Facebook. But I guess he wants more. Presumably more control over the media would be helpful with any presidential run. He doesn't want to just buy a paper like other billionaires. Maybe Facebook should buy Twitter? He's tempted. After all, Facebook is already a news source for nearly half of all Americans.

"Why are you guys recommending compromising with traditional media? It's an industry locked in a death spiral. We don't need to accommodate. You're not thinking big enough," Mark says, chiding Elliot for pushing partnerships and profit-sharing models with media. Concessions for the culprits. "You're compromising with a dying industry rather than dominating it. Crushing it."

Mark has this will to survive above everybody, and it feels like he is always plotting to kill off those things that get in his way to ensure his survival.

"You don't want to go to war with these guys," Elliot says.

Mark disagrees. He doesn't hide his frustration with Elliot as he explains that the way digital technology is going will ultimately result in the extinction of the media industry as we know it now. "The way I see it, we've got three obvious options: I buy the 'failing *New York Times*,' the paper of record, and remake the news ecosystem through that, but putting Facebook at its heart. Make it truly digital. Fix it from the inside out. Make it the first effective digital publication. The other option is to come at it the other way to try and rebuild the fourth estate. I don't buy a newspaper, I make one. From the ground up. Hire engineers and journalists and rebuild it at Facebook. Remake the entire news ecosystem here. Maybe I put in some Chinese walls for independence or maybe I don't."

"Make it truly 'digital first,'" Elliot ponders, absentmindedly playing with the zipper on my portable breast pump case.

"Yes. Appoint a Facebook editor, but make something new. Not the fourth estate, a fifth estate. But a fifth estate that has Facebook at its center. You know—something that recognizes and grows the role Facebook plays alongside these other power structures in society."

"A digital fifth estate." Elliot's warming to it. "A home for everyone now that we've removed these gatekeepers."

"Or your option, this terrible status quo. Facebook continues on this path of compromising around the edges with these failing media entities, we continue to play an increasingly large role in controlling and directing traffic and wait for them to die off over time. I don't see what this gets us. We're just losing time."

The sheer scale of the contemplated power grab silences us all. He'd control how the news is made, as well as the algorithm that targets and distributes it. What stays up and what doesn't. Who is on the platform and who isn't. Which would certainly come in handy if he runs for president.

I try to piece together how we got to this point in the less than forty-eight hours since we set off for Peru. What I settle on is this: Mark had no intention of running for president when he arrived at the airport without his passport. I think he really was blindsided by the accusation that Facebook was responsible for Donald Trump winning the election, and his anger at being blamed was real. But on the flight to Peru, as Elliot painstakingly explained piece by piece how the Trump campaign used Facebook to win, Mark became convinced that Facebook did play a decisive role. That realization was forefront in his mind as he played at world leader at APEC, chairing that bubble-bath session with all the prime ministers and presidents, realizing the extent to which he and his platform truly were kingmakers and how he would outlast almost everyone there. Sought after for selfies by men who run countries. He already thought of himself as the most well-known person of our generation in the world, and this experience supercharged that belief. Obama's dressing down provoked a "who does he think he is" response in Mark,

petulance rather than introspection, a desire to flex power, not contrition. As Mark contemplated his future—his legacy and the coming
year's personal challenge—I think he came to this dark conclusion: if
Trump can do it, so could he.

After all, not only does Mark now have Trump's playbook, he
owns the tools and sets the rules. And he has something no one else
has, the ability to control the algorithm with zero transparency or
oversight. The power to control what Facebook users see. To throw
someone like Trump off Facebook. He already has his personal team
"maximizing his reach and engagement" or whatever euphemism is
appropriate for whatever it is they do. I assume they're the reason he
has four times more followers than Trump and more than any other
political leader in the world.

Also, he's loaded. He could run for president and never ask anyone for a dime.

Mark goes back to planning the various states he wants to visit.
He wants to go to a farm, a factory, a church, a community center.
He wants to meet with Black leaders, opioid addicts, autoworkers. He
wants to eat fried foods in Iowa and barbeque in Texas. He wants to go
to a rodeo, drive some heavy machinery, wear a hard hat.

The jet staff tell us to get ready to land. As I take my seat next to
Mark and the plane starts to descend, Mark asks me what I think. I
feel my insides tumbling. I want to tell him this is the beginning of
the end for me. I had fooled myself into thinking APEC might be
some kind of reckoning. In fact, it was the opposite. I've seen some
hard truths I can't unsee, about Mark and where he's going. This is
the last foreign trip I invent for him, the last time I travel with him.
I've spent many years now, flying around the globe and helping him
learn how to navigate the world of prime ministers and presidents. I
don't want this to become who I am. I didn't sign up for where he is
now trying to go. I know I can't do it anymore.

This trip is one of many moments where Mark could have gone a different way. Could have been convinced by a different path. But something else kicked in. After all the headlines saying he was in denial about the election, after being shit on by Obama, he dug in. He's not built to take criticism like that and genuinely try to understand and fix the problems the 2016 election exposed, wield his power responsibly. That's not who he is. He's defiant. He'll show them. And in the middle of all that, he stands on a stage full of the most powerful people in the world, and they dote over him like some boy king. All of that came together and solidified in this new vision of himself that's both comforting and sort of thrilling. He'd run for the most powerful job on earth. If Facebook can propel someone into the White House, why not him?

And now we're sitting here side by side on a plane and he's asked me what I think. Where to even begin? Do I try to talk him out of this plan to run for president? Do I point out all the ways it probably won't make him happy or end well for anyone? Do I tell him how he's changed since I've met him? He was a single-minded maniac, sure, but it was all about building something, making a tool to change the world. The way he saw politicians back then—he had no time for them, would never want to be one of them—I prefer that to the way he is now. Over these five years, I feel like I've seen him face so many choices and lose touch with whatever fundamental human decency he had when we started. Do I say that? How? How can I say any of these things to him?

The plane is descending. Time's running out. Here we are. Mark's looking at me expectantly. What do I think, he's asked me.

I look him in the eyes and say, "Rosebud."

Mark gives me a blank look.

"What are you talking about?"

"You know, Rooooosseeeebuuud."

Mark looks baffled. Oh god. This was a very bad idea.

"*Citizen Kane?*"

I start to wonder if he's being deliberately obtuse.

"*Citizen Kane.* You know, the movie," Elliot says. He's sitting across from Mark. We're in a pod of four facing chairs. Strapped in for landing.

Still Mark doesn't get it.

"Hearst," I say, by way of explanation.

Mark cocks his head and looks at me quizzically.

Elliot clearly can't believe I've gone down this road, but tries to help me out. "I think what she's saying is that if you do this and you control the publishers and you run for office, that makes you a modern-day William Randolph Hearst," he explains. "You know, with the publishing and the politics and the . . ."

"Oh," Mark says softly. "Is that a bad thing?"

What a question. Neither of us takes that one on. Mark smiles wanly, still confused, but shakes it off as the plane touches down on the runway.

We're back on the tarmac, where we were forty-eight hours before. Everything's the same but everything's different.

"Good trip, everyone. Lots to think about," he says.

We all unbuckle our seatbelts and wait for him to go. After he exits, we gather our things and leave the plane ourselves.

37

Man of the People

In the months that follow, Mark sets out on a road trip through the small towns of Iowa; works a Ford assembly line outside Detroit, Michigan; celebrates Pride in Omaha, Nebraska; attends Sunday service at Emanuel African Methodist Episcopal Church in Charleston, South Carolina; drives a tractor at a dairy and beef cattle ranch in Blanchardville, Wisconsin; visits a shrimp boat in Bayou La Batre, Alabama; does NASCAR ride-along laps with Dale Earnhardt Jr. in Charlotte, North Carolina; sits with a group of recovering heroin addicts in Dayton, Ohio; and tours a drilling rig at one of the main fracking sites in Williston, North Dakota.

Each stop is carefully scouted by an advance team. And then beautifully documented by one of Mark's photographers, including Charles Ommanney, whose job for nine years was photographing George W. Bush and Barack Obama. The results of these efforts are posted to Mark's Facebook page and then "optimized" to ensure his many millions of followers see them. Mark's also started to optimize himself, eschewing the fatty fast foods for fresh cut fruit and putting time into working out every day.

Officially he denies he's running for president, but what else is this very time-consuming side hustle? Why the focus on battleground states? He hires the consultants who got Obama and Bush elected—

David Plouffe and Ken Mehlman—to his foundation. He publishes a six-thousand-word manifesto full of global aspirations.

His speeches take on a new tone, like what a kid thinks a president sounds like:

> Our greatest opportunities are now global—like spreading prosperity and freedom, promoting peace and understanding, lifting people out of poverty and accelerating science. Our greatest challenges also need global responses—like ending terrorism, fighting climate change and preventing pandemics. Progress now requires humanity coming together not just as cities or nations but also as a global community.

And,

> The occasion is piled high with difficulty, and we must rise with the occasion. As our case is new, so we must think anew, act anew.

If I had any doubts about Mark's intention to become a presidential candidate, his response to some bad press in Hawaii wipes them away. Mark owns a lot of land in Hawaii. He started with seven hundred acres of beachfront property in Kauai. Then he launched lawsuits against hundreds of Hawaiians who may have held titles to small plots on his estate, under an old Hawaiian law, to force them to sell their land to him. Many do not wish to sell. Mark was doing all this quietly, through three shell companies, but then the fact that he owned the companies was revealed by the *Honolulu Star-Advertiser*. "This is the face of neocolonialism," a law professor pronounces in one of the articles. The *Vanity Fair* headline reads, "Man of the People Mark Zuckerberg Sues to Keep Native Hawaiians Off His Kauai Estate." An Inertia editorial says, "So now it looks as though not only is Zuckerberg suing a bunch of native Hawaiians over land that's been in their families for generations, but he's suing DEAD people. What a dick move!"

This is the sort of media coverage that months ago Mark would have brushed off. I've seen him weather all sorts of bad press, going back years, and he never seemed to care. But now he's on the phone to Elliot, all worked up. I overhear them. Mark tells Elliot to do something about the headlines and Elliot explains that would be difficult because they seem to be true. (Ha!) Then Mark declares he's just going to get rid of the entire estate, sell everything he has in Hawaii. He just wants to make this go away. Elliot's confident he'll change his mind; Mark's not used to giving up on things he wants. He's never okay losing any battle, and he cares way more about his home in Hawaii than he does about Settlers of Catan or Ticket to Ride.

Sure enough, within days he's found a workaround. He officially announces that he's dropping the lawsuits, and Elliot tells me they have a plan. Later I learn that a retired professor has purchased the disputed land from his own cousins for millions of dollars. He openly brags of being paid $6,000 a month by Mark Zuckerberg to do the deals and keep people off the land, the cousins tell reporters.

So the attempt to quash the bad press is not entirely successful. But he tried. Over the years, I've seen Mark take a lot of criticism, but I've never seen him so concerned about how he's being seen by the public. Just like, you know, a politician.

He also has Facebook's board approve a new stock structure that would allow him to run for office. The filing with the Securities and Exchange Commission expressly allows Mark to leave Facebook for up to two years without losing control of the company if his absence is "in connection with his serving in a government position or office." I assume the two years would cover the period Mark would be taking on the—presumably time-consuming—endeavor of campaigning to be president of the United States. Then, if he won, he'd step down as CEO. A lawsuit subsequently reveals that some of Facebook's board members were concerned about the time commitment of this side gig and told Mark they were struggling with "how to define the gov't service thing without freaking out shareholders that you are losing commitment," but Mark fought hard and won. He's wedded to his plan. The day the special committee recommended that Facebook's board approve the new system, according to court documents, board member Marc Andreessen texted Mark, "The cat's in the bag and the bag's in the river."

Mark replied, "Does that mean the cat's dead?"

Andreessen answered, "Mission accomplished," adding a smiley face.

And while Mark continues to look at other jobs, so do I. Calling people I know, having conversations about positions at Google, Cloudflare, and think tanks. Nothing solidifies and I can't quit Facebook without a place to go, because I need the health insurance. In the year since Xanthe's birth, my medical situation has gotten pretty frightening. My body is producing precancerous growths in my bowel. Doctors cut them out, but as soon as they do, more form. I had twelve growths cut out soon after Sasha's birth. But still they continue to grow. This shouldn't be happening to someone my age, they tell me, but they really don't understand what's causing it. I wonder if this is some kind of legacy from my shark attack, because the shark ripped through my bowel, but the doctors say no.

My doctors send me to a "genetic counselor" who says that it appears I have something called Lynch syndrome. I'll need some more tests to confirm but I'm told that if they don't remove my bowel, I'll get bowel cancer. I'm given pamphlets that start,

A diagnosis of cancer raises complex emotions and questions. Among these are questions such as "What caused my cancer?

Will I have to face cancer again? Are my family members at increased risk of cancer?"

The way the specialists speak so casually of the likelihood of cancer makes living without health insurance inconceivable, especially with two children.

38

Let Them Eat Cake

The day Donald Trump is inaugurated, I'm flying home from Davos with Sheryl, Elliot, Sadie, and other Facebook staffers.

By now, Tom has a spreadsheet. Every time I announce I have to leave him and the girls for another work trip, he says, "Well this is going in the spreadsheet," in a determined way before conspicuously updating it. He never tells me what the spreadsheet is for or what happens if there are too many entries. But I know it won't be good. To make matters worse, he's concerned by everything going on within Facebook, but can't report on it at his newspaper because of the conflict of interest obligations he's under. He's set a deadline for leaving San Francisco, which we both know really means leaving Facebook, but with the ongoing health stuff, the incessant work, and the tiny children, I'm finding it hard to make the time to figure out a way out and still deliver what everyone needs day-to-day.

Thankfully, Davos has become routine. The hardest part these days is managing Sheryl's ever-increasing desire to be in the spotlight. After months of negotiations, I'd secured a lineup she was satisfied with, making sure she was on the right panels, went to the right parties, and had more time with the microphone than her female frenemies. All of us accompanying Sheryl are well trained enough to know Sheryl's expectation that we sit in the front row, applaud loudly, and provide admiring feedback on her words or, as I've come to think of them, her emperor's clothes. Any deviation from this risks her chewing you out after.

But on this trip, I decide I won't sit in the front row and won't praise her after each event. It's one of my tiny acts of resistance. It feels rebellious. I know it aggravates her. Autonomy disturbs a certain kind of powerful person, and Sheryl has never accepted independence among her advisers. Even those she is icing out. Her team races to be the first to craft complimentary comments on her Facebook posts even after we've drafted them ourselves, to share any positive feedback from "important people" after a public appearance, and to be as obsequious as possible about her events. It creates a strange reality around her.

And so I'm surprised at this 2017 Davos when—during Sheryl's final panel—some of her closest advisers start a WhatsApp group while sitting in the front row to complain about how bored they are and include me. They joke about livening up the panel by asking about filter bubbles or Facebook's role in news monetization and the other hot-button issues for Facebook right now. Then they turn to criticizing Sheryl, her scowl, how she always pivots to the same three inane anecdotes about people using Facebook, including an Indian small business called Pigtails and Pony. It's jarring because these are some of her most trusted lieutenants, her most obsequious cheerleaders.

Afterward, they rush up to her, quick to heap praise, telling her how she eclipsed Christine Lagarde, Meg Whitman, and the other panelists.

Over the time I've been at Facebook, I've watched people who disagree with Sheryl and Mark become marginalized and exit. The people who enable remain and Sheryl rewards them with an astonishing amount of money. Perhaps I was expecting some kind of honor among thieves. I didn't realize that they do say what they think, just not to her.

That's another thing that's weighing on me, the money. Like most tech companies, Facebook offers equity grants. And since the time I joined pre-IPO, these have become seriously valuable. My bosses earn astonishing amounts of money, the sort of money that ensures they will never need to work again. My equity grants are definitely not at that level (probably because I didn't know what equity was when I started at Facebook and so never negotiated or asked for more), but after years at Facebook they are worth serious money. Potentially millions of dollars. Meted out over four-year cycles. But only if I stay at the company. That's hard to grapple with as the main earner in our household. Leaving could potentially mean losing all of that.

Maybe that's why they do it. Either way, open dissent isn't an option with Sheryl. People actively hide bad news or situations they know she won't like because they've seen her shoot the messenger.

Unfortunately for Sheryl, Facebook is generating a lot of bad news. Elliot and Joel are quick to tell me that I shouldn't mention these things to her, whether it's the fact we still haven't resolved the issue that led to her arrest warrant in Seoul years ago or we still haven't found a way to launch Facebook for kids—"Project Family." No one wants to get shot.

We're in Sheryl's private jet flying home from Davos. It's my first time on a plane with her since the flight—one year ago—where she asked me to bed with her. She's been chilly with me since then. I've worked with her a lot less, and every interaction feels loaded.

Soon after takeoff, she approaches the younger women—Sadie, me, and another one of her assistants—inviting us to the bedroom at the back of the jet. At first, none of us respond. Then, strangely, Elliot says he wouldn't mind a nap. What is he doing? Anything seems possible, including that he just wants a nap.

Sheryl calls Sadie over. They whisper for a bit, then Sadie comes back to me and confides that Sheryl finds Elliot "creepy," before tidying up her stuff, closing her computer, and going back to the bedroom with Sheryl.

She's calling Elliot creepy while asking her subordinates to go to bed with her?

While we work, extraordinary scenes are unfolding at Donald Trump's inauguration in Washington, DC. Hundreds of thousands of women in the streets protesting there, with many more in hundreds of cities around the country, the largest single-day demonstration in US history. And it all started with a Facebook post.

When Sheryl emerges from the bedroom hours later, I'm excited to fill her in on the largest women's protest in our lifetimes. She's fresh off a Davos panel about women's leadership where Elliot called her the "unofficial self-appointed world dean of women."

Sheryl picks over some fresh cut fruit that's been arranged for her, still in her pajamas, which are silky and perfectly tailored. I breathlessly start to tell her about the history she missed while she slept. She looks bored immediately. I press on about the Women's March, how people are marching everywhere, tiny towns, red states and blue, and not just in America. She cuts me off, changing the subject to her weekend plans, meeting up with friends, the possibility of going dancing sometime in the future, redecorating her ski house, something about her apartment in Los Angeles, and some story about her boyfriend Bobby and how he's trying to buy a private jet or staff for a private jet or something. She seemingly could not care less.

Sadie passes champagne and cake around this private jet. One of Sheryl's three assistants arranged this to toast a "successful Davos."

Sadie used to work at the Lean In organization, and I try to enlist her help in getting Sheryl to show some interest in the Women's March.

Sadie starts in with, "Don't you think it's amazing?" when Sheryl shuts her down. She's not even a little bit curious.

"You're gonna come dancing with us, aren't you, Sadie?"

Sadie gives me a look that tells me to drop it. There's silence while Sheryl sips her champagne and picks at the cake.

"What was she wearing?" Sheryl asks. I'm so relieved that she's engaging that I don't totally understand the question. I start to tell her about the pink hats that are showing up in marches all around the world. Sadie's making eyes at me to stop.

"No, no, not that," she scolds. "What did Melania wear?"

Here she is on her private jet, champagne in her hand, her back to a big-screen TV showing thousands of women with signs and banners. It takes all my self-control not to exclaim, "Let them eat cake!"

"I don't know," I answer. It had not occurred to me to look at what Melania Trump was wearing.

"Sadie, will you find out?" she says.

I retreat to the back of the jet and stay silent for the rest of the flight home.

39

Facebook Feminist Fight Club

It turns out I'm not the only one who noticed Sheryl's silence on the Women's March. Far from it. Nearly two hundred female employees who work under Sheryl have recently created a secret Facebook group, the Feminist Fight Club (FFC).

The existence of the FFC is a relief. I'm not alone. Unhappy workplaces are conspiracies of silence. But once you get outside the sycophantic leadership bubble, this place is roiling with discontent. The ethos of Facebook, like America, is one of rugged individualism right down to the product, which personalizes, atomizes, and weaponizes despite being based on community and networks. Similarly, Lean In is premised on personal responsibility in the face of structural issues. But the FFC is different. And how stupid of me to think I was alone in this. I'm working with incredibly smart people who are facing the same systemic issues I am. Of course, there is some form of group or collective. In this one, you can watch its members try to reconcile the Facebook they hoped for and the Facebook they experience.

The FFC manages to make enough noise on women's issues that management is forced to respond, and naturally they do this in the most Facebook way possible. They announce #ally bot, a "bot that promotes ally behaviors within the company by letting you thank your colleagues for being allies." A top aide for the chief technology officer explains that the bot is for men to use when they see other men supporting women. "If I'm in a meeting and I see another dude be an ally I could say 'hey that was great keep that up.'" The bot "gives the recipient a shiny new Ally badge on their internal Facebook profile" once their name has been added with the hashtag #ally in the #ally bot.

The bot keeps score and is linked to the performance review system—meaning men will be receiving a highly visible input to the system that will affect pay, promotions, and stock options and can be easily gamed by any men who decide to hand each other #ally hashtags. When the FFC figures this out—how it's intended to incentivize and reward men and not women—the comments pick up a tone of incredulity and despair. One woman posts, "Doesn't it seem like this is an undue amount of credit for men who are hitting the bare minimum of decency?"

"You don't get a cookie for not being a scumbag," another FFC member writes.

"Where's my 'I got sexually harassed at work' badge?" someone else posts.

Thanks to the FFC, women are starting to talk more openly about the harassment at Facebook. When I take a business trip to one of our overseas offices, one of my coworkers pulls me aside as soon as I arrive. We'd worked together for years and I'd noticed her cheerful personality change when she was moved under a new boss, a balding pale man around the same age as Joel. She closes the door and issues a quick warning about him, her face reddening as she says, "Don't be alone with him. Stick to the open-plan office and don't let him talk to you about sex stuff." Later, the same man begins an affair with a young coworker who wanted to join the team he was leading. She subsequently left the company. He's still there.

I know that an open office or even being thousands of miles apart won't spare anyone from having your boss "talk to you about sex stuff," and because of the FFC we know that this is happening office to office and in between. I heard about incidents from Korea to India to Australia to California and beyond. The worst of which involved hospitals and police reports, coupled with prepared statements that "Facebook takes these issues seriously." The bulk of the rest protected by a silence. A silence born of the knowledge of what happens to those women who speak up beyond these urgent whispered warnings. It doesn't help them advance, let's just say. That's why these whispered warnings have developed. The belief that the people who do this will be protected is part of what enables powerful people to go on abusing that power. There's a growing realization among the FFC that we're going to be saved not by the captains of Facebook but by the crew. If we're going to be saved at all, that is.

I decide I have to do something about how Joel is making me feel. I'm hearing so many stories from other women about complaints they have made. I am concerned that others may have complained about Joel and that my silence would also impact them and ensure nothing changes. I can't do nothing. I want to be able to do my job without having to google "dirty sanchez."

I decide to talk to Elliot. I know HR will just protect Joel. Mark's out running for president. And Sheryl, who advocates for women in the workplace day after day, in bestselling books, TED talks, and panels around the world? I remember her once writing in a message,

> I always believe that when companies and people have to say things over and over it is because they want them to be true but they are not. When I was at McKinsey, they always said they were "non-hierarchical" because they were so hierarchical.

Google is "not political." One of our favorite candidates who almost joined us was "highly ethical."

So that's obviously complicated.

I tell Elliot about Joel's behavior, Joel's scheduling meetings and work for me during maternity leave, and the systemic problems of sexual harassment across his department. Elliot seems both unsurprised and unconcerned. He listens to me, nods along, says next to nothing. When I'm done talking, he tells me he's sure all of this is solvable and will work itself out. And the meeting's over. He couldn't make it clearer that he doesn't want any part of this. I rise and walk to the door. Elliot starts typing on his laptop.

"And if it doesn't work itself out?" I ask.

Elliot looks up from his laptop and stares me straight in the eyes. "Well, that would be a shame, but I'd be happy to write you a reference."

It lands like a physical blow.

Weeks pass, and I worry Elliot's going to fire me at any moment. Then I spot another way I can take action. Separate from all this, Facebook's lawyers are looking into some things Facebook's doing in the Philippines after I raised concerns about whether the company violated the Foreign Corrupt Practices Act. During that investigation, I realize there's an opportunity to put some things on the record, with company lawyers. Just in case I am fired.

I tell them about Joel's behavior and the fact that he made me work during maternity leave. I tell them I've informed Elliot.

Within days, one of Joel's team invites me out for a drink. This person is often Joel's mouthpiece so the invitation scares me, but I decide to say yes, understanding that a message is going to be delivered to me one way or another. We meet at a bar not far from where I live. It doesn't take long to get to the point.

"How's the investigation going?" they ask casually.

Since the investigation is supposed to be strictly confidential, I play dumb, hoping my poker face comes through for me.

Undeterred, they say, "Joel is loyal to his people. He looks after them. He's a marine. He values loyalty."

The message seems to be: Joel won't fire me if I keep my mouth shut.

Days later, the person running the investigation asks me what I want them to do about Joel. Do I want the investigator to look into the issues related to Joel that I put on record? I'm surprised at the question, because I naively assume that if Facebook's lawyers are aware of his behavior, they'd have some sort of protocol that would tell them whether they have to investigate. They wouldn't be asking me.

Before responding to the investigator, I go back to Elliot. I ask him directly: If I shut down this investigation right now, then Joel's creepy behavior will stop? He nods yes.

I go back to the investigator and tell him that Joel sent a message about the investigation and the importance of "loyalty" and "looking after people who are loyal," and for that reason, if it's up to me, I do not wish to trigger an investigation.

It feels like retaliation from Joel begins almost immediately. He informs me that he's halving my job. I can choose between running Asia or Latin America, but no longer both. There's no explanation given, other than that he has made a decision, although it is obvious to me.

Of the two options, there's no question which one has more responsibility, growth, and importance for the business. It's Asia. But Joel insists that if I pick Asia, I have to run China as part of the job.

He knows how strongly I oppose Facebook's China policy and that I don't want anything to do with it.

I can't bring myself to work on China. I shock Joel and Elliot by choosing to run Latin America and Canada. It's less responsibility and importance.

This surprises them. They really had expected me to take on China. They want to force me to submit. They counter that they'll only give me the smaller job if I lead the search to find someone to run Asia. So, for the time being, I continue to run Asia.

The real kicker, though, is China. Even in this interim period, they insist that I work on China.

40

Greetings from Beijing

In the past, when I expressed dissent about what Facebook was attempting in China, I was removed from the China team. Now, in a totalitarian move I suspect the Chinese leadership would admire, as a result of dissent in other areas, I am being installed to run it, against my will. A test of loyalty to the regime.

China has always been first in the "things I don't want to know" about Facebook. I'd rather not know the worst about this place I've devoted so many years of my life to. My plan is to hire someone and get out of Facebook.

It's January 2017. Only weeks since Mark's trip to Peru and his decision to start his US political tour. Joel, Mark, and Vaughan all travel back and forth between the US and Beijing and have been doing so for years. Joel would send emails titled "Greetings from Beijing." I didn't pay much attention. Other than moments that make the news, like when Mark went for a smoggy jog through Tiananmen Square and posted about it.

I know Facebook's advertising business in China is growing—even while we're blocked—because Chinese businesses are buying ads on Facebook. It's possible, through resellers, for them to target ads to people outside China and to people who travel to China. In fact, China is Facebook's second-largest market, accounting for an estimated $5 billion of revenue at this time and roughly 10 percent of Facebook's total revenue, trailing only the US. That's while the company is banned. So I know China matters a great deal to Facebook.

But as I take over the day-to-day running of Facebook's China policy from Joel, their strategy is so opaque, there's no obvious place to find out what's happened so far. After a not terribly informative coffee with Vaughan, I figure my only option is to sift through random documents to try to understand the situation.

So I sit down to read.

In the three years since Mark sent out his email to top managers declaring that getting into China was Facebook's top priority, his desire to make this happen has only grown, according to the documents.

To make it happen, Facebook's put important people on the payroll, including a former deputy secretary of the treasury, Bob Kimmitt, who's now the lead "independent" director on Facebook's board. Mark gets advice from Henry Kissinger and Hank Paulson.

I'm curious—why would China allow Facebook in? I soon find a set of documents that sets out Facebook's pitch. The first is titled "China—Our Value Proposition." It's mostly the corporate feel-good "we'll boost your economy and help you prosper" bullshit. They promise to help China increase its global influence and promote "the China dream," support innovation and job growth, and advertise Chinese products to people around the world.

But the "key "offer is that Facebook will help China *promote safe and secure social order.*" And what does this mean? Surveillance. They point out that on Facebook, the profiles represent real people with their real names, and that "we adhere to local laws wherever we operate and develop close relationships with law enforcement and governments."

In the most benign reading of this, Facebook is saying: millions of your citizens will post information about themselves publicly that you can view and collect if you want. In the least benign reading—

the way I read this—Facebook is dangling the possibility that it'll give China special access to users' data. Authoritarian states need information on everyone at every level of society, and Facebook can provide a treasure trove.

That pitch signals Facebook's intent to work hand-in-glove with the CCP to help enforce its will on its people:

Facebook seeks to create an online environment that is *civilized*, which is why we respect local laws as well as *harmonious* which is why we remove offending content. We agree with Minister Lu Wei when he said: "We must stick to the bottom line and exercise governance in accordance with the law" and "Liberty means order. The two are closely linked. . . . Liberty cannot exist without order."

I can't imagine Mark saying that to US citizens.

And who will do this surveillance on Facebook in China? Who'll be responsible for going through user posts and private messages looking for each and every piece of content that the Chinese government wants removed and expunging it? Does this include private messages between Americans and Chinese citizens? Who will use Facebook's technology to search for faces at the government's request? Who'll turn those people in? Be accountable to the CCP? Who gets their hands dirty? The stakes of this are grim. Support for banned opinions can lead to harassment and arrest and worse.

Take instructions from the Chinese government and do this surveillance on its own users? Or a Chinese company can do it, in some sort of joint venture with Facebook supplying the technology? I soon find a document where our China team weighs the pros and cons of Facebook doing this itself.

On the pro side, Facebook's leadership believe they would have more direct communication with the government, there'd be simpler coordination since they wouldn't have to deal with a business partner, and Facebook would own more of the China operation. This is something that's important to Mark because he doesn't want to give away equity or ownership for his China operation if he can avoid it.

The con side is more complicated. They list several:

- "Govt may be less forthcoming in its communication to us" [than to a Chinese partner]
- "increased human rights, media and public condemnation for censorship and user data practices"
- "Congress may demand visibility into content moderation requirements" [in other words, US lawmakers might want to know what's on the blacklist of things the Chinese government won't allow on Facebook]
- "More leverage for other Govts seeking similar treatment"

But the thing that gets me is where Facebook's leadership states that one of the "cons" of Facebook being the one who's accountable for content moderation is this:

- "Facebook employees will be responsible for user data responses that could lead to death, torture and incarceration."

Which seems bad but somehow keeps getting worse. In the edit notes, I see that Joel has edited out the part about death, torture, and incarceration and replaced it in the final document, so instead it reads,

- "Facebook employees will be responsible for directly responding to requests for data from a government that does not respect international standards for human rights."

And yet, despite the fact that our employees would be responsible for death, torture, and incarceration (however Joel might want to word it), the consensus among Mark and the Facebook leaders was that this was what they'd prefer:

> We'd prefer more content/data control and communication with the Govt over the limited protections we'd gain from being able to say that our partner is responsible for taking down controversial content and responding to Govt requests for user data.

Ugh.

I knew that Facebook's leadership could be utterly indifferent to the consequences of their decisions, but it never occurred to me that it would go this far.

41

Our Chinese Partner

"Aldrin" was the code name given to the project to get into China. They named it for Buzz Aldrin, the astronaut who landed the first manned spacecraft on the moon. After the Chinese government decided that Facebook needed a Chinese partner if it wanted to operate in China, Hony Capital, a Chinese private equity firm, was brought in and given the code name "Jupiter."

Hony would store all Chinese user data in China and Hony would establish a content moderation team that would be responsible for working with the Chinese government. That team would censor a blacklist of banned content and deliver user data that the Chinese government requested. Hony would monitor all the content in China, with the authority to remove that content even if it did not originate in China. Facebook would build facial recognition, photo tagging, and other moderation tools to facilitate Chinese censorship. The tools would enable Hony and the Chinese government to review all the public posts and private messages of Chinese users, including messages they get from users outside China. This seems particularly outrageous. What followed was years of exchanges and visits between Facebook and Chinese representatives hashing out the particulars of facial recognition, photo tagging, and other moderation tools. Briefings from Facebook's experts about artificial intelligence, virtual reality, and augmented reality. Facebook invites Huawei—a company that's widely accused of being a tool of Chinese government surveillance—to join Facebook's Open Compute Project. Facebook offers to teach China about internet infrastructure, so Chinese companies can compete better with US firms like IBM and Cisco (Cisco's the American company that built China's internet firewall).

Under direction from Mark, Facebook assembled a large team, including some of its most senior and respected engineers, to work up what the Chinese Communist Party (CCP) wanted. They start building new censorship tools for Hony to use to scour through people's messages and posts and converting everything into simplified Chinese.

I find detailed content moderation and censorship tools. There would be an emergency switch to block any specific region in China (like Xinjiang, where the Uighurs are) from interacting with Chinese and non-Chinese users. Also an "Extreme Emergency Content Switch" to remove viral content originating inside or outside China "during times of potential unrest, including significant anniversaries" (like the June 4 anniversary of the Tiananmen Square pro-democracy protests and subsequent repression).

Their censorship tools would automatically examine any content with more than ten thousand views by Chinese users. Once this "virality counter" got built, the documents say that Facebook deployed it in Hong Kong and Taiwan, where it's been running on every post.

And there's a draft letter for Mark to send to the head of the Cyberspace Administration of China (CAC). In it, he's solicitous:

We have already worked with the San Francisco Chinese Consulate to take down terrorist sites that are potentially dangerous for China, and we will be happy to work more closely with all of your Embassies or consulates around the world to fight against terrorism around the world.

What horrifies me is that the sorts of things that China considers terrorist sites are human rights advocates or Uighurs or Falun Gong or people supporting Tibet. The CCP even purchases Facebook advertisements to spread propaganda designed to incite doubt about human rights violations against the Uighurs. Facebook should not be allies in China's war against what it considers "terrorism." I hope this letter was never sent.

At the other end of the scale, I find an email where a team member admits that a lot of the censorship might be pretty petty:

> How much and what types of Chinese user-generated content are we preventing the world from seeing? Very likely, much of the relevant content not only does not violate our Community Standards, but is not even illegal in China, just objectionable to the authorities (e.g., names and commentary casting high party officials and their families in a bad light).

Breaking Facebook's fundamentals on content is one thing; data is another. As Vaughan writes to Elliot, "Filtering content is important, but having server/data in China is even more important so the Chinese government would be able to control/see it."

From the start, the Facebook team agrees that Facebook will store Chinese user data in China under their terms. When other countries have asked for this—Russia, Indonesia, Brazil—Facebook has refused. I personally had told presidents and officials at the highest level of government that we would *never* do this, reproachfully adding that we only locate our servers and data centers in countries where we believe the government would never try to access them or seize them.

When it comes to the Chinese government getting access to all the data in Facebook's data warehouse, a report offers drily, "Note that this will happen." This is the kind of government access to user information that we'd aggressively fought against providing to the US government, even after receiving National Security Letters demanding it in specific cases. When Edward Snowden revealed that the NSA had hacked into Facebook to spy on its users in 2013, Mark called President Obama to express his frustration over government surveillance and "the damage the government is creating for all of our future." He and Joel went to the White House to meet with Obama about it, with Mark saying, "The government kind of blew it on this. They were just way over the line." Not long after, he was offering a much better deal to the Chinese.

The infrastructure that underpins the internet is on such a big scale—submarine cables, data centers—that it requires significant investment, planning, and execution. When Facebook started its major projects to get into China, it also started working with Google and a Chinese firm, Pacific Light Data Communication, to build an undersea cable that would land in China to support its Chinese operations. Facebook would be pioneering the first undersea cable to directly connect China and the US. It was clear there would be very significant risks that China would intercept this data. And not just Facebook's data. The cable was designed to carry a large chunk of all internet traffic. It's why no one else had ever connected the two countries in this way. Facebook knew this and didn't care. Well, more than that, they wanted it for Mark's number one priority: China. They invested serious money building a data pipeline to China, a project the US government blocked over concerns about the CCP's access to data many years later.

One of Facebook's few supposed red lines is that China will not get any access to the data of users who are located outside China. But, unsurprisingly, the documents tell a different story.

Facebook "will deploy Points of Presence (PoP) servers with the goal of speeding up the experience for users in China." Facebook has PoP servers like this all over the world. Basically, they speed up service by bringing data closer to users. As I understand it anyone outside of China who's in touch with someone in China could have their data stored on a PoP server. Under Chinese law, the government could access those servers.

That wasn't the only worry about non-Chinese user data being exposed to the CCP. Another document, titled "Aldrin Security Risks," outlines the risks that the Chinese content moderators could feed data on non-Chinese users to the government either directly or by sharing their credentials. This, coupled with espionage reaching further into Facebook's network, was a real concern. Facebook's leadership had been briefed on recent activity attributed to Chinese espionage, including attempts to compromise the corporate networks of WhatsApp and other messaging services. And attempts to compromise Facebook account passwords, penetrate secret groups, and install malware on mobile devices and desktop computers. Facebook's risk assessment experts say all those things are not just possible but highly likely to happen.

The complicity with the Chinese government is so extensive that the team concludes it's highly likely that the US government will see the data warehouse in China as a target for its own intelligence collection and compromise it. I'm stunned at this. Facebook is working so closely with China that now it'll have its own government breaking into its systems as if it were a foreign adversary? And that's just a given of doing business, rather than a serious red flag that you're on the wrong path?

As I read through page after page, I see the sort of briefings that would warm the hearts of every government I work with. We never share this type of information, and believe me they've asked. But here are detailed explanations of precisely how the technology functions, of algorithms and photo tagging and facial recognition. All the secrets of the trade that I thought would never be revealed to anyone outside Facebook. Facebook is providing engineers to demonstrate, offering ideas on how to adapt the settings to meet the Chinese government's needs. It's white-glove service for the CCP.

The ugly fact is that these are many of the things Facebook has said are simply impossible when Congress and its own government have asked—on content, data sharing, privacy, censorship, and encryption—and yet its leadership are handing them all to China on a silver platter.

They know none of this looks good. Facebook was so worried about a leak, they wanted a contact at the CAC for "leak co-ordination." Because "if it leaks we won't be able to keep doing what we're doing." One risk assessment document contemplates how word might get out:

A disgruntled current or former employee leaks additional details about how we are treating data to highlight differences in what we say to the public vs what we do.

But what did they mean when they worried about *highlighting differences in what we say to the public versus what we do?*

42

Respectfully, Senator

They needed a plan to deal with the problems they'd have if the world found out about what they were planning in China. The problem was they knew they couldn't tell the full truth. And how to solve this conundrum in difficult situations, like being questioned by Congress? That's what makes these documents so intriguing.

They got very close to launch. There's a detailed rollout plan for Facebook's entry into China. It starts with the announcement of a Facebook Representative Office in China, supported by a Nicholas Kristof column they hoped to get him to write for the *New York Times* with a "simple and modest argument": internet is not going to change China, exposure to the rest of the world will, and what we're doing will contribute to that.

The Facebook team appears to be aware of how bad its plans for China might look. So much so that when they worked up some hypothetical headlines for what the news coverage might be, they included these gems:

- "Chinese Government uses Facebook to spy on its citizens"
- "Facebook hands over data on Chinese citizens to the Chinese Government"

- "Facebook grants backdoor access to Chinese user data"
- "China now has access to all Facebook user data"

Worried about damaging Facebook's brand with users, advertisers, and lawmakers, they ran focus groups on these headlines and others, with Facebook users in Atlanta, Phoenix, London, and Berlin. My favorite finding in all of the consumer research decks was this:

- "The idea that Facebook cares about people's privacy is not believable anywhere."

Millions of dollars are siphoned into China launch efforts. There's money to give to groups who will be supportive, groups they want to fund in order to "neutralize" organizations that might criticize Facebook like Human Rights Watch, Reporters Without Borders, and Freedom House.

When the team asks Mark what he'd consider a successful launch in China, he's conservative:

If we look at one of the worst countries we're performing in (Russia), even getting 20% of the internet population in China will equate to more users than Russia.

Congress would want to know what technological advances Facebook is briefing the CCP on, what technological information has been transferred since they first started secretly working together in 2014. China is renowned for its development of homegrown copycat technologies. Congress needs accurate information to develop regulations and policies on national security and technology. The stakes are high. And Joel knows this. That's why he identified "managing opportunities in China with consequences for brand, relationships with government and the Internet" as one of the biggest challenges of his role.

To anticipate the reaction from Washington lawmakers, Joel's team work up a United States Impact Analysis. It warns that "it's good politics for members of Congress to be tough on China and to look like they're protecting 'the more than 50% of each Member's constituents who use Facebook.'"

> We should expect intense criticism on Capitol Hill and hearings in at least the Foreign Affairs, Judiciary, Commerce, and Intelligence and Homeland Security Committees, in both the House and the Senate, as well as letters from multiple Members.

The team points out that "members of the intelligence community who opposed us on surveillance reform will attack us for hypocrisy," perhaps remembering Mark's outraged call to President Obama after the Snowden leaks and his other protests about US government surveillance.

> They'll claim we rolled back US intelligence actions that were privacy protected, and didn't result in human rights abuses, but now we are willing to hand data to the Chinese government if we can profit off it.

With these criticisms and others in mind, Mark's talking points were prepared. He would argue, basically, "that our service in China operates under the same constraints as other Chinese social media platforms." The Chinese users would know better than to post anything dangerous on Facebook or anything they didn't want the government to see.

Which may be true for some Chinese users. But who knows? It's not like Mark or Joel or Vaughan has spent enough time in China to know how well people will censor themselves in their social media posts and private messages to each other. And it misses a bigger problem. Totalitarian regimes move the line on what's admissible. Something that seems safe to post on Facebook today—support for some idea or leader or book or musician or movie—could change tomorrow or in a year and users would pay the very steep price. Whatever we and they believe today may not be the case tomorrow. There is no security for anyone to rely on in a regime like this.

The goal for companies is, as I understand it, to answer the questions Congress has without committing perjury. Mark prepares for the mock congressional hearings, or "Murder Board sessions," with questions he's likely to face. The questions are tough, and the team coaches him to sidestep nearly every one. Even with this evasive approach, Vaughan is not satisfied and instructs the team, "On balance, I think we should be less emphatic about how clear our disclosures will be."

The team's advice is that Mark should not directly admit that Facebook wrote the censorship software in collaboration with the Chinese Communist Party.

Is it true that you're writing, controlling, and applying the censorship software?

i) No, that is not entirely accurate. Our partner, Jupiter, will make decisions on content restrictions in accordance with Chinese laws and obligations. [Jupiter is the code name for Hony Capital, Facebook's joint venture partner.]

ii) For the security of our users around the world and the integrity of our service, Facebook will own the technology that Jupiter will use to manage content review in China. This is the same kind of technology we use to enforce our community standards around the world.

It's not the same kind of technology Facebook uses around the world.

The whole answer definitely feels like stretching the truth, given that Community Standards around the world do not require a "Chief Editor" and a staff of hundreds of people to enforce government censorship and protect the families of leadership on software created by Facebook.

On this next question, Mark is to say that it's not what he would prefer but Facebook's mission comes first.

Why are you willing to give the Chinese de facto bulk data access to China user data, but you fight U.S. requests aggressively even where the data might be needed to protect U.S. national security?

Facebook opposes bulk data access by any government. . . . Although the law on this issue in China—as well as other countries—is not what we would prefer, we believe in our mission of building bridges and connecting people globally. To do that, we offer our service in countries whose policies we sometimes find objectionable. . . .

There are a number of questions gamed out about what Facebook will do if China takes certain actions. For example, what if it demands code or encryption keys? One question reads, "Do you have any 'red lines' you won't cross?" To all these questions, Mark is coached to say, basically, Facebook will evaluate those things if and when they happen.

In response to the very pointed question, "How is this not providing a gateway into your network and making your non-China user data more vulnerable to hacking?" they suggest Mark stonewall. He's to tell them that the only data that'll be stored in Chinese data warehouses will be that of Chinese users, and that the Chinese won't have access to the rest of Facebook's data. Which obviously ignores the whole issue of the access to US and other citizens' data on PoP servers. But if Congress says the specific magic words and he's asked directly, "Will any non-China user data be in China?" he will concede and acknowledge the existence of the PoP servers:

> Like most companies who operate a large global network serving millions around the world, we use a variety of systems to make our service faster, and some of these will be deployed in China. As a result, there may be instances where some pieces of content from non-China users are located on these systems for short periods of time.

Or will he say this? Joel tags these bullet points in a comment, saying first, "Not sure we need to say this yet"—meaning, maybe don't admit this. Then he leaves a comment, "For further discussion." No one suggests telling the truth, that his own security and legal experts have said that China will have access to the PoP servers and there's nothing Facebook will do to protect US and other citizens from that.

There seems to be no compunction about misleading Congress. Presumably because the team assumes they'll never be caught out. Senators will need to ask exceptionally specific questions to get close to any truth.

At one point, the team genuinely considers the possibility that the US Congress will compare Facebook's entry into China to being complicit with the Nazis. If Mark is asked if he's abetting crimes against humanity, he's basically supposed to say, "That hurts my feelings."

How is this different from being complicit with the Nazis?
Respectfully, Senator, that is an unfair comparison and I resent the implication that doing business in China is akin to abetting crimes against humanity. China is one of the United States' largest trading partners and has lifted millions of its people out of poverty and grown its economy quickly.

Mark is eventually asked about China in a Senate hearing in April 2018. Senator Catherine Cortez Masto, a Democrat from Nevada, asks,

> The Chinese government is unwilling to allow a social media platform—foreign or domestic—to operate in China unless it agrees to abide by Chinese law. First, a social media platform must agree to censor content and conversations in line with directives from China's information authorities. And second, businesses that collect data from Chinese individuals can only store that data in China where, presumably, it would be easier for the Chinese government to access, via legal means or otherwise. You've made no secret of your desire to see Facebook available once again in China. Could you please reveal to the Committee whether you are willing to agree to either of these requirements?

Mark's answer is mostly a lot of blahblahblah about how, because Facebook is blocked in China, "we are not in a position to know exactly how the government would seek to apply its laws and regulations" to the platform. This is not true. The Chinese Communist Party has told them exactly how it would apply its laws and regulations. And Facebook has developed technology and tools to meet their requirements and tested them together with the CCP. Then he says,

> No decisions have been made around the conditions under which any possible future service might be offered in China.

He lies.
After the congressional hearing Facebook's stock price rises.

43

Move Fast and Break the Law

When Mark is asked by the China team how long Aldrin will be a priority for Facebook, he says, "The longer we don't get in, the more important it becomes as a priority for the company as we knock out other hi-pri issues."

I need to hire someone as fast as possible and then get out.

But who do you hire for this role? I struggle with this. Whoever steps into this job will be the person working most closely with the Chinese government contacts for anything related to Facebook. They'll live in China. Ideally, they'll be a Chinese national.

One of the documents I found said that a risk with this project is that the "Chinese government arrests a Facebook employee who has access to the blacklist and is accused of sharing the list under the State Secrets Law. Facebook employee spends the rest of their life in prison or worse."

The person I'm supposed to hire is definitely at risk. Should I ask them if they're prepared for that? They're leverage. And by now, I've seen enough to know how little Mark weighs the interests of Facebook's incarcerated employees.

And I think even Vaughan gets where I'm at. I'm not even told when Vaughan's team does their regular meetings with the CAC to discuss Facebook's China entry, but I find the notes from these meetings later. The official they'd been meeting with before everything blew up in 2015 is gone. That man—Lu Wei—was the head of the CAC. Mark referred to him as "our guy" and thought he'd be the one to get Facebook into China. Vaughan told everyone Lu Wei had staked his career on the Facebook deal and the Asia team said, "Minister Lu Wei is hanging his hat on this endeavor just like Mark is and . . . this decision will shape his career for better or worse." But Lu Wei abruptly stepped down in 2016. And was imprisoned shortly after on corruption charges. The photo of Lu Wei visiting Facebook's headquarters and viewing President Xi's book on Mark's desk was included in a lot of the state media coverage of his downfall. This is the same book, *The Governance of China*, that Mark gave to a number of his top lieutenants.

Apparently, Facebook wasted no time in resuming negotiations with the new director of the CAC, Zhao Zeliang. As Sheryl framed it, the focus of Facebook's work at this time was strengthening "our government relations" with the Chinese Communist Party. Detailed briefings with CCP officials on the new tools it's building for the Chinese Communist Party. Zhao wants to know how Facebook will cooperate with the Chinese government to "arrest bad people if Facebook can't identify whether a person is good or bad." In this scenario, Facebook needs to "cooperate with the CAC to block content from (not yet legally bad person) from showing up in the feed." The team sets to work on this, knowing that this content is probably just protecting CCP officials and their families. Before long they are fulfilling Zhao's request to show that the censorship tool can do keyword and entity blocking, part of the extensive testing the CCP is setting Facebook.

Zhao appears to be less of a fan of Facebook than Lu Wei, lecturing the Facebook team that "since US election last year [2016], many say [the] social networks especially Facebook influence [the] outcome with fake news." He tells the team that China is different from the United States and it does not want unverified information sources to affect its political processes.

Something he does want is: Guo Wengui. Guo is an exiled Chinese billionaire businessman who became a political activist and frequently criticizes the Chinese government. Zhao asks whether the content on Guo's Facebook page counts as fake news. If so, and if a complaint is made, will measures be taken? He tells the China team there are people who don't want Facebook in China:

So we need to take measures and do more in such situations to demonstrate we can address mutual interests.

He explains that Facebook needs to tell them what it can do about Guo, and there are three possible responses:

1. There is nothing we can do
2. There is something we can do
3. We can do even more than expected

In case that is not clear enough, he states explicitly that if there's nothing Facebook can do about Guo's page, it'll "impact on our cooperation," but "if handled well, this can be a force to help our cooperation." Zhao explains that there are people who ask him why he is pushing this deal with Facebook if Facebook can't do anything about Guo. The meeting notes then list three possible options:

1. Shut down the account
2. Block his content from Chinese users
3. For specific articles or video posts, if a Chinese organization reports, can we remove or do anything?

Zhao tells the team about GitHub, a site with very active discussion boards, owned by Microsoft. He tells them that he knows GitHub's leadership and when someone "started slandering" President Xi, the CAC filed a report with the GitHub CEO, the content was removed, and GitHub let them know it was because of their relationship with the Chinese government.

I wondered why Zhao is even bothering to meet with Facebook. But in this particular meeting, he says the quiet part out loud. Guo is not in their control, and he is "just one example." He explains,

> Last year a BBC article said the most influential organization today is not a newspaper or tv. Facebook is not just a technology platform. The content on Facebook guides public discourse.

Later he elaborates,

> Facebook is the most influential platform (or let's say media) in the world so China should have access.

For China, that's the upside of continuing to actively negotiate with Facebook for access to China. They get a lever they can pull on the "most influential media in the world" to shut down the things they don't like—including the free speech of activists living abroad—and Facebook will do its bidding. And with Guo, they are using the leverage they have created, linking it directly to Facebook's ability to enter China.

Facebook blocks Guo's page in April 2017. I don't hear about it till I read it in the *New York Times*. Facebook doesn't tell the *Times* about the pressure—or the quid pro quo—from the head of the CAC. They explain the shutdown of Guo's account as an accidental act of God. Their story is that it's a random bug in the software that coincidentally struck exactly the person China said would need to be suspended to help it's "co-operation with Facebook." That is until the *Times* started asking questions:

> A Facebook spokeswoman said that the company's automated systems had erroneously suspended Mr. Guo's account and

that once the company was able to investigate the error, it had restored the profile. The precise reason for the suspension would be difficult to determine, the spokeswoman said, adding that publicizing the reasons could allow others to manipulate the system.

Perhaps they were aiming for irony on the question of being public about manipulation of the system.

The *Times* also notes, "Some Chinese activists have complained about accounts being sporadically suspended on Facebook and other sites without explanation." Hmm.

On this occasion Guo's account is restored within days.

Five months pass, and then Guo's thrown off Facebook permanently in September 2017. This happens around a week after China blocks WhatsApp—one of Facebook's most important bets for growth internationally. I know the fundamental challenge that an important country blocking Facebook presents to Mark. A member of the China team tells me the removal of Guo from Facebook was Mark's decision. He'd initially wanted a middle ground, a temporary suspension, but given China's demands and the stakes, he ultimately decided to do the full suspension.

Weeks later, Facebook's general counsel is asked under oath about Facebook's treatment of Guo's account by the Senate Intelligence Committee.

Senator Rubio: My question—so what I want to be clear is, was there any pressure from the Chinese government to block his account?

Colin Stretch: No, Senator. We reviewed a report on that account and analyzed it through regular channels using our regular procedures. The blocking was not of the account in its entirety, but I believe was of specific posts that violated our policy.

Rubio tries again:

Senator Rubio: But you can testify today that you did not come under pressure from the Chinese government or any of its representatives, or people working for them, to block his account or to block whatever it is you blocked?
Colin Stretch: I want to make sure I'm being precise and clear. We did receive a report from representatives of the Chinese government about the account. We analyzed that report as we would any other and took action solely based on our policies.

This is not precise or clear. Facebook was under direct pressure from the Chinese government. Told explicitly there would be a quid pro quo, that the way they handled Guo would affect whether Facebook would be allowed into China. The reports were not analyzed "as we would any other." Actions were not taken *solely based on Facebook's policies*. China demanded action. Raised Facebook's China project. And Mark blinked. And blocked.

In May 2017, I'm told that Facebook has launched two apps in China. This is surprising news because Facebook and its apps have not been licensed or authorized to operate in China in any way, despite every effort from Mark and the team. What's more surprising is that the only reason I'm told about this is that a *New York Times* reporter has somehow learned about these apps and is preparing a story. I'm supposed to help the comms team figure out what to say to him. When Vaughan lays out some facts in an email to us, one of my favorite comms people writes just to me,

"Oh Jesus. I just read it. WTF am I supposed to do with THAT?"

For years, Facebook had tried and failed to get a Wholly Foreign-Owned Entity (WFOE) license or a representative office that would allow Facebook to operate in the country. Apparently, this is no deterrent to the team. They created a shell company incorporated in Delaware named Leaplock. Leaplock creates a subsidiary in China. They call it IvyCo after Ivy Zhang, Facebook's head of business development in China—who's a Chinese citizen and has only been working for the company a few months. They obscure Ivy's employment arrangement by taking her off of Facebook's payroll and making her an employee of a Chinese human resources company. Neither Leaplock nor IvyCo has a WFOE or a representative office. Officially, Ivy is the owner of IvyCo, and the only employee of IvyCo.

Facebook takes two apps it has deployed around the world—Moments and Flash—and makes minor adjustments to remove Facebook's name from everywhere in the apps and Terms of Service. Then it launches them in China.

Moments is a photo-sharing program that is renamed Colorful Balloons for China. Flash is Facebook's Snapchat clone. They modify the logos of the apps, but not very much despite Vaughan claiming these apps were "designed for China."

It's unclear if they're storing user data for these apps in China but I doubt they are. Facebook already has a global infrastructure to serve Moments and Flash. Moments gathers facial recognition data of all its users, but there seems to have been no consideration about whether they'd be turning this data over to the Chinese government if asked, or whether they would censor content at the request of the Chinese government. If I'm right about this, the level of illegality is staggering. It would mean that the user data is stored on Facebook's servers outside China, in violation of Chinese law. And that Facebook has launched apps in China without any disclosure to investors, employees, the Federal Trade Commission, or even Congress, all of whom have taken a close interest and asked questions about what Facebook is up to in China. Facebook keeps saying it is "studying and learning about China," not telling the truth that it is operating apps there.

As soon as I learn about all of this, I go straight to Joel, assuming he's unaware that this has happened. The series of decisions that led to such a clownish attempt at subterfuge are incomprehensible to me. And I'm not alone. I know that one of the senior lawyers at Facebook has flagged concerns about the launch of apps in China. But Joel's fine with it.

"Are Mark and Sheryl okay with it?" I ask.

He admits that they weren't aware of it. I tell Joel that they need to know. He tells Vaughan to write a memo for Mark and Sheryl. The draft begins, "Over the past couple months we've quietly released Moments and Flash in China." Turns out these are not even the first apps we've launched in China. Facebook has also released Boomerang, Layout, Hyperlapse, and MSQRD. Again, in all cases they have completely hidden this.

I am surprised to read, "We've done this with the tacit approval and encouragement of the CAC." He also states,

> The CAC unofficially and verbally recommended that we not use the Facebook name, and that the distributor be a Chinese entity for social apps. The CAC has implied that they want us to succeed—but they don't want the apps to attract undue public attention, and could shut them down if that were the case.

Reading this I wonder if it's true that the Chinese know about the apps; it's entirely possible they knew and are in cahoots with this subterfuge. But it's also completely plausible that the "tacit approval" from the CAC is the barest possibly-lost-in-translation head nod from a random official. I like Vaughan, but he can be a cowboy sometimes.

The memo to Mark and Sheryl gets delivered. In my regular weekly meeting with Joel, I ask, "Has Vaughan been fired yet?" He tells me Mark and Sheryl are fine with what Vaughan's doing.

Of course they are.

The secret launch of Flash then becomes, in Vaughan's words, "a priority for Mark." The way Mark sees it, "the biggest risk is that Facebook gets stuck with a small business in China and all the costs outside China," so he's aggressively pushing every lever to get in, no matter how dodgy.

The way Vaughan's memo frames things, the big issue with these apps isn't the Chinese government but "critical media attention from the Western press." To be ready for this, the comms team puts together a plan.

This reactive comms plan is here in prep for the worst case scenario when and if we have investigative journalists sniff out all the information on the points below.

The plan starts with some possible headlines we might be facing when the news breaks:

"Facebook sets up sketchy shell companies in an effort to get inside China"

"Zuckerberg will stop at nothing to get into China. Inside the story of the web of deceit that Facebook has spun to get a piece of the world's most lucrative market."

"Facebook will do anything to get into China, except use the name Facebook"

This is bad. It gets worse. As the *New York Times* reporter is about to publish his story I learn two things: someone at Facebook is leaking to the *New York Times*, and something is very wrong with the documentation used to register the company that is launching the apps in China. I go straight to Facebook's lawyers. I explain that the *New*

York Times has discovered that the address used in the registration documents for this Moments/Colorful Balloons app is fake. There's no office there. And there's a bigger issue with the registration documents. IvyCo's subsidiary Youge Internet Technology, which is officially launching this Facebook product, also has Ivy's husband as a registered director. Unbelievably, it appears they have registered this shell company as a couple. I have no idea who her husband is, but he is definitely not employed by Facebook and no one at Facebook appeared to anticipate his involvement at all. There's some suggestion that he's trying to get business with Facebook, and I guess registering yourself as a director of a product being illegally launched would give you some leverage in those endeavors.

In the hours leading up to publication of the *New York Times* story, everyone involved in the China project is in full-blown panic. Debbie messages me, "OMG this china thing is a shit show."

"Yes—how can I help?" I respond.

"Represent me when I kill Vaughan. Bring rosé to my house."

One of those instructions is easier to follow than the other. The story publishes. But it doesn't have some of the key details and is not as bad as Facebook feared.

I'm told that Chinese officials are upset about the leak to the *New York Times* and that "Facebook has to get its house in order." The apps are shut down. But months later Ivy's name is added to more Facebook applications with the Chinese government: applications for an Oculus license in China and a start-up incubator Facebook sets up in 2018 to give out $30 million to small businesses in China. After all, it's worked for them so far. This is after Facebook had simply launched Oculus and its apps in 2014 with the strategy of not seeking a license and "playing dumb." China eventually grants a license for Oculus years later when Ivy applies and approves registration for the Facebook subsidiary designed to give out tens of millions to China's small businesses, although the subsidiary's registration disappears from the public record under mysterious circumstances. I don't know what happened to that $30 million.

Beyond all this, Facebook's chief financial officer has flagged serious concerns from the tax team around public statements the company's making about Facebook's China advertising revenue, its second-largest market after the United States. Which Vaughan is forced to concede "is challenging" because "what we do in accounting will impact the important tax negotiation we hope to have shortly." The CFO's also concerned about all the hiring Facebook is doing in China.

This leads me to discover yet another issue, this one with our employees in Beijing. Facebook's chief representative in China—who used to report to Joel and now reports to me—is working there illegally. They don't have the correct work permit and—beyond that—Facebook is required to have a local subsidiary if it wants to employ *anyone* in China, which it does not. I ask one of our lawyers to look into this, and she writes explaining that if Facebook's chief representative in China decides to point out the ways Facebook is breaking the law to Chinese authorities, they could cause "significant harm" to Facebook.

> As I see it, they have the ability to "bring the house of cards down" by simply raising a grievance—any grievance—in relation to their employment in China, e.g. failure of FB to pay appropriate social security contributions, incorrect tax reporting, absence of company regulations, claim for additional bonus, etc.

What's strange is that no one seems to have considered how hiring Facebook's chief representative in China this way might "bring the house of cards down."

I guess no one's considered it because Facebook's chief representative in China is not the only one; other parts of Facebook are staffing up teams in China. Facebook has had office space for employees in China for years now. In response to concerns from Facebook's CFO, Vaughan claims this has all been "blessed" by legal, but this is quickly shot down by one of Facebook's most senior lawyers with a "clarification" that it was "*not* blessed."

Facebook is operating illegally in China. One of America's biggest publicly listed companies is completely indifferent to the rules.

44

Emotional Targeting

B y now, it feels like the day-to-day at Facebook is lurching from one dismaying shit show to the next. Mark and Sheryl seem completely removed. Focused on presidential runs or promoting new books or commencement speeches or whatever.

In April 2017, a confidential document is leaked that reveals Facebook is offering advertisers the opportunity to target thirteen-to-seventeen-year-olds across its platforms, including Instagram, during moments of psychological vulnerability when they feel "worthless," "insecure," "stressed," "defeated," "anxious," "stupid," "useless," and "like a failure." Or to target them when they're worried about their bodies and thinking of losing weight. Basically, when a teen is in a fragile emotional state.

Facebook's advertising team had made this presentation for an Australian client that explains that Instagram and Facebook monitor teenagers' posts, photos, interactions, conversations with friends, visual communications, and internet activity on and off Facebook's platforms and use this data to target young people when they're vulnerable. In addition to the moments of vulnerability listed, Facebook finds moments when teenagers are concerned with "body confidence" and "working out & losing weight."

At first blush it sounds pretty gross, sifting through teens' private information to identify times when they might be feeling worthless and vulnerable to an advertiser flogging flat-tummy tea or whatever other rubbish.

But apparently Facebook's proud of it. They've placed a story in Australia explaining how the company uses targeting based on emotions: "How Brands Can Tap into Aussie and Kiwis [sic] Emotions: Facebook Research," which touts how Facebook and Instagram use the "emotional drivers of behavior" to allow advertisers to "form a connection." The advertising industry understands that we buy more stuff when we are insecure, and it's seen as an asset that Facebook knows when that is and can target ads when we're in this state.

It's a reporter for an Australian newspaper who's gotten his hands on one of the internal documents about how Facebook actually does this, and he reaches out for a comment from Facebook before publishing. That's when I hear about it. I didn't know anything about this and neither did the policy team in Australia. It's an advertising thing. I'm put on a response team of communications specialists, members from the privacy team and measurement team, and safety policy specialists that's supposed to figure out what to say publicly.

No one in that group, other than me and my Australian team, seems surprised that Facebook made an advertising deck like this. One person messages the group, "I have a very strong feeling that she [the Australian staffer who prepared the deck] is not the only researcher doing this work. So do we want to open a giant can of worms or not?" And they're right. At first, we think the leaked document is one Facebook made to pitch a gum manufacturer to target teenagers during vulnerable emotional states. Then eventually the team realize, no, the one that got leaked was for a bank. There are obviously many decks like this.

The privacy staffer explains that teams do this type of customized work targeting insecurities for other advertisers, and there are presentations for other clients specifically targeting teens. We discuss the possibility that this news might lead to investigations by state attorneys general or the Federal Trade Commission, because it might become public that Facebook commercializes and exploits Facebook's youngest users.

To me, this type of surveillance and monetization of young teens' sense of worthlessness feels like a concrete step toward the dystopian future Facebook's critics had long warned of.

A statement is quickly drafted and the response team debates whether Facebook can include the line, "We take this very seriously and are taking every effort to remedy the situation," since in fact this is apparently just normal business practice. A comms staffer points out what should be obvious: that "we can't say we're taking efforts to remedy it if we're not."

This prompts other team members to confirm his take, revealing other examples they know of. Facebook targets young mothers, based on their emotional states, and targets racial and ethnic groups—for example, "Hispanic and African American Feeling Fantastic Over-index." Facebook does work for a beauty product company tracking when thirteen-to-seventeen-year-old girls delete selfies, so it can serve a beauty ad to them at that moment.

We don't know what happens to young teen girls when they're targeted with beauty advertisements after deleting a selfie. Nothing good. There's a reason why you erase something from existence. Why a teen girl feels that it can't be shared. And surely Facebook shouldn't then be using that moment to bombard them with extreme weight loss ads or beauty industry ads or whatever else they push on teens feeling vulnerable. The weird thing is that the rest of our Facebook coworkers seem unbothered about this.

My team and I are horrified; one of them messages me, "Also wondering about asking my apparently morally bankrupt colleagues if they are aware of any more. The Facebook advertising guy who is cited in the [Australian] article has three children—I talked him through his kid being bullied—what was he thinking?"

I'm still struggling to get a better picture of what we're dealing with here. So I ask for an independent audit by a third party to understand everything that Facebook has done like this around the world, targeting vulnerable people, so I can try to stop it. Who has this information and how many advertisers has it been shared with? The team is not enthusiastic. Elliot nixes any audit and cautions against using the word "audit" at all, even as an ask like mine, saying that "lawyers have discouraged that description in similar contexts." He doesn't say why but I'm guessing he doesn't want to create a paper trail, a report with damning details that could be leaked or subpoenaed. Years later I would learn that British teenager Molly Russell had saved Instagram posts including one from an account called Feeling Worthless before committing suicide. "Worthless" being one of the targeting fields. This only emerged due to a lawsuit that revealed internal documents acknowledging "palpable risk" of "similar incidents."

The initial statement Facebook gives the Australian journalist who discovered the targeting and surveillance back in 2017 does not acknowledge that this sort of ad targeting is commonplace at Facebook. In fact, it pretends the opposite: "We have opened an investigation to understand the process failure and improve our oversight. We will undertake disciplinary and other processes as appropriate."

A junior researcher in Australia is fired. Even though that poor researcher was most likely just doing what her bosses wanted. She's just another nameless young woman who was treated as cannon fodder by the company.

When that doesn't stop media interest, Elliot says, "We need to push back hard on the idea that advertisers were enabled to target based on emotions. Can you share to group so Sheryl et al can i) see the article, ii) understand next steps." Joel wants a new, stronger statement, one saying that we've never delivered ads targeted on emotion. He directs that "our comms should swat that down clearly," but he's told that it's not possible. Joel's response: "We can't confirm that we don't target on the basis of insecurity or how someone is feeling?" Facebook's deputy chief privacy officer responds, "That's correct, unfortunately." Elliot asks whether it is possible to target on words like "depressed" and the deputy chief privacy officer confirms that, yes, Facebook could customize that for advertisers. He explains that not only does Facebook offer this type of customized behavioral targeting, there's a product team working on a tool that would allow advertisers to do this themselves, without Facebook's help.

Despite this, Elliot, Joel, and many of Facebook's most senior executives devise a cover-up. Facebook issues a second statement that's a flat-out lie: "Facebook does not offer tools to target people based on their emotional state." The new statement is circulated to a large group of senior management who know it's a lie, and approve it anyway. It reads,

On May 1, 2017, The Australian posted a story regarding research done by Facebook and subsequently shared with an advertiser. The premise of the article is misleading. Facebook does not offer tools to target people based on their emotional state.

The analysis done by an Australian researcher was intended to help marketers understand how people express themselves on Facebook. It was never used to target ads and was based on data that was anonymous and aggregated.

I take a couple of days off for a family trip and to celebrate Xanthe's birthday, and the response team continues on without me. I'm glad to miss it.

One of the top ad executives for Australia calls me late one night to complain. Why are we putting out statements like this? he wants to know. "This is the business, Sarah. We're proud of this. We shout this from the rooftops. This is what puts money in all our pockets. And these statements make it look like it's something nefarious." It looks bad in front of our advertisers, he says, for Facebook to pretend it's not doing this targeting. He's out there every day promoting the precision of these tools that hoover up so much data and insight on and off Facebook so that it can deliver the right ad at the right time to the right user. And this is what headquarters is saying to the public? "How do I explain this?" he asks. And thirteen-to-seventeen-year-olds? "That's a very important audience. Advertisers really want to reach them. And we have them! We're pretending we don't do this?"

As if to back him up, just three days after the false denial, on an earnings call Sheryl touts Facebook's ability to target based on sex and age, stating, "We think that targeting and measurement are significant competitive advantages for us. . . . Just in basic targeting itself, just age and gender, we're 38% more accurate than broad-based targeting according to Nielsen in the U.S. And that's just age and gender."

I know I'm on vacation and I have a valid excuse to stay out of this, to not put any grit in the machine or damage my standing with leadership. I know anything I do or say at this point will not change the choices leadership is making. I know it's in my best interest to just stay silent. To not sabotage myself.

But then before I can think too hard about it, I'm confronting Elliot. Relaying the call I had from the ad executive and my own concerns that we're lying to the public, more angrily than I mean to. Why, I ask Elliot, can't we just stop targeting depressed teenagers, and anyone else in a vulnerable emotional state? We'll still make a lot of money. It can't be that much of our business.

Elliot's amused.

"If you and he both hate this—for opposite reasons—we must've gotten this exactly right."

45

A Fish Rots from the Head

Trust is gone between staff and leadership at Facebook. The lingering discontent over Facebook's role in Trump's election, the Feminist Fight Club's issues, and the broader silence and lack of contrition about the harm Facebook is causing globally have changed how so many people feel about working here. Before all this, you felt proud to be at Facebook. That's gone.

People feel like they're complicit. Internal Facebook groups are starting to see posts from employees asking if they could move to different teams where they could "try not to be morally implicated." It's harder to recruit. In fact, prospective hires are telling recruiters to never contact them again, that they'll never work for Facebook. That's new.

But the leadership at Facebook doesn't seem to get it. Sheryl despairs after meeting with the new crop of interns that they're focusing on the wrong questions, with their insistence on asking about morality and culture. She is seemingly unaware of the generational shift as Generation Z enters the workforce. "Why aren't they asking about the business?" she fumes. "Not a single question on that."

Management meetings now regularly include discussions of how to manage mental health and morale issues. Elliot holds a "fireside chat" (sans fireside) to boost morale on his team—which is now hundreds of people. During this pep talk, a few weeks after Davos, he declares that the elites at Davos are out of touch but Mark and Sheryl are different from other business leaders because of their "moral authority." He's grasped that the issue of moral authority is being discussed by the people who work at Facebook; what he's missed is that the employees are wondering where it is. That's how clueless he seems to be about how we're feeling. "A fish rots from the head," whispers a friend after she catches me rolling my eyes.

After Trump begins his term, Joel and Elliot set up "diversity brown bag sessions" to address the growing discontent over race and gender bias. When Joel attends these sessions, he's visibly uncomfortable. Usually he takes up space, his body languid and voice commanding, but here he's angular and awkward, his voice deferential, back to Bush's "angular dude." Mostly these meetings are pretty bland. Issues are raised in the most noncombative language possible, when they're raised at all. It's a room full of very political people who are not fools. This is less a forum to boldly hash out the diversity issues facing the department and more of a pantomime pretending to do that.

So it's quite surprising in the middle of one of these brown bags when an FFC member speaks up. "What responsibility does Facebook have when one of its employees has sexually harassed another?"

It's as if a current of electricity goes through the room. Joel looks stricken. FFC members catch each other's eyes, like, okay, now it's on.

Before Joel can answer, one of the other senior men in the room jumps in. "When will women focus on work and stop talking about diversity already?"

That shuts it down. The room seems to deflate. One of the HR staff launches into some boring process response about who to report sexual harassment to and how seriously Facebook takes it and we move on. Nothing is going to change.

I think many of the employees are fine with that. Most of the company is made up of white and Asian men who don't seem to have a problem with how things have been going. The entitlement in the Facebook offices flows as freely as the prosecco from the Prosecco Tap that's installed in one of the Facebook office kitchens. When there are complaints of gentrification around Facebook's Menlo Park campus, driving up rents and forcing longtime residents out, they post things that could have been lifted from the pages of *Atlas Shrugged*, like, "I take exception to think that I am part of the problem, I won't be villainized for my own successes in life." And, "These people just want our gobs of money."

At Facebook, the veil of civility is very thin.

When Charlottesville happens—with neo-Nazis marching and a woman killed—a few people propose questions about it for Mark's weekly Q&A session. Mark answers the questions that get the most votes, and a question on the overcrowding of the Facebook campus gym gets far more than Charlottesville, the rise of the alt-right, and the new challenges those pose for Facebook. A year earlier, the Southern Poverty Law Center had provided Facebook with a list of two hundred hate groups with Facebook pages, most of them in violation of Facebook's Terms of Service, which prohibit hate speech. But Facebook had done next to nothing. The Unite the Right Facebook page promoting the Charlottesville rally was up for a month before Facebook removed it, the day before the event. The FFC wants to hear Mark address all this, but we don't have the votes to make that happen. Most of the company would rather talk about the gym.

Mark and Sheryl, meanwhile, respond to the public outcry against Facebook—the deluge of headlines that say we're making the world worse—by calling it a "witch hunt" or "scapegoating." People who criticize Facebook employees "just didn't understand." They act like we're the victims.

It reminds me of the way a nationalist movement responds to criticism. Nationalism always begins with the claim that you're on the principled, moral, righteous side of things. That's always just a given at Facebook. You're an insider. Even now, there's a lot of self-congratulatory talk about how we're connecting the world and not everyone understands our mission. And Mark often uses the weekly company Q&A, which some wanted to rename "Question Mark," to mythologize the past. He tells stories about how people thought he was crazy not to sell Facebook when Yahoo offered him a billion dollars, or how the company introduced the newsfeed and everyone was so upset but ultimately people learned to love it. How he was so clever to buy WhatsApp (he doesn't mention the spyware Onavo that showed him which apps to buy by giving him confidential usage data, making acquisitions like shooting fish in a barrel). It's us against the outsiders and haters, whether that's the media, academics, or other companies. It's us versus them. And as with nationalism, there's something cleansing in this narrative pushed from the top, something comforting about being in the right, an organized innocence.

So the schism widens between employees who feel that Facebook is wronged by its critics and those who feel that Facebook needs to right its wrongs in the world.

Despite its public statement to the contrary, Facebook was long aware that its research, models, and programs sought to optimize user engagement at all costs. Facebook employed a series of "addictive by design" features specifically targeted and tailored to exploiting the vulnerabilities of young users, while hiding the risky and harmful nature of such features. Forcing every lever to drive engagement and drive that addiction.

There is one hope. The powerful algorithms that are contributing to atomized societies could be weakened because they have the potential to cause so much harm that they hurt the bottom line. In an internal memo titled "Mapping a Vector Space in Motion," Facebook's chief technology officer, Andrew Bosworth, urges senior management to change Facebook's focus on engagement at all costs, pointing out that it is irresponsibly influencing behaviors, including negative behaviors. Acknowledging Facebook's centrality in all of it.

> We [Facebook] make the weather. . . .
> Lately, however, we have been thinking more deeply about how the content we show not only responds to existing affinities but also reinforces or shapes future affinities, potentially by clustering people and cutting off some points from other points prematurely. . . . We have been prematurely optimizing and we are driving towards a local maxima and . . . what we have to do is relax the optimization a bit. Take a hit on time spent and engagement and let things flow with greater exploration.

Boz showed that Facebook's senior management knew exactly what Facebook was doing. Then he argued that Facebook should step back from all this "optimizing and driving," instead letting people have greater input and more control over the content they see.

But nothing changed.

After the election, and with all the other problems coming to light, they could've decided to genuinely clean things up. Instead they create some window-dressing "fact checking partnerships" and, before long, some of the main "partners," Snopes and the Associated Press, pull out. "They've essentially used us for crisis PR," Brooke Binkowski, the former managing editor of Snopes, tells the *Guardian*. "They're not taking anything seriously. They are more interested in making themselves look good and passing the buck. . . . They clearly don't care." A different fact-checker who had long worked for Facebook vents their frustration to the *Guardian*: "They are a terrible company and, on a personal level, I don't want to have anything to do with them."

Even the office feels different. One day there's a commotion in the large open space where the policy team works. I run over from my desk and see a woman convulsing on the floor. She's foaming at the mouth and her face is bleeding. She must've hit something when she fell from her desk. And she's being completely ignored. She's surrounded by desks and people at computers and no one's helping her. Everyone types busily on their keyboards, pretending nothing is happening. She's spasming violently, bringing her dangerously close to mobile filing drawers with sharp metal edges.

I and two members of the FFC who are both relatively new to the team push aside the furniture and call 911 but can't provide the basic information the dispatcher needs. History of seizures? The woman's age? Her name?

"Are you her manager?" I ask a woman at a nearby desk who seems to be studiously concentrating on her computer, while a woman convulses in pain at her feet.

"Yes. But I'm very busy," she says brusquely.

"Are you serious? What's her name? Does she have epilepsy? How can we help her?"

The woman looks surprised. "She's a contractor. I don't have that sort of information. Her contract's coming to an end soon. I suggest you call HR."

We do. They refer us to a company that manages contractors. The representative for that company doesn't pick up. The woman continues to convulse.

This is not what it was like to work here when I began in 2011. There was a boisterous, happy energy to the place. The idea that someone could be in pain, writhing at your feet, and just be ignored, that was unthinkable. The guys in the office could be obnoxious or fratty, but I never doubted that they would've jumped in. They did have that much basic human decency. But now everyone around me seems completely detached. Shut down. Anxiously looking at their screens, eyes on the job. I don't want that to become who I am.

46

Myanmar

We're not just treating each other badly in our own headquarters. We're also doing some real damage out in the world. And I'm failing when I try to get the people in charge to care.

Take Myanmar. By now, it's not that I expect anything good or responsible from Facebook's leadership. There was a time when I could make that happen, but I know I can't influence the things that matter now. It's hard for me to hold on to the difference between knowing when to perservere and knowing when to quit. I keep telling myself I can do more to change things inside than I can out. So I'm trying to work the rotten system to achieve what little I can to make things better. In this case, I'm trying to do something very simple. I want to hire a human rights expert to manage Myanmar. But even this is not going well.

Myanmar exemplifies how damaging Facebook can be. But to understand this and why I can't hire someone to fix it we need to go back in time. Since my visit to Myanmar four years ago, things have deteriorated there. And Facebook has played a big role in this unraveling.

Myanmar is the one country where Mark's dream for Internet .org kind of came true. Since my time there in 2013, it went from having virtually no internet to everyone on mobile, totally skipping desktops. And on mobile phones, Facebook *is* the internet for nearly everyone. Facebook made deals with the local telecoms to preload phones with Facebook, and in many plans, time spent on Facebook wasn't counted toward your minutes.

So in Myanmar, if you're on the internet, you're on Facebook, and because of this, Myanmar demonstrates better than anywhere the havoc Facebook can wreak when it's truly ubiquitous. The best way I can describe what's happened there is a kind of lethal carelessness. At every turn, when Facebook's leaders see how Facebook is inflaming tensions and making an unstable and frightening political situation much worse, they do . . . nothing.

We got our first real glimpse of how badly things can go in 2014, nearly one year after I met with the junta. In April 2014 I and some others on the policy team hear that there is virulent hate speech circulating in Myanmar. Most of it is targeted at the country's Muslim minority, the Rohingya. Mobs are burning down mosques. We go to the content team that's responsible for removing hate speech and ask if there's more we can do to address it, and we're told no. They've just hired a new Burmese contractor to manage this; everything is fine. Facebook's head of content policy says, "I can confirm our Burmese rep has plenty of bandwidth." We push for more details and they provide a breakdown showing that they only have four or five reports of hate speech in the queue, which is nothing.

A few months after this exchange with the content team, a riot is triggered by a Facebook post and the junta blocks Facebook on July 4, 2014. The post claimed a Buddhist woman had been raped by a Muslim man, a tea shop owner. Much later a UN report concludes that the story is fabricated. But it went viral after it was shared by a Buddhist monk who's often described as the "Burmese Bin Laden," Ashin Wirathu. Wirathu had been jailed in the past for inciting religious hatred, and he was beginning to figure out how to weaponize

Facebook. (And yes, I know the phrase "Buddhist monk" conjures something very different from "terrorist" for most people, but members of the Buddhist majority in Myanmar have persecuted Rohingya Muslims for decades.)

I get an email telling me the junta wants us to remove Wirathu's posts about this alleged rape. Because they're causing real-world violence—riots are ongoing, Buddhist mobs are attacking Muslim shops, people are dying—the posts seem like a clear violation of our standards. But the content operations team—which is based in Dublin—doesn't want to take down the posts. The case officer tells me she doesn't think they violate our rules, but she can't find anyone who speaks Burmese, and Google Translate doesn't do Burmese, so she can't say for sure.

I pull in someone more senior, and he reaches out to that same contractor they'd hired a few months before—a Burmese guy based in Dublin—to review the material. Five hours pass.

"How long do you think this will take?" I ask. There are riots in the streets over this. I really need these posts to come down.

"Unfortunately no idea," the senior guy responds. "He's offline, I have pinged him on FB and hope he sees it and gets back to me."

"Do you have a contact phone number for him?" I write. "This is an emergency."

The senior guy calls him. The Burmese contractor is at a restaurant and I'm told he'll go home and "should have access to a PC in fifteen minutes." He'll comb through the posts to try to see what is being said, and if we would action it or not. Nearly two hours pass, and the senior guy confesses that the contractor does not have his work laptop and he himself is on the road but he'll get to it when he gets home later. I feel both responsible and completely impotent.

"When will you be in a position to do this? We really need to move quickly," I urge.

After receiving no response, I find a way to get other people to take down the posts from California, but to do that we need the senior guy to send the links that have been reported. Finally he does, the three posts are removed, and four minutes later we get notification that Facebook was unblocked in Myanmar, despite the fact that it's 4:30 A.M. there.

This cannot be the system Facebook relies on when people are dying. If posts are causing riots in the streets, we can't be depending on some random contractor in Ireland who's out to dinner and can't find his laptop.

Based on this and the experience over the last few months, I suggest to both leadership and the content teams that we need to rethink how to handle Myanmar, and figure out what we did wrong and how we fix it. This does not go over well. The head of the content team emails that her people "did exactly what they were supposed to do. This content, on its face, did not violate our policies. . . . Those 3 posts contained factual reports and calls to political action—not hate speech." I point out that this doesn't matter under our own guidelines, which state clearly that we remove content "when we perceive a genuine risk of physical harm, or a direct threat to public safety." Triggering real-world violence like riots violates our rules. They think they can ignore this because it's happening in Myanmar, but as with the elections of despots, if Facebook can enable it in one place, the pattern will surely repeat unless it is actively prevented. This gets me nowhere. The head of content policy doesn't want to do more training, and doesn't see anything wrong with how this was handled. In fact, they want to send a "quick note reassuring the CO [content operations] folks that they did the right thing here." They tell leadership,

"To be clear on CO's responsibilities here . . . [the] team did exactly what they were supposed to do. This content, on its face, did not violate our policies."

I disagree. At this point in 2014, Myanmar is too explosive—grappling with hate speech, fake news, and mob violence, struggling to become a democracy—for us to treat it like any other country. Millions in Myanmar think of Facebook as the internet, and we have only one person who speaks Burmese in Facebook's operations team. That's it. One person. Compared with the hundreds for China. One man in Dublin, who isn't even on staff, to resolve all of the hate speech roiling Myanmar.

The note thanking the content operations team for how they handled this gets sent anyway.

So even though the content operations team doesn't want to figure out what's going on with reported content in Myanmar, at least my team and I can try. Within weeks, we learn just how crudely Facebook is functioning in Myanmar. For example, we've never posted our Community Standards in Burmese, so it would be impossible for anyone to know what's allowed and what isn't. Basic architecture of the site—the like button and most importantly the reporting button that you'd use to alert Facebook to problematic content—is not in Burmese (or shows up as corrupted characters). And—biggest and most surprising of all—Facebook is incompatible with the Burmese language. Facebook's site could be translated into Burmese at any point. It's just . . . not a priority.

In addition to all this, Myanmar is one of the few countries that doesn't run on Unicode. This Unicode is the universal standard for encoding text on computers. As a result, if you're in Myanmar, you can type posts in Facebook and read them as recognizable Burmese characters. But for anyone outside Myanmar, the letters are just an unreadable jumble.

How do you moderate the content when you can't read it? We go to the head of internationalization at Facebook, who tells us that she and engineering are very aware of this problem with Burmese, and it's eminently solvable. In fact, she'd tried to address it a year before this, but nobody would listen. She just needs someone to prioritize it and assign engineers. Myanmar is a huge potential market for Facebook, with over sixty million people. A few weeks after the riot, I go to Elliot and Javi and the head of content policy and others to plead my case. In the wake of the riots, now we can see how deadly Facebook can be in Myanmar. We need to do a better job monitoring hate speech on the platform. So we need everything in Unicode. Nobody cares. I'm told, "I would love to prioritize getting this done. . . . I just don't think we can justify that given the other things in our pipeline." By contrast, there's no problem spinning up huge teams of expensive engineers to build a Facebook tool to facilitate Chinese censorship.

This would become a consistent refrain whenever my team and I ask for something for Myanmar.

Faced with the absurd situation that Facebook can't actually post in Burmese on its own platform, my team translates the Community Standards and a tip sheet on how to report questionable content, and we print it as a handout. A leaflet. Like it's the year 1776 and Thomas Paine has this great commonsense idea about independence from Great Britain. That's how we're going to get the word out. We go to the comms team to ask for their help in getting this to people in Myanmar. We're told no. "Myanmar isn't a priority country in SEA [Southeast Asia], which means we don't have any PR resources on the ground."

And then, the kicker in June 2015: while trying to help groups and activists report abusive content on Facebook, my team starts noticing that users appear to be using unofficial Facebook apps that don't offer a reporting function. This is something that civil society had been trying to tell us, but it seemed so preposterous that we didn't believe them initially. Then we learn that the official Facebook app is still unavailable for download in Myanmar and, as a result, unofficial versions of the app get shared through friends and at mobile shops. It seems impossible to report the hate speech, racist posts, or content intended to trigger violence even if they could solve the language and Unicode issues.

This explains why we've had a steady flow of complaints from the junta, civil society, activists, and others all complaining about fake news, hacked accounts, and racist, violent, threatening content on the site. They said it's impossible to report these posts, and in the few cases they managed to get a report through, no one took action. They clicked on a button and nothing happened. It also explains why the content team confidently assured me throughout 2014 that users in Myanmar weren't filing reports about questionable content. Of course they weren't filing reports. Of course we took no action. Our users weren't using apps capable of any of that.

As if that's not troubling enough, a new problem emerges in May 2015. By slowly piecing together the decisions being made by the now two Burmese contractors who are doing all the content moderation in Dublin for the content reports that manage to make it through all those issues, my team and I start to suspect that one of them is allowing a lot of racist content onto the site. He's allowing a slur for Muslims that's the equivalent of the N-word—*kalar*—and defending its use, even in posts calling for people's blood. He's removing more posts by civil society groups and peace activists than government and anti-Muslim accounts. Worried he might be in cahoots with the junta, we raise this with the content team, who tell us there's nothing to worry about.

We inform our bosses and plead with them to do something, anything, to make the content team address it, but nothing comes of that. We ask them to ban the word *kalar,* if they won't deal with the moderator. They refuse. (Years later, after untold harm, Facebook finally bans the slur.)

With few other options, my team sets up clandestine meetings with nongovernmental organizations in Myanmar that track what's posted on Facebook, to gather information to make our arguments internally. It feels weird and disloyal to collaborate with groups outside Facebook to solve an issue within Facebook, but I don't see what other choice we have. One of the groups has been monitoring the

posts and accounts Facebook takes down, keeping records on big
Excel spreadsheets, and it confirms that our moderators are not removing racist and nationalist content that should come down, and
they're taking down other content they shouldn't.

We set up secret Facebook groups where civil society organizations can communicate directly with us about whatever problems
are not getting addressed on the platform. They send us examples of
posts where government ministers spread hate speech and talk about
how they'll ensure Muslims won't be able to vote in the upcoming
election. Or junta-backed candidates encouraging their followers to
burn a mosque to the ground.

This all heats up as Myanmar heads toward its first fully free,
fully contested election in decades, scheduled for November 2015,
an election where millions will be voting for the first time. A month
before the election, the civil society groups use the secret group to
tell us that liberal candidates opposing the junta have been removed
from Facebook en masse. Their accounts have been suspended in response to mass reports saying the accounts are fake. Our platform is
so dysfunctional in Burmese that there's no way to verify accounts.
My team gets them reinstated.

At the same time, the junta starts to arrest civil society members
for their Facebook posts.

More than anything, it feels like we're flying blind. This extremely
fragile country is heading into a contentious election while struggling
with hate speech, violence, and ethnic tension that Facebook appears
to be enabling. It's like a newborn that needs extra care. In a country
where most people treat Facebook as though it is the internet, leadership have assigned only two full-time Burmese staffers and it is unclear
whether they are employees or contractors (and two bonus contractors for the week of the election), and they're all based in Dublin, so
not in the right time zone to monitor all the posts. To properly cover
the country as well as we cover, say, Germany, we'd need hundreds

of skilled moderators. And in China we had promised four hundred, initially rising to over two thousand Facebook employees. I know the size of the Myanmar staff is woefully inadequate, so my team and I do what we can. On the cusp of the election, I divide up the clock with a teammate in Australia so there's always someone from our team monitoring any reports to Facebook and our secret groups even in the middle of the night, the fear of catastrophe ever present.

In the end, the election goes peacefully, with only rare and isolated incidents of violence in the run-up. The National League for Democracy sweeps into power in a landslide, driving out the junta. But as we head into 2016, it's still unclear whether the military will respect the results and step down.

After the election, the hate speech and fake news on Facebook continue, worse than we've seen in any other country. The junta is supposedly transitioning to democracy but that seems to be backsliding, and we genuinely can't tell where they stand on all this. Sometimes they ask to collaborate to fight hate speech, but we don't know if that's sincere or if they're doing it as an underhanded way to crack down on their political opponents. We're in over our heads. We don't understand the role Facebook is playing in the country. And much of the platform still isn't working as it should in Myanmar. We need to get someone on the ground to figure it out and start to work on solutions urgently, every day. Or at least that's what I think. The leadership of Facebook is utterly indifferent.

Then I think I've struck lucky. I've managed to find someone with exactly the right expertise. And when I say "the right expertise," I'm not just referring to his extensive human rights experience. I've learned by this point that hiring for a senior position at Facebook follows certain unspoken rules. If you want someone to actually influence the policy and political decisions that are ultimately made by Joel and Elliot, they'll have a greater chance of success if they're male, older, white, and a Harvard graduate. Facebook's leaders want someone just like them. The ultimate trump card is if they're friends with Joel, Elliot, Marne, Sheryl, or especially Mark. A few years ago, one of the Republicans in the DC office—an old Capitol Hill veteran with a dry sense of humor—sat me down to explain.

"Sarah, you know your boss Joel. He's a Jew who went to Harvard."

"Yes," I said uneasily, worried that we're drifting into some anti-Semitic conversation I don't want to be part of.

"And his boss."

"Elliot."

"Yes—a Jew who went to Harvard; and his boss . . . a Jew who went to Harvard. And her boss . . ."

"A Jew who dropped out of Harvard?" I venture.

"You're catching on," he said. "So you see, one of these things is not like the other."

"You mean me?"

"Yeah," he said. "You're not like these people. And you'll never be like them. And the sooner you grasp this, the better."

Facebook is an elite product, born in an elite college, fronted by elite Harvard grads who show up for other elite Harvard grads, who are decision makers in all sorts of places. A pragmatist accepts that and moves forward. And so, back in 2016, I decided that until I walked out the door for the last time, I would try to work the system, because for so long I still believed I could do more good inside than out, by doing things like hiring good people. I accepted that I failed to get the changes Myanmar needs, and I'd probably continue to be ignored, but I started the process to hire a Harvard man who might be able to fix Facebook's problems in Myanmar in a way that I can't. Someone who could focus exclusively on Myanmar without responsibility for hundreds of other issues. Someone who'd wake up every day and devote all their efforts to the problems Facebook is causing in Myanmar. Someone leadership would listen to. Hiring someone with responsibility for Myanmar is obviously the right thing to do.

The guy I find is a human rights expert based in Thailand, with a master's from Harvard, and—bingo!—a friend of Elliot's. Years before this, Elliot had suggested I try to find work for him at Facebook. He's dated a member of the policy team and she vouches for him, satisfying the requirement of casual nepotism that runs through most of the senior team, and we have an opening in Thailand that I can expand to include Myanmar, getting around the sad fact that it would be impossible to convince Facebook's leadership to hire someone just for Myanmar.

The process of hiring this guy drags on for months. Finally, I'm in my regular weekly meeting with Joel in February 2017. Everyone else has signed off on hiring him. I come back to Joel and say it's time to make this happen. Things in Myanmar seem darker and more confusing each day. We're good to go. The candidate is good to go. Let's do it.

For the first time since I started this long process of trying to hire someone for Myanmar in 2015, and with this particular Harvard man since May 2016, Joel levels with me.

He tells me it's time to move on and get over it. He concocts a bureaucratic reason to say no: that it would be wrong to "install my guy" in this job because I'm only in charge of Asia temporarily. Never mind that I started this hire long before there was any suggestion I was temporary. Never mind that we need someone in-country and we're not going to find a more qualified candidate. He tells me not to raise the issue again.

Over the next few months, the hate speech and inflammatory posts in Myanmar only increase. Journalists and activists are being arrested for things they post on Facebook. Civil society groups raise an alarm about the rampant misuse of Facebook services in Myanmar, saying things like,

I think it's critical to recognize that Facebook is being used deliberately, systematically, and very *effectively* to target not just

peace and interfaith activists, but also journalists and anyone
who deviates from the dominant [junta] narrative.

Facebook's security team documents a widespread pattern in
which people's accounts are being hacked and taken over in Myanmar. They discover a secret Facebook group with 571 members that
seems to be a site for planning and sharing information for spearfishing
attacks on verified users and pages. This group seems to be doing another thing the civil society activists warned Facebook about: they're
taking over the verified accounts of anyone in Myanmar with a large
following and pumping out content, lurid photos, fake news, incendiary memes, and propaganda, pretending to be them. Spreading
rumors to both Muslim and Buddhist groups that an attack from the
other side was imminent. Anything that would spread hatred and
fear, making people vulnerable and wanting the protection of the
military. And of course Facebook would elevate all this content because it received so much engagement.

So Facebook knows this is happening, but it doesn't mean it does
anything about it. When my team recommends taking down posts
that are destabilizing or coded hate speech—or posts that might lead
to real-world violence—the content operations team often throws
up its hands, saying the posts don't violate local laws, so there's no
reason to take them down. When a fake news story goes viral in June
2017, saying that the democratically elected president of Myanmar is
resigning, my team recommends as usual that we take it down, worried it'll further destabilize the country. And as usual, the content
team and legal team leave it up. Frustrated, the person on my team
handling Myanmar responds,

There is a commonly held belief that the military or someone
is trying to undermine democracy in Myanmar. We have identified hundreds of accounts trying to destabilise things. Secu-

rity operations is currently reviewing. . . . Are we going to let
our service be used to destabilise . . . ?

The answer is apparently yes.

The unthinkable happens. In late August, the military launches
a campaign of atrocities against the Muslim population that the UN
later describes as genocide and crimes against humanity. At least ten
thousand people are murdered. The clinical language of the UN report
on this somehow makes it all seem more horrible. They interviewed
over eight hundred eyewitnesses and victims of the violence.

> Children were killed in front of their parents, and young girls
> were targeted for sexual violence. . . . Rape and other forms
> of sexual violence were perpetrated on a massive scale. . . .
> Sometimes up to 40 women and girls were raped or gang-
> raped together. . . . Rapes were often in public spaces and in
> front of families and the community, maximizing humilia-
> tion and trauma. Mothers were gang raped in front of young
> children, who were severely injured and in some instances
> killed. . . . Women and girls were systematically abducted,
> detained and raped in military and police compounds, often
> amounting to sexual slavery. Victims were severely injured be-
> fore and during rape, often marked by deep bites. They suf-
> fered serious injuries to reproductive organs, including from
> rape with knives and sticks. Many victims were killed or died
> from injuries. . . .

> Others [men and women] were killed in arson attacks, burned
> to death in their own houses, in particular the elderly, persons
> with disabilities and young children, unable to escape. In some
> cases, people were forced into burning houses, or locked in
> buildings set on fire.

Over seven hundred thousand Muslims fled the country.

What the world will learn later is that the military had set up a
massive operation—at least seven hundred people—to spread misinformation and hate on Facebook. This was revealed by a reporter
named Paul Mozur in the *New York Times*. Sources in the military's
secret operation told him how they created and took over verified
accounts that had huge followings—fan accounts for pop stars and
celebrities, the Facebook page for a military hero—and used them
to pump out false, inflammatory posts. "Troll accounts run by the
military helped spread the content, shout down critics and fuel arguments between commenters to rile people up."

As Mozur points out, "It's among the first examples of an authoritarian government using the social network against its own people."

Facebook's response to Mozur? The company issued a statement
saying, "It had found evidence that the messages were being intentionally spread by inauthentic accounts and took some down at the
time. It did not investigate any link to the military at that point."

Which raises the question, What was Facebook's role in all of this?
The UN report on the human rights violations in Myanmar devotes
over twenty pages to the critical role Facebook played in spreading
hate. It catalogs the different kinds of derogatory language investigators found in posts, memes, and cartoons—including several variations on the ethnic slur *kalar*, the word our team tried and failed to ban
for years because we couldn't convince the decision makers at Facebook to take action. It lists the different anti-Muslim narratives found
on Facebook: posts that portray Muslims and Rohingya as a threat to
the Buddhist character of the country and Burmese racial purity; posts
that characterize Muslims as terrorists, criminals, and rapists; posts
that claim they "breed like rabbits" and will overtake the population.
Organizations with an explicitly racist agenda like MaBaTha, led by
the extremist monk Wirathu, have an active Facebook presence. Death

threats, harassment, and calls for violence aren't just against Muslims "but also against moderate commentators, human rights defenders and ordinary people who have views that differ from the official line." All of these are issues Facebook had been aware of for years.

The UN investigators point out many of the other issues we'd tried and failed to convince Facebook's leaders to address: the woefully inadequate content moderation Facebook provided for Myanmar; the lack of moderators who "understand Myanmar language and its nuances, as well as the context within which comments are made"; the fact that the Burmese language isn't rendered in Unicode; the lack of a clear system to report hate speech and alarming unresponsiveness when it is reported. The investigators noted with regret that Facebook said it was unable to provide country-specific data about the spread of hate speech on its platform, which was imperative to assess the problem and the adequacy of its response. This was surprising given that Facebook had been tracking hate speech. Community operations had written an internal report noting that forty-five of the one hundred most active hate speech accounts in Southeast Asia are in Myanmar.

The truth here is inescapable. Myanmar would've been far better off if Facebook had never arrived there.

I've spent a lot of time thinking about what unfolded next in Myanmar, and Facebook's complicity. It wasn't because of some grander vision or any malevolence toward Muslims in the country. Nor a lack of money. My conclusion: It was just that Joel, Elliot, Sheryl, and Mark didn't give a fuck. Joel was a veteran of George W. Bush's White House. An issue in Syria would be met by a wave of his hand and, "Drop a bomb on it. I don't care." A joke, but also who he was. He was the man in charge of those countries for Facebook. And when it came to Myanmar, those people just didn't matter to him. He couldn't be bothered. There was no greater principle ever offered.

People outside big companies sometimes wonder and speculate

about how these sorts of decisions happen. This is how it happened at Facebook.

And it wasn't just Joel. None of the senior leaders—Elliot or Sheryl or Mark—thought about this enough to put in place the kinds of systems we'd need, in Myanmar or other countries. They apparently didn't care. These were sins of omission. It wasn't the things they did; it was the things they didn't do.

47

It Really Didn't
Have to Be This Way

Things are bad, but the one saving grace so far has been that Joel and I are not in the same office or even the same state. So his behavior has so far been limited by geography to creepy questions and taking our one-on-one meetings in bed. But Elliot is about to host everyone who works for him at an offsite, which means Joel will be in town. I'm worried. I fear something is going to happen.

Joel has recently interviewed for a cabinet position with Trump but remained at Facebook as the key conduit into the Trump administration. With Trump's ascension, he's become increasingly powerful. Closer to Mark. Weighing in on not just policy issues but product issues. Core decisions for the company. This means that decisions about political speech, content, and the algorithm all go through Joel. It seems to me like a ratcheting up of the inherent conflict of interest that has always underpinned his job. Joel's responsible both for lobbying government and for making key content and product decisions that keep Facebook in good standing with the Trump administration.

He doesn't wear this newfound status lightly.

Through two days of presentations, meals, and group activities, it's very awkward with Joel. He drops a napkin at the opening night reception and he waits and stares at me till I figure out that he's expecting me to kneel to the ground and pick it up for him. He makes weird comments about Tom. "Is Tom gonna let you out tonight?" "You're going home to Tom now?"

Following a presentation from a famous Silicon Valley venture capitalist who tells us it's great that governments around the world are starting to regulate technology because that will entrench Facebook's advantage, the offsite culminates with a blowout dinner and karaoke session at the Hiller Aviation Museum. I deliberately arrive late, wanting to limit my in-person exposure to Joel to the bare necessities. We're almost finished with the team photos when I feel Joel staring at me. I'm standing with some of the women in our team. Joel calls out, "Sarah Wynn-Williams is looking sultry tonight."

I freeze. I'm not. In fact, it's hard for me to think of a time in my life when I've looked less sultry. I'm vampirish from sleep deprivation. Up at all hours doing calls with Asia, plus a one- and three-year-old at home who don't like sleeping. Work life and home life are punishing. I haven't lost the weight from the second pregnancy. I'm dressed like a nun and devoid of makeup to avoid any unwanted attention from my boss. But I guess that's not the point. This is as much about power as anything else. In fact, Sheryl later posts,

> The 1992 presidential race was once summed up in a pointed phrase: "It's the economy, stupid." Today, as headlines are dominated by stories about sexual harassment and sexual assault at work, a similar phrase comes to mind: "It's the power, stupid."

And in this situation, I have none.

I try to get as far from him as I can, and head to the middle of the dance floor. The white, libertarian Ayn Rand fanboys and

Republican politics guys from the policy team are taking turns onstage with embarrassing stilted karaoke renditions of the raps from *Hamilton*.

One of the senior women in our team comes over.

"Did you hear Joel call you sultry?" she says, looking concerned.

"Yeah, I'm trying to just ignore it," I tell her, but it's a relief to know that others can see what's blatantly obvious, right in front of them.

She says something sympathetic, which I can barely hear over the rap battles, about not being sure if she likes drunk Joel and places a hand on my shoulder. I feel grateful. Then she drifts away to another part of the dance floor.

Then Joel comes over, beer in hand, doing some pretty embarrassing dad dancing. It doesn't take very long before he's behind me, grinding into me.

I feel like an abject object. I momentarily disassociate and in my mind I'm transported to crowded subway cars in New York on hot sticky days where bodies are crammed together and it takes moments for your head to isolate the different body parts pressed against you. Moments more for the alarm to register.

I flee as fast as I can to the safest place I can think of, which is right next to Stacey, the HR person, who's standing by the bar, wine in hand. She confesses that it's not her first and invites me to continue drinking at her place after the offsite, then instructs me to look around.

It's a writhing mass of drunk corporate lobbyists and staffers. Stacey pulls me in closer.

"You would not believe the things these people tell me," she confides. "Just because I know exactly how much every last one of them is paid, they think they've got to tell me everything. Unbelievable things. Like whatever you think, worse. Things you shouldn't tell me or shouldn't tell anyone."

Maybe she's had a few wines and is about to spill some amazing gossip. Or maybe she has sensed what I wanted to tell her. Maybe she saw me and Joel on the dance floor and is warning me off discussing it, because she doesn't want to do what she'd have to, if I told her. Whichever it is, that moment convinces me not to confide in her now about Joel.

But I can't let it go. I feel sick. Because I feel it isn't going to stop. There's an inevitability to it now. If Joel behaves like this in front of our coworkers, calling me sultry, pushing himself up against me basically in front of everyone we work with, it means more is likely to come. Surely, it will only get worse. This isn't the end. Standing there on the edge of the dance floor, I decide I have to get out immediately. No more procrastinating.

While I redouble my efforts to find a job elsewhere, in the meantime I ask Javi if I can move to his department, the growth team. Javi loves the idea and sets up interviews with his team, who are all supportive and anxious for me to start as soon as possible. It's just a few months since Trump's election, and I suggest we could focus on fixing Facebook's systems for elections—for content moderation, geoblocking, and more—before elections in Germany, which are fast approaching. People aren't focused on the collision of technology and elections yet. Like when I pitched to Marne, they don't really see it as a job. But they're worried Facebook isn't complying with German election law. These are problems I know I can help fix, and I'm able to convince Javi and his team that I would bring value to their team beyond just Germany.

I know something's up when things don't move fast.

At the same time I pitch this transfer, Eric Holder's report on sexual harassment at Uber is getting a lot of attention in Silicon Valley. This came out in the wake of the revelations by a whistleblowing engineer named Susan Fowler, who wrote a blog post detailing how she'd been treated by her bosses at Uber, and the failure of Uber's HR department to help her. One of Holder's big recommendations is specifically about allowing people to transfer away from bosses who they report are harassing them. At Uber, supervisors were blocking transfers, trapping women with those they were complaining about. I assumed that with this in the news, and Sheryl Sandberg still one of our most visible executives, my transfer would go through.

I was wrong.

Javi and I try everything to make the transfer happen quickly, but eventually Javi says the only way through is to plead directly with Elliot so he unblocks it. I don't know if it's Joel or Elliot who's stopping the transfer, but it never happens.

Elliot and I meet in his office. He admits that he "knows it's been tough for me with Joel." Then he blindsides me by asking whether my new role with Javi will involve working with the policy team at all, because "that might be a problem."

That's when I understand he's not going to let me do this.

"I don't want to put you in a bad position," I tell him. "I'm trying to do the best thing by everyone. You know me. I'm just trying to do my job. I've behaved with integrity throughout all this, and I don't think that can be said of everyone, and it seems unjust that I should have to leave my job with nothing to go to because of Joel's behavior."

I mean every word. It doesn't seem fair that I should have to sell our house, which we had purchased based on the equity I had been granted but would not receive if fired; move our children again after moving here at Mark's request; go back into the insecurity of renting. Losing the equity is punishing financially. And it seems unjust that I should have to worry about health insurance with everything going on with my health, which Elliot is very aware of. It seems such a steep price to pay for someone else's behavior. But I know I am entirely at the mercy of Joel and his bosses.

"You know I'm going to have to let HR know," Elliot says, meaning, I assume, he's going to dismiss me.

I tell him that I thought we had a deal. I'd keep doing my job, I'd shut up about Joel's behavior, kill the HR investigation into him, and Elliot would make the behavior stop. But things have gotten worse.

Elliot doesn't take the bait. All through this conversation, he's careful to say very little.

I tell him it's not just me. It's a much broader problem at the company.

"I need to understand what has gone on here," Elliot responds, which is surprising because he knows exactly what's been going on.

Elliot turns his back to dismiss me and the conversation is done.

I leave that meeting and, in an act of extravagance, get an Uber to Sonoma, where friends have organized a long weekend away with our families. Tom and the girls are already there.

The driver drops me off and I've not quite finished punching in the security code on the gate when I feel a stabbing pain behind my left knee. It's quickly followed by another and another, like a fistful of knives thrusting in and out of the soft unprotected flesh below one of my best professional dresses, which I carefully selected for my meeting with Elliot. It's soft white; I wanted the visual association of innocence and purity that white conveys.

Reaching down, I feel firm bodies and crunchy wings and realize that I'm being attacked by a swarm of wasps that are now zeroing in on the backs of both my knees. I try to swat them away and get stung on my hand. Then I attempt to pick them out of my flesh one by one, but they overwhelm me and I crash down to the ground, writhing in agony. I'd been brought low by a lot of things, but it's the wasps that bring me to my knees. Or rather they're in my knees and behind my knees and I have no choice but to drop farther still. I roll in my beautiful white dress on the dusty country ground, kicking my legs in the air and screaming.

Eventually, I'm relieved to hear movement behind the gate. Tom's walking toward me surrounded by children who are screaming and crying. He gets in our dilapidated car alone and edges carefully out of the main gate. I think he's going to open the car door and pull me in and away from the wasps. The crippling pain in both my knees means that I can't walk or even stand. So I drag myself along the ground toward the car, part human, part wasp swarm.

Just as I reach the car, Tom accelerates, driving off down the narrow dusty road. The large metallic gates clang shut in automatic efficiency, leaving the children behind, their screams still in the air.

At this point it is perfectly plausible to me that Tom has simply had enough of trying to support me through painful situations that are out of his control and is driving off into the sunset. I almost don't blame him.

As the wasps continue to attack, the venom from their stings behind my knees causes my skin to redden, swell, and throb hot with pain. I allow myself to consider whether this is rock bottom. I stop trying to remove the wasps or prevent their stings. It doesn't matter what I do; I'm outmaneuvered, overpowered, overwhelmed.

Eventually Tom and the car come back into sight. He drives up, leaning over to open the car door. Apparently, the only way he could open the gate and keep it open long enough for us to enter was to get the car outside a certain distance from the gate and push the remote. He helps drag me into the front seat, wasps and all. I quickly shut the car door, trapping some of the wasps in the car.

"Sorry, I meant to mention the aggressive wasp nest before you got here but I've been dealing with the children's wasp stings and a child's near-drowning situation."

I take in the fact that this could have been avoided and turn to him slowly.

"Would you believe this isn't even the worst part of my day?" I respond. As the truth of that statement hits me, a tear escapes. Tom looks at me, incredulous, and then down at my dirty, swollen, red body, white dress covered in grime. He takes in what I just said and we both start to laugh. My tears don't stop. I'm no longer sure if I'm laughing or crying.

Friends who have fallen for Sheryl's *Lean In* schtick earnestly recommend going to her with my concerns. I get where they're coming from—this is an issue she's chosen to take a high profile on. Around this time she is quoted in a *Bloomberg* article recommending a zero tolerance policy to harassment and saying, "I think it's great when people lose their jobs when it happens, because I think that is what will get people to not do it in the future. And I think it's a leadership challenge. As a leader of a company, there needs to be no tolerance for it. People respond to what is tolerated and what is encouraged." But having witnessed how she treats her own staff—not to mention her intimate relationship history with Joel, a relationship where he often stays at her house when he visits the Valley—and how often her actions differ from her words, I know that's not viable.

Heidi Swartz, the company's chief employment lawyer, tells me that they're opening an investigation into my experience with Joel. Elliot then lets me know he has concerns about my performance. My research has prepared me for the likelihood that speaking up might lead to this, but the reality of it still stings.

Oddly, Elliot and Stacey say the main performance issue is that I didn't hire people and expand my team fast enough. Over the years I've hired many people and built a large team around the world without incident, but recently Joel, as the final decision maker, has been actively blocking my hires. Not just the human rights job in Myanmar but a half dozen others.

I put together a deck documenting all the hires Joel has blocked and pass it on to Elliot and Stacey. When I meet with them, Elliot admits he hasn't looked at it, or any of the regular recruiting updates I've sent him, and I realize what a farce this is. The fix is in.

The investigation rolls out as badly as you could imagine. Very quickly it seems to switch from an investigation of Joel, or the facts, to an investigation of me. For example, the "sultry" comment. People who were there confirm he said it. But then the investigator tells me in an accusatory way that Joel was looking at a photo of me when he said it. As if that would make the comment okay rather than weirder, and I was somehow at fault for not knowing or disclosing this fact.

I start to provide the investigators with documents and names of witnesses they can talk to. So I'm genuinely shocked when the investigator emails her findings, letting me know that the investigation has cleared Joel. Their position is that the review he gave me was not actually a review, but that he was sharing feedback for the period before I went on maternity leave (even though nearly all of what was discussed occurred during maternity leave, and even though Joel acknowledged the timing was "not ideal"). Because I had asked to "stay involved" in certain matters at the start of my maternity leave it was felt okay that I had been asked to work during my maternity leave (I am fairly sure most employers would have not contacted me after I had come near to death and been in a coma but who knows!). Apparently, Joel did not remember asking me about breastfeeding or my bleeding (hard conversations to forget, you'd have thought) and as there was no one to evidence these comments—nothing to see here! Oh, and apparently they had been discussing the separation of APAC and LATAM for years—the fact that it was only after I complained that this was actioned felt not worthy of too much investigation. In summary, my "challenges" with Joel were found to be a result of communication issues and "concerns around my performance." I'm stunned.

I tell the investigator how surprised I am that they closed out

the investigation before they'd received or reviewed all the documentation and information I said I would supply or spoken to the people
who would corroborate that information. I hadn't even handed over
the dirty Sanchez email yet. The speed with which they closed out
the investigation and the way they glossed over my complaints about
behaviors certainly suggested that anything I did now supply would
not have made any difference.

Not long after receiving the investigation report, I have my regularly scheduled six-month performance review. This one's with
Elliot, not Joel like usual, and then I realize Heidi is joining it. For
a minute it doesn't compute. Then I realize why the company's
chief employment lawyer is sitting there for my "performance review."

It's less of a savage attack on my career and more of a quick eu-
thanasia. Elliot and Heidi fire me in a perfunctory manner moments
into the meeting. Elliot doesn't even look sheepish. My laptop is con-
fiscated. I'm not allowed back to my desk to retrieve the personal
items that had built up over the years at the company. I ask about a
reference. I'm told that's a question for my manager. Joel. I ask to say
goodbye to my team and beloved assistant and I'm told no. Instead,
I'm walked out of the building by a security guard.

Standing in the driveway in front of the building, waiting for a taxi
to take me home, I have an awkward conversation with the company's chief security officer, Alex Stamos, who has no idea why I'm
standing there stunned. He asks me if I've figured out a way to stop
working on Facebook's entry into China. He knows my views on
Facebook's plans there.

"You could say that, yes," I tell him.

"Congratulations!" he exclaims, and my taxi pulls up.

I get in and the driver quickly pulls onto the Bayfront Expressway.

Through the rearview mirror I take one long last look at Facebook's gargantuan headquarters as we speed past the scrubby marshland surrounding it and onto Highway 101.

I'm stunned by the firing. I saw the possibility, sure. But it's all so abrupt.

Mostly I'm scared about what comes next for me and my family.

48

Just Business

So that's how it ended for me at Facebook. I faced the behavior so many women at Facebook and other tech firms have faced. I wasn't silent enough. But if they hadn't thrown me out, I wouldn't have lasted much longer at the company anyway. I had told myself I could do more on the inside than the outside, but realistically, being the grit in the machine wasn't working.

I think all the time about how the company looked to me before I joined. All the possibility of it, the promise of connecting everyone in the world. How I was so sure that Facebook would change the world for the better. The Facebook I saw then has been corrupted.

In the early days, when I traveled anywhere in the world with Mark, people would approach us and pour out heartfelt stories of how the platform changed their lives; how they reconnected with someone who became their husband or wife; how they made new, life-changing friendships; how it helped them start their businesses; how they were all alone—immigrants to a new country like me, gay kids in conservative towns, people with rare diseases and no one to talk to about their care—and found community on Facebook. It felt promising and vast, and sometimes actually historic.

Now I'm consumed by the worst of it. The grief and sorrow of it. How Facebook is helping some of the worst people in the world do terrible things. How it's an astonishingly effective machine to turn people against each other. And monitor people at a scale that was never possible before. And manipulate them. It's an incredibly valuable tool for the most autocratic, oppressive regimes, because it gives them exactly what those regimes need: direct access into what people are saying from the top to bottom of society.

It really didn't have to be this way. I can't state that strongly enough. If I had to sum up what seven years of watching the people running this massive global enterprise taught me, it's that something else was possible. They really could have chosen to do it all differently and fix so much of what's been destructive about Facebook. At every juncture, there was an opportunity to make different choices; China, Myanmar, elections, hate speech, vulnerable teens. They could've made it right again. A different path was possible. And in the long term, it would've been in their own self-interest too. Facebook, the business, the brand, and the company, would be better off. We all would be better off.

And my bosses seemed deeply and blindly unconcerned about any of this. In fact, just the opposite. Turn after turn they encouraged it. In China, they specifically built the software to order. In America, they put staff in with the Trump campaign to help them stage the war of misinformation, trolling, and lies that won him the election. And in Myanmar, they enabled posts that led to horrific sexual violence and genocide. A lethal carelessness.

That's what this company is, and I was part of it. I failed when I tried to change it, and I carry that with me.

You'd hope that people who amass the kind of power Facebook has would learn a sense of responsibility, but they don't show any sign of having done so. In fact I see the opposite. The more they see of the consequences of their actions, the less of a fuck Mark and Facebook's leadership give. Instead of fixing these things, this ongoing suffering they caused, they seem indifferent. They're happy to get richer and they just don't care. It feels crude to put it that way, but it's true. They profit from the callous and odious things they do. Which seems so crazy. They could've tried to fix these things and still been insanely rich and powerful. They were in the rare situation where the money was there in abundance. They could have afforded to do the right thing. They could have told the truth. They could have exercised basic human decency. It was all within their power. Instead, they focused on commencement speeches, vanity political campaigns, vacation properties, raising artisanal Wagyu beef from macadamia-eating cows, whatever their latest plaything was.

And it seemed that none of these choices, these decisions, these moral compromises, felt particularly momentous to Facebook's leadership.

They didn't seem to lose sleep over any of it.

It's simply what they did day-to-day.

Just business.

Epilogue

The next time I laid eyes on Joel was nearly a year later. Brett Kavanaugh's Supreme Court nomination hearing. Where Kavanaugh's grilled by Congress over allegations of sexual assault. Christine Blasey Ford's testifying when the TV camera pans out. Joel's two rows behind Kavanaugh; his wife, Laura, is in the front row. He's there showing support for Kavanaugh. On company time, of course. I wasn't the only person watching coverage of the hearing who noticed. This provoked something of an outcry at Facebook among the rank and file. So, Joel apologized and said he was grateful for the feedback from employees. And then the day after this apology he and Laura threw a celebratory party for Kavanaugh at their palatial home. Friends from Facebook got in touch to see how I was feeling. Facebook's lawyers got in touch to warn me to be silent. Joel's still at Facebook, now Meta. Promoted and even more powerful. Central to core decisions like what to allow on Facebook in the lead-up to the January 6 riots or how Facebook should engage in the efforts to engineer a ban of emerging rival TikTok. Running the largest lobbying effort by a public company in the US. Mark's chief consigliere in Washington, DC.

Elliot's gone. He fell on his sword after reports emerged that Facebook had hired a Republican opposition research firm, Definers, to covertly sway public opinion against competitors, activists, and policy experts who have spoken out about Facebook. Part of Facebook's broader efforts to dig dirt on people who criticize the company. They attacked George Soros, smearing him with anti-Semitic conspiracy theories. It later emerged that, despite denying any knowledge of dirty PR tactics and Elliot taking responsibility, Sheryl Sandberg had been involved in Facebook's efforts to target Soros.

Sheryl's gone too. For someone who built her profile leaning into her career, it's not clear what her next career step is or why she left. There were reports that in the months before her departure in June 2022, she was facing "internal scrutiny" for multiple things including her use of corporate resources for personal projects such as her Lean In foundation and Facebook employees' work writing and promoting her book. The *Wall Street Journal* characterized it as a "broader review of Ms Sandberg's personal use of Facebook's resources over many years." The allegations under investigation also reportedly included Sheryl using Facebook resources to kill a story about her then boyfriend Activision CEO Bobby Kotick, which would have surfaced allegations of harassment (which Kotick had always denied) and a temporary restraining order (lifted shortly after it was made). Sheryl is now campaigning against the silence around sexual assault following the October 7, 2023, attacks in Israel.

Mark? He's done apologizing. Instead he's wearing shirts with EITHER A ZUCK OR NOTHING emblazoned across them in Latin, commissioning sculptures of his wife "in the Roman tradition," and vowing to fight Elon Musk in a cage match. Beyond that, Mark's main preoccupation has been the metaverse, Facebook's play in building and colonizing the next digital frontier, augmented and virtual reality. Mark went all in on the metaverse, so committed to it he changed the name of the company, spending tens of billions of dollars on its creation. And now that is his brand. Which is curious. The metaverse is looking more like Internet.org, or Facebook's efforts in hardware—the Facebook phone, the Facebook Portal, Building 8—or Facebook's crypto currency. Although building Facebook more than two decades ago proved he could have the right idea at the right time, these subsequent efforts (the ones where he builds rather than acquires based on data from spyware) show he is also capable of the opposite.

No matter—like everyone else, he's into AI and Facebook's, now Meta's, stock is being carried along in the bubble.

And this matters. But I'll come back to that.

As for me . . . Another baby. I know. The medical professionals were aghast. Telling me "there's no literature," which wasn't actually a sign to write this book as I initially thought, but a way of letting me know that there is no medical research on how to approach birth after an amniotic embolism. Or as one doctor bluntly put it, "Everyone who has what you had is dead, and if they're not dead, there's no way they're having another baby." Obviously, this did not please Tom, who very selfishly was against me dying, as well as decisions that might increase the likelihood of this, like a high-risk pregnancy. And, like Zika, it made me feel like I was carrying a grenade alongside my baby. The baby's birth is another story. But now this baby is here. And healthy. And has brought so much joy. Exhausting joy.

What else? After my friend and former Facebook coworker Ifeoma Ozoma cowrote and cosponsored California's Silenced No More Act, legislation that protects employees who speak about harassment and discrimination even if they've signed a nondisclosure agreement, I reached out. We worked with advocacy organizations Open MIC and Whistle Stop Capital to run shareholder resolutions on this issue at major tech companies including Apple, Google, Amazon, Microsoft, and of course Facebook. They seek to hold companies to account. I also advanced a shareholder resolution on issues related to Facebook's engagement with China over the last decade. But it's very difficult when the company has this much centralized power. Mark has unassailable majority control through dual class share structure.

I also submitted an extensive whistleblower complaint to the Securities and Exchange Commission. I believed that the government needed to know the truth. That Congress, shareholders, employees, and all of us were lied to. Another story. But, at the risk of leaving this story incomplete, one I won't go into here.

What else? Like the early days of Facebook, I've been drawn to AI, which is wild with geopolitical and policy issues. And will be the next great clash of technology and governments. Since the end of my time at Facebook, I've thrown myself into working on different aspects of AI policy, but the one where this clash was most apparent was between China and the United States.

I began working on something called "the Track II Dialogue on Artificial Intelligence (AI) in National Security Development and Application of Artificial Intelligence-Enabled Military Systems." The jargon disguises something much more interesting: unofficial negotiations between the US and China on AI weapons. Trying to answer some of the most fundamental existential questions: Should a human be involved before nuclear weapons are triggered? Should lethal or nonlethal AI weapons operate under human oversight or control? or What rules need to be in place to avoid inadvertent escalation with the use of AI enabled weapons systems in Warfare? All questions humans have never had to deal with before.

And this is vital because the rapid rate of development of AI weapons systems has outpaced any agreement on how they should be used. At the same time as geopolitical tensions have ratcheted up.

Anyone who has worked closely with technology can tell you how buggy it can be. How an innocuous snippet of code can break a robust system. How technology can behave in ways that the humans in charge could never expect. How technology can create unexpected harms.

That's one thing when it's a social media platform that serves over three billion people. And quite another when it's second-strike capability in the South China Sea. That is, the automated ability to launch a devastating nuclear retaliation after absorbing a disarming first strike.

We live in an era when intelligent weapons can autonomously identify and kill human targets without human input.

Before this hot war, there is a cold battle over AI already being fought. At the heart of it is whether closed AI models or the open-source model pursued by Mark, Meta, and others is the best path for humanity.

There's no question about what China would prefer; as Facebook's China team used to say, "The Chinese love open source."

Some AI experts in the West see a closed model as critical. They believe that an open model like Facebook's will allow China to overtake US dominance in AI. Sam Altman says, "China will force U.S. companies and those of other nations to share user data, utilize AI to develop new ways of spying on their own citizens or create next-generation cyberweapons to use against other countries."

Mark disagrees: "Some people argue that we must close our

models to prevent China from gaining access to them, but my view is that this will not work and will only disadvantage the US and its allies. Our adversaries are great at espionage, stealing models that fit on a thumb drive is relatively easy, and 'most tech companies are far from operating in a way that would make this more difficult.'"

To work out the safe way forward, we need to understand the relationship that Facebook actually has with China, its second-largest source of its revenue behind the US. To have an honest and open accounting of what technology and what data they've already shared.

These are still the same careless people. They've changed the name of the company from Facebook to Meta. But leopards don't change their spots. The DNA of the company remains the same. And the more power they grasp, the less responsible they become. I experienced the first tentative meetings between Mark and world leaders. And witnessed the exploration and embrace of power that has continued to expand. Now Meta is one of the world's most powerful companies. The direction it sets continues. And now we're living in the world that has been shaped by these people and their lethal carelessness.

To say nothing of the future. If we don't address what has been covered up, we'll repeat Facebook's mistakes.

This time the stakes are too high.

Acknowledgments

Thank you to the people who decided that this mattered to them and did whatever it took to make it happen.

To Christy Fletcher, who skillfully navigated more than her fair share of twists and turns, along with her UTA team of Claire Yoo, Melissa Chinchillo, and Yona Levin. Thank you for your counsel and steadfast support.

To Cathryn Summerhayes and the brilliant Curtis Brown team of Edina Imrik, Georgie Mellor, Annabel White, and Katie Harrison.

To Megan Lynch, who had such conviction in this from the first word. Her grit, ambition, and expertise made the impossible happen. Whatever the publishing version of statecraft is, Megan and her Flatiron team of Marlena Bittner, Malati Chavali, Kara McAndrew, Kate Keating, Morgan Mitchell, Chris O'Connell, Tim Greco, Jennifer Edwards, John Edwards, Christine Jaeger, Tom Stouras, Louis Grilli, Jon Yaged, and Deb Futter have perfected it.

To Mike Harpley and the outstanding Macmillan team of Poppy North, Kim Nyamhondera, Ríbh Brownlee, Lyndon Branfield, Stuart Dwyer, and Joanna Prior.

To Professor David Runciman, who always advocated for the book even when I didn't. Thank you for the Tocqueville anecdote and your insight.

To my friends from Facebook, thank you for your decency during dark times and beyond.

To Ifeoma Ozoma, for doing something about it.

To Catherine Nicol, so much of this grew from work stories I both loved and hated telling you. And that continued throughout this process where your trusted advice was essential. Thanks for being such a great friend throughout it all.

To my friends and first readers Tamineh Dhondy, Dr. Katharine Smales, Jamie Joseph, Rebecca Jenkin, Chloë Østmo, and Ruth Wynn-Williams, both my life and this book are so much better because of you.

And, of course, to Tom and our three little pistols, thank you for everything.

About the Author

Sarah Wynn-Williams is a former New Zealand diplomat and international lawyer. She joined Facebook after pitching a job and ultimately became director of global public policy. After leaving the company she has continued to work on tech policy, including artificial intelligence.